The Duke of Wellington's Regiment
(West Riding)

The Royal Irish Regiment
(27th Inniskilling) 83rd, 87th and
Ulster Defence Regiment)

CAP BADGES
OF
THE BRITISH ARMY

The Devonshire and Dorset Regiment

The Cheshire Regiment

The Royal Welch Fusiliers

The Royal Regiment of Wales
(24th/41st Foot)

The Royal Gloucestershire,
Berkshire, and Wiltshire Regiment

The Worcestershire and
Sherwood Foresters Regiment

The Staffordshire Regiment
(The Prince of Wales's)

The Light Infantry

The Royal Green Jackets

The Royal Gurkha Rifles

The Queen's Gurkha Engineers

The Queen's Gurkha Signals

The Queen's Own Gurkha
Transport Regiment

The Parachute Regiment

Special Air Service Regiment

Army Air Corps

Royal Army Chaplains Department
(Christians)

Royal Army Chaplains Department
(Jewish)

The Royal Logistic Corps

Royal Army Medical Corps

Corps of Royal Electrical and
Mechanical Engineers

Adjutant General's Corps
(SPS and ETS Branches)

Adjutant General's Corps
(Provost Branch – RMP)

Adjutant General's Corps
(Provost Branch – MPS)

Adjutant General's Corps
(ALS Branch)

Royal Army Veterinary Corps

Small Arms School Corps

Royal Army Dental Corps

Intelligence Corps

Army Physical Training Corps

General Service Corps

Queen Alexandra's Royal Army
Nursing Corps

EX LIBRIS

RENNIE · CVLLODEN · INVERNESS

BRITISH

ARMY

2000

Falklands, March 1999. HRH The Prince of Wales, Colonel of The Welsh Guards, casts a wreath on the waters of Bluff Cove in memory of the 55 members of the Regiment who died on 8 June 1982 on board the Logistic Landing Ship *Sir Galahad* (see page 43) and, as Colonel-in-Chief of The Parachute Regiment, for the 20 men of that Regiment's 2nd Battalion who are commemorated in the Battle of Goose Green War memorial. RAF MOUNT PLEASANT

ST. JAMES'S PALACE

This excellent book is about one of the greatest features of our country: the British Army.

At the end of the Second World War four and a half million men and women were serving in the British Army and there were few families in the land who did not have an Army connection. The transition from Empire to Commonwealth and, more recently, the ending of the Cold War, have seen the British Army go through several major reorganizations which have resulted in a massive reduction in the number of serving men and women. Today the established strength of the Regular Army stands at 102,300 all ranks.

These changes to our Defence policy and posture have, sadly, resulted in the disbandment or amalgamation of many distinguished Regiments and Corps which were formerly household names. An inevitable consequence of this contraction in size is that members of the public no longer have widespread personal contact with serving soldiers and are, therefore, less familiar with the composition of the British Army as we enter the new Millennium.

This very comprehensive book aims to help rectify this situation. It describes, in their own words, the history and antecedents of the 58 Regiments and Corps who now make up the British Army 2000. I am sure you will find it a most attractive and informative publication. The proceeds will go to the Army Benevolent Fund which directly supports those members of the Army - past and present - or their families and widows who find themselves in situations of hardship or real need.

CHIEF OF THE GENERAL STAFF

THE ARMY AND THE ARMY BENEVOLENT FUND - THE LINKS

The links between the Corps and Regiments of the British Army and the Army Benevolent Fund are unique. Each supports the other. The **Army Benevolent Fund** is the Army's central charity committed to the welfare of Army, and ex-Army personnel and their families. Therefore the Army Benevolent Fund works in **partnership** with Corps and Regimental Benevolent Funds and in **co-operation** with other service charities in identifying, investigating and, primarily, giving financial support to eligible cases in **real need** amongst the Army and ex-Army community.

For a number of reasons, for example increasing life expectancy, the demands on the Army Benevolent Fund are continuing to rise and are predicted to do so well into the next decade. It is in all our interests to ensure that there are funds available to enable the Army Benevolent Fund to continue to give help when and where it is most needed in the years ahead. Awareness provides the oxygen for any charity and all of us serving in the Army owe it to those serving now and of course those who served in the past to do so as much as we can to support our own central charity. Our soldiers are great fund-raisers and there are frequent examples of large sums of money being raised by units and individuals in a variety of imaginative ways.

That being so, all the proceeds of this book, which I greatly commend, will go to the Army Benevolent Fund.

The Army Benevolent Fund

41 Queen's Gate
South Kensington
London
SW7 5HR

MESSAGE
from
FIELD MARSHAL LORD INGE GCB,
PRESIDENT OF THE ARMY BENEVOLENT FUND

The history of the British Army and its Regiments and Corps is one of service, sacrifice and valour. It is also one of frequent and major change, reflecting the dynamics of foreign and defence policy on one hand and the dramatically changing face of the battlefield on the other. The British Army has handled these changes with great imagination and fortitude. But there is one thing which has not changed and remains essential to success in battle and that is the moral component of fighting power – THE BRITISH SOLDIER. It was the great Field Marshal The Viscount Slim who said that the greatest soldier he had ever known was not some general but was the British Soldier. It is the British Soldier who has made and who continues to make our small Army so greatly respected throughout the world. His 'fighting spirit' is built on our unique Regimental and Corps system.

This Regimental system which has been so flexible in embracing change while at the same time defending those core elements which gives the British Army its special ethos characterised as it is by selfless commitment, physical and moral courage, self discipline and respect for others. This ethos is fundamentally important and yet is so difficult to describe. It is certainly not a policy, nor is it a science. It is a mixture of emotional and intellectual and moral values. It is about comradeship and team spirit, it is also about integrity and it is about the high quality people that one is fortunate enough to work and to serve with. It is also about tradition. Some people scoff at tradition and how right they are if tradition is taken to mean that you never do something new or for the first time. But how wrong they are if you regard tradition as a standard of conduct handed down to you below which you must never fall then tradition instead of unsettling you will be a hand rail to steady and guide you when the going gets rough.

Britain is rightly proud of its army and it was General Sir John Hackett who said in his wonderful book, 'The Profession of Arms';-

'What a society gets in its Armed Forces is exactly what it asks for, no more and no less. What it asks for tends to be a reflection of what it is. When a country looks at its fighting forces it is looking in a mirror; if the mirror is a true one then the face that it sees will be its own.'

The proceeds from the sale of this book go to the Army Benevolent Fund which gives enormous reassurance to our soldiers, ex-soldiers and their families, that 'We Will Never Forget Them' if they find themselves in need of help and support. Since the Fund was set up in 1944 it has helped many thousands of people – and the demands on its funds continue to increase and pose a considerable fundraising challenge. Many of our old soldiers and their families need your help.

P. A. Inge

THE ARMY BENEVOLENT FUND gratefully acknowledges the generosity and interest of the following organisations and individuals who made the publication of *British Army 2000* possible.

A

Aardvark Clear Mine Ltd	64
Alcan Rolled Products UK	70
Pat Allsop Charitable Trust	111
Alvis Vehicles Ltd	66 & 85
Arjo Wiggins Fine Papers Ltd	88
Aquafresh & Aquafresh Flex S K & B	116
Avesta Sheffield Ltd	27

B

Ballymena Borough Council	74
Barclays PLC	8
B·A·T Industries PLC	34
Bearmach PLC	11
Rowan Bentall Charity Trust	69
Binder Hamlyn	18
A F Blakemore & Son Ltd	48
Bombardier Aerospace Shorts	100
Bovis Ltd	108
British Aerospace Defence Systems	115
British Aerospace Plc	47
British Engines	23
The British Petroleum Company p.l.c.	97
David Brown Defence Equipment Ltd	12
Burmah Castrol PLC	79

C

Cadogan Estate Group	37
Calor Gas Ltd	105
The County Council of the City and County of Cardiff	10
Cazenove & Co	36
Charter plc	35
Chelsea Building Society	76
Cheltenham & Gloucester plc	76
Coca-Cola & Schweppes Beverages Ltd	72
Colgate Palmolive (UK) Ltd	117
Computing Devices Company Ltd	108
His Royal Highness The Duke of Cornwall	42
Courage Ltd	99

D

De Beers Diamond Trading Co (Pty) Ltd	9
The Delfont Foundation	113
Dorset County Council	26 & 56
The Drambuie Liqueur Company Ltd	12 & 44 & 45

E & F

EKA Ltd	75
Elida Fabergé Ltd	122
Ernst & Young	25
Robert Fleming Hldgs Ltd	13

G

Gallaher Ltd	119
GEC Marine	49
Gibb Ltd	30
Guardian Royal Exchange Group	21

H

Hackett	15
Halifax plc	83
Hall & Woodhouse Ltd	32
J & W Hardie – The Antiquary Scotch Whisky	65
Healey & Baker	28
Hello ! Magazine	41
Highland Distillers – The Famous Grouse	87
Highland Distillers – The Macallan	89
Hillsdown Holdings plc	19
Sir Julian Hodge Foundation	71
The Hoover Foundation	68
HSBC Bank	73
Hunting Engineering Ltd	114

I & J & K

ICI PLC	29
IMI plc	84
Imperial Tobacco	77
Industria Engineering Products Ltd	98
Industrial Fastners Ltd – Infast	120
Kidde Graviner Ltd	108

L

Laing's Charitable Trust	31
Land Rover International	Front & Back Endpapers
Lincolnshire County Council	54
Lloyds Bank Plc – Cox's & King's Branch	110
Lovell Construction	80

M & N

Marconi Electronic Systems	109
J & H Marsh & McLennan Ltd	51
Mars UK Ltd	
Bernard Matthews P.L.C.	55 & 112
Method Publishing Company Ltd	88
Next plc	122
The Duke of Northumberland	50

P

Pearson plc	38
Perkins Engines Company Ltd	16 & 58
Pfizer Group Ltd	106
Pilkington plc	53
Procter & Gamble Ltd	22

R

Racal Electronics plc	33
Rathbones	52
RBS Trust Bank	56
Reckitt & Colman Plc	107
Rio Tinto plc	10
Rolls-Royce plc	40
Rothmans UK Holdings Ltd	
N M Rothschild & Sons	96
Royal Bank of Scotland plc	90
Royal Mint	43
Rushmoor Borough Council	121

S

Salisbury District Council	102
Scottish Hydro-Electric	86
Shell International Limited	95
Shepherd Building Group	61
Simrod Optronics Ltd	118
Singer & Friedlander Group PLC	57
John Smiths Ltd	62
The Earl of Stockton	123
Suffolk County Council	55
Bernard Sunley Charitable Foundation	93
The Sun – News International plc	46
Surrey Heath Borough Council	104

T

Telegraph Group Ltd	94
TI Group plc	24

U & V

Vaux Group plc	58
Vendome Luxury Group PLC	82
Vickers P.L.C.	17
Unilever PLC	103
United Biscuits (UK) Ltd	39
United Distillers & Vintners	92

W

Waitrose Limited	76
Paul C R Wates	20
Colonel The Duke of Westminster OBE TD DL	67 & 101
Garfield Weston Foundation	14
Wilkinson Sword Ltd	59
Willis Corroon Group	81
Worcester City Council	78
Ray Ward Gunsmiths Ltd	63

X & Y & Z

Yorkshire Bank PLC	60
The William Allen Young Charitable Trust	91

Dustjacket design: 'Camouflage, Ceremony and Compassion' by Elizabeth Grant. Pictures by Alan Symes London Press Service

Published by: SEAGULL S.A. P O Box 122 Helvetia Court South Esplanade St Peter Port Guernsey Channel Islands GY1 4EE

Typesetting: SetSystems Ltd 12 Market Walk Saffron Walden Essex CB10 1JZ

Origination, printing and binding: Tien Wah Press (PTE) Ltd 4 Panden Crescent Singapore 128475

All sales and distribution: The Army Benevolent Fund 41 Queen's Gate South Kensington London SW7 5HR Tel: 0207-591 2000

Copyright © the Army Benevolent Fund 1999

ISBN: 0 9518229 1 8

FIRST EDITION

CONTENTS

EARLY HISTORY UP TO 1850

The Life Guards

The Life Guards, the senior regiment in the British Army, were formed at the Restoration in 1660 by Charles II.

They first saw action at the battle of Sedgemoor in 1685 and subsequently in the Jacobite wars of 1689–93 and during the War of Austrian Succession at Dettingen (1743) and Fontenoy (1745).

The 1st and 2nd Life Guards, after participating in the Peninsular Campaign, formed the front charging line of the Household Cavalry Brigade at Waterloo.

The Blues and Royals

The Blues and Royals were formed in 1969 from an amalgamation of The Royal Horse Guards (The Blues) and The Royals Dragoons (The Royals).

The Royal Horse Guards (The Blues)

The Royal Horse Guards trace their origins to a force raised by Cromwell prior to the second invasion of Scotland. After the Restoration King Charles II renamed them the 'Royal Regiment of Horse in January 1661.

The Regiment saw almost continuous service in Flanders, The Boyne, the War of Austrian Succession and the Seven Years War during which the Regiment was commanded by the celebrated Marquis of Granby.

The Regiment went on to see service during the Peninsular Campaign, fighting at the decisive battle of Vittoria (1813), and as part of The Household Cavalry Brigade at Waterloo.

The Regiment was especially favoured by King George IV with the Duke of Wellington being made Colonel of the Regiment and Gold Stick in 1813 and elevated to the status of Household Cavalry in 1821.

The Royal Dragoons (1st Dragoons)

The Royal Dragoons trace their origins to a troop of horse raised by proclamation of Charles II in 1661 to form part of the garrison at Tangier and were known as 'The Tangier Horse'.

The Regiment served in the War of Spanish Succession, the War of Austrian Succession and in the Spanish Peninsula before performing with distinction at the Battle of Waterloo where the Regiment captured the Colour, surmounted by an eagle, of the French 105th Infantry Regiment. The Eagle is now commemorated in the Regimental cypher and worn on the sleeves of all uniforms.

NINETEENTH CENTURY POST WATERLOO

The 1st and 2nd Life Guards and the Royal Horse Guards (The Blues)

During the nineteenth century, Squadrons of The Life Guards and The Royal Horse Guards served in a composite Household Cavalry Regiment in Egypt in 1882 taking part in the famous moonlight charge at Kassassin and the more decisive battle of Tel el Kebir. At the turn of the century another Composite Regiment was formed to fight in South Africa first taking Rensburg and subsequently in action to relieve Kimberley, taking part in the battle of Paardeberg, the advance to Pretoria and the battle of Diamond Hill.

The Royal Dragoons (1st Dragoons)

The Royals saw action in the Crimea as part of the heavy Cavalry Brigade, with whom they charged at Balaclava in 1854.

The Boer War was marked for The Royal Dragoons by hard service with few highlights. After a conventional campaign in Natal in 1900 they spent the rest of the war taking part in Kitchener's drives in the Transvaal to round up Boer guerrillas.

FIRST WORLD WAR

The 1st and 2nd Life Guards and The Royal Horse Guards (The Blues)

At the outbreak of the 1st World War a Composite Regiment consisting of a squadron of each Regiment embarked for France. During its short life of three months the Regiment was awarded battle honours at Mors, Le Cateau, The Marne, The Aisne, Messine and Armentieres and was reduced to a mere 65 men.

In October 1914 the remainder of the Household Cavalry were sent to Belgium where they saw action at the battle of Ypres, in the battle of Langemarch where they manned the trenches and around Zandvoorde where The Life Guards lost two Squadrons.

In September 1916, the Household Battalion, an infantry battalion with Household Cavalry Officers and NCOs with men, was formed. Their first action at Sailly-Saillisel cost them 300 casualties. In 1917 they added the honours of Brookseinde, Poelcapplle and Passchendale. In 12 months it had suffered a total of 20 Officers and 437 men killed in action.

The three Regiments lost their horses early in 1918 and were re-equipped as Machine Gun Regiments (GMGRs). All three GMGRs took part in many actions over the year including Assas, Warlay, battles of the Scarpe and the Hindenberg Line and Wassigny.

The 1st and 2nd Life Guards combined to form The Life Guards in 1922.

The Royal Dragoons

At the outbreak of the 1st World War The Royals were in South Africa. By October 1914 the Regiment was in Flanders, where they fought in the trenches at the first and second Battle of Ypres, at Loos in 1915, opposite the Hohenzollern line in 1916 and against the Hindenberg line in 1917.

Post war, The Royal Dragoons after a short spell in Ireland, were posted to Egypt in 1927 and thence in 1929 to India. They returned home again in 1936 after another short spell in Egypt.

Life Guards and the Blues and Royals change duties – mounting The Queen's Life Guard, Horse Guards, Whitehall. London.

Right: Falklands War – 2 Troop B Squadron enter Port Stanley.

SECOND WORLD WAR

Household Cavalry

The 2nd World War marked the first time in history in which the Regiments of Household Cavalry were really composite. 1st and 2nd Household Cavalry Regiments were formed.

1st Household Cavalry Regiment

1 HCR went to Palestine with horses in January 1940 and were motorised in the spring of 1941. They stayed in the Middle East until they converted to Armoured Cars in 1942.

They then went to the Western Desert and took part in the Battle of El Alamein in late October 1942. After a spell in Syria they were shipped to Italy and were in action near Arezzo and in the advance to Florence finishing in dismounted actions in the Gothic Line. In October 1944 the Regiment, after a short spell in England, went out to NW Europe remaining in Holland until April 1945 when they entered Germany.

2nd Household Cavalry Regiment

After starting as a training Regiment, they were converted into an Armoured Car Regiment in the Guards Armoured Division.

The 2nd HCR landed in Normandy in July 1944 and were in the van of the British advance having some notable successes. They were the first to cross a number of rivers and captured three bridges over the Somme. They were the first into Belgium and to enter Brussels on the 3rd of September 1944.

In April 1945, when the Regiment was employed in the Nijmegen sector a troop found a bridge over the River Ems, unblown but strongly held. The bridge was subsequently stormed by the Guards Armoured Division.

The Royal Dragoons (1st Dragoons)

Starting the War in Palestine, where they were mechanised, at the end of 1941, they were sent to the Western Desert where, during the battle of El Alamein, troops of The Royals managed to infiltrate behind the enemy.

After a short time back in England the Regiment crossed over to Normandy in July 1944 and took part in the rapid advance through France, ending up on the German border in September. Immediately after the German surrender in May 1945, The Royals liberated Copenhagen.

POST WAR to 1992

The Life Guards

At the end of the war The Life Guards Armoured Car Regiment was formed out of the 1st Household Cavalry Regiment in Germany. Between 1946 and 1948 they served in the Middle East on internal security duties.

In 1952 they were sent to Germany but within two years they were back in Egypt with squadrons in Aden and Cyprus. They were stationed off and on in the Middle East until returning to Germany in 1960 for 2 years.

After a spell in England the Regiment were flown out to Malaya, Singapore, Borneo and Hong Kong. They returned to England in 1968 when independent squadrons served in Northern Ireland, Norway, Denmark, Greece and Turkey.

The Life Guards became a Tank Regiment and relieved The Blues and Royals in Germany 1971. During the next twenty years they took it in turn with The Blues and Royals to be in Windsor as an Armoured Recce Regiment

or in Germany as a Tank Regiment. During this period the Regiment served twice in Northern Ireland and independent Squadrons also served in Northern Ireland and Cyprus on a number of occasions. In 1990 the Regiment was deployed on operation Desert Storm in the Gulf and was awarded their latest Battle Honour.

The Royal Horse Guards (The Blues)

At the end of the war The Blues and Royals Armoured Car Regiment was formed out of the 2nd Household Cavalry Regiment. For seven years the Regiment served in Germany with a squadron in Berlin.

In 1952 the Regiment returned to Windsor, but was sent to Cyprus in 1956 where they stayed until 1959 only to return to Cyprus for three months in 1960.

Germany was again the Regiment's station from 1962–66 returning to England at the end of that time. The Regiment became part of the Strategic Reserve in England whilst independent squadrons were stationed abroad, one with The Life Guards in Singapore and another in Cyprus.

The Blues were amalgamated with The Royal Dragoons to become The Blues and Royals in 1969.

The Royal Dragoons (1st Dragoons)

The Royal Dragoons spent the first five years after the war in Germany returning to Chester briefly in 1950. In 1951 the Regiment embarked for Egypt where they spent three years on internal security duties. In 1954 The Royals returned to Germany for five years before being sent to Aden, with troops from the Western Aden Protectorate hill forts, the Trucial States and the Oman.

In 1960 the Regiment moved to Malaya and Singapore for a two year tour. The Royals returned to England and converted to Centurion tanks at Tidworth before moving to Germany as an Armoured Regiment in 1965. They stayed there until they amalgamated with The Blues in 1969.

The Blues and Royals

The amalgamated Regiment stayed in Detmold until 1971 and for the next twenty years they swapped over with The Life Guards every few years between Windsor and Germany.

During their time in Windsor as an Armoured Recce Regiment, indepoendent squadrons were posted to Cyprus and Northern Ireland on a number of occasions. Whilst they were in Germany they took on several 6 months tours of Northern Ireland as well as their Armoured Role.

In 1982 two troops went with the Task Force to the South Atlantic and were awarded the Falkland Battle Honour.

1992 ONWARDS

The Household Cavalry Regiment

In 1992 as part of 'Option for Change' The Life Guards and The Blues and Royals merged into a Union and formed two composite Regiments. The Household Cavalry Regiment (HCR) at Windsor, an Armoured Reconnaissance Regiment, with two squadrons of Life Guards and two Squadrons of Blues and Royals and The Household Cavalry Mounted Regiment (HCMR) of two squadrons doing the ceremonial role.

The Regiment was awarded The Wilkinson Sword for Peace in 1997 for their humanitarian work in Bosnia during the previous year.

1st THE QUEEN'S DRAGOON GUARDS

1st The Queen's Dragoon Guards (QDG) was formed on 1st January 1959 by the amalgamation of the two senior regiments of the Cavalry of the Line, the 1st King's Dragoon Guards and the Queen's Bays (2nd Dragoon Guards), both raised June 1685. The battle honours emblazoned on the Regimental Standard are testament to their long and distinguished histories. Surprisingly and despite over two hundred years of service, up to the time of the Boer War in South Africa, only Warburg (1760) is common to both. Her Majesty Queen Elizabeth The Queen Mother, who had been appointed Colonel-in-Chief of the Queen's Bays 1937, continues to hold the same appointment in the present Regiment.

Since 1959 QDG has served in varied operational theatres. Two squadrons were in Borneo in the armoured reconnaissance role and saw service in Sarawak in 1965 and 1966, engaged in convoy escorts, border patrols, ambushes and gaining the support of local tribes.

In the summer of 1966 QDG together with its Air Squadron of helicopters moved to Aden and was widely dispersed throughout South Arabia with one squadron in the Persian Gulf. Internal security duties for the Aden squadron consisted of extensive patrolling in the urban areas in armoured cars and the guarding of key points. Patrols frequently came under small arms, grenade and mortar attacks by terrorists as well as anti-armour weapons. Up country in the mountainous areas a squadron carried out escorts and patrols, again coming under attack on several occasions. In early 1967 it was engaged in the withdrawal back to Aden. In July of that year 'A' Squadron took part in the re-occupation of Crater.

Following successive periods in Germany and England equipped with firstly Centurion and then Chieftain main battle tanks, the Regiment carried out its first two operational tours as infantry in Northern Ireland in 1974 and 1976 in the Londonderry and Armagh areas respectively. In 1978 as a result of Army restructuring, QDG re-roled and became an armoured reconnaissance regiment again and further tours in Northern Ireland by individual troops ensued followed by a full two-year tour for the whole Regiment from 1980 to 1982 in Co Tyrone.

In January 1983 'C' Squadron was sent to Cyprus, part of which joined the United Nations Peacekeeping Force. The remainder were deployed with their Ferret scout cars to the Lebanon as the British contingent to the Multinational Peacekeeping Force in Beirut, which was attempting to maintain peace between the various warring factions. 'A' Squadron took over from July to December to continue the work of patrolling and guarding as well as providing protection for the Ceasefire Committee.

With QDG in England in 1985, 300 years of distinguished service by the Regiment and its forbears was celebrated with many events, the highlight of which was a major parade in the presence of the Colonel-in-Chief. In July the Regiment was granted the freedom of the City of Cardiff in recognition of it being the Cavalry Regiment of Wales and the Border Counties, from where it has recruited the majority of its soldiers since 1959. Two squadrons subsequently served further tours with the United Nations in Cyprus.

In 1987 Her Majesty Queen Elizabeth The Queen Mother completed her fiftieth year as Colonel-in-Chief and honoured her Regiment by opening its new museum in Cardiff Castle. QDG returned to Germany and was based at Wolfenbuttel near the former inner German border at the time of reunification.

'A' Squadron was warned for service in the Gulf in September 1990 as the medium reconnaissance element of 7th Armoured Brigade. Over the following months additional QDG soldiers were deployed in support of other units and formations. When preparations for the land offensive began, the squadron provided the reconnaissance screen in front of 4th Armoured Brigade and then operated independently in support of the artillery group raids. As part of the reconnaissance group 'A' Squadron led through the breach crossing of the Iraqi defensive line on 25th February 1991. It was then engaged in the fighting eastwards over the next three days leading 7th Armoured Brigade through Iraq to the Basra road north of Kuwait City, which was strewn with Iraqi dead and destroyed or abandoned equipment. A composite squadron meanwhile went to Northern Ireland and ever since independent troops have been deployed to the Province. ADG also provided the last reconnaissance troop sent to Belize.

Following a short period in England and as a result of the *Options for Change* reorganisation of the Army, ADG returned to Germany reverting once again to armour, equipped with Challenger tanks. With the break-up of the former Yugoslavia and consequent civil war, the main part of the Regiment deployed to Bosnia in June 1996 for six months as part of the British led MultiNational Division South West, in armour and armoured reconnaissance, with one squadron arriving in September as a mechanised infantry company – three roles adopted simultaneously. The Regiment returned to England from Germany in 1998.

The many other aspects of regimental life have been actively encouraged over the years and QDG officers and soldiers have enhanced the Regiment's and the Army's reputation by representing Great Britain at the Olympic Games and in international competitions in a variety of sports. Numerous adventurous training expeditions have brought excitement and travel to many countries. As with all Regiments, QDG is proud of its traditions and customs. The 'Waterloo' battle honour is celebrated every year on or close to 18th June, when the officers and senior ranks dine together in the Warrant Officers' & Sergeants' Mess to commemorate the event in 1815 when, with food short following the battle, they shared out their rations and ate together.

One of the Cavalryman's characteristics, evolved over many centuries of warfare, is that of flexibility. This short history of 1st The Queen's Dragoon Guards over a period of just under forty years demonstrates how essential that quality continues to be and why the Regiment has always and will always live up to its reputation to be 'First and Foremost'.

The Queen's Dragoon Guards A squadron, 1st The Queen's Dragoon Guards, attack on Objective 'LEAD', Iraq, 26 February 1991.

CYNGOR SIR ADINAS A SIR CAERDYDD
THE COUNTY COUNCIL OF THE CITY AND COUNTY OF CARDIFF

RIO TINTO plc

Top: The King's Dragoon Guards at Waterloo – 18 June 1815.

Bottom: The Queen's Bays (second Dragoon Guards) brewing up by their General Grant tanks, Gazala May 1942

THE ROYAL SCOTS DRAGOON GUARDS
(Carabiniers and Greys)

The Silver Eagle on the plaque 'Waterloo' surmounting the crossed carbines, which constitute The Royal Scots Dragoon Guards cap badge, perpetuates the long and colourful history and traditions of three Cavalry Regiments raised in the late 17th century.

The Royal Scots Dragoon Guards derive their cherished position as Scotland's senior Regiment and her only regular cavalry from the first troops raised in 1678 by order of King Charles II. In 1681 they were formed by General Thomas Dalyell of the Binns, near Edinburgh into the Royal Regiment of Scots Dragoons, later to become the Royal Scots Greys. They had patrolled the Highlands wearing stone grey coats and before embarking for Flanders in 1694, mounted on Grey horses, were reviewed in Hyde Park by William III.

In 1971 the Greys amalgamated with the 3rd Carabiniers, whose predecessors from 1685 to 1922 were the 3rd Dragoon Guards (Prince of Wales's) and 6th Dragoon Guards (The Carabiniers). For their support of King William at the battle of the Boyne and other actions the 9th Horse (later 6DG) were honoured in 1691 with the title of The King's Carabiniers, derived from the cavalry 'carabin', now denoted by the crossed carbines on the cap badge.

Fifty of the eighty-nine battle honours awarded to the Regiments for gallant service in wars over three centuries are displayed on the Regimental Standard. They fought through Marlborough's campaigns, winning their first honour at Blenheim. The Greys were awarded the privilege of wearing the grenadier cap – unique among the cavalry – for their defeat of the 'Regiment du Roi' at Ramillies. The 3rd Dragoon Guards fought in the Peninsular War, returning to England in 1814, when Napoleon was banished to Elba. His escape to France led to the battle of Waterloo the following year where the Scots Greys in the Union Brigade made decisive cavalry charges but suffered heavy casualties. Sergeant Charles Ewart captured the Eagle and Standard of the French 45th Regiment. In commemoration the Eagle and title 'Waterloo' form part of the present cap badge. Ewart lies buried at Edinburgh Castle where the Eagle and Standard are on display at the Regimental Museum, and Ansdell's painting 'Fight for the Standard' hangs in the Great Hall.

In the Crimea, on 25 October 1854 the Greys provided two of the leading squadrons of the Heavy Brigade when 300 men successfully held back 3000 Russian Cavalry. For bravery at Balaclava Victoria Crosses were awarded to Sergeant-Major Grieve and Private Ramage. The third VC in the Regiment was awarded posthumously to Lieutenant Colonel Geoffrey Keyes MC who led the famous commando raid on Rommel's HQ in North Africa in 1941.

In the latter half of the 19th century the regiments saw service in the Indian Mutiny, Abyssinia, Afghanistan, Egypt and the Matabele War. All three were involved in the Boer War at the turn of the century, and suffered heavy casualties in the trenches during the Great War. The onset of the Second World War brought mechanisation, desert warfare and campaigns in Europe and the Far East. In 1941 the Scots Greys were the last Regular Cavalry to lose their horses, although a few Greys are retained today for ceremonial occasions.

During the battle for Imphal in Burma, on 13 April 1944, B Squadron 3rd Carabiniers with the 1st Dogra Regiment attacked Nunshigum, a hill vital to the security of the Allied Forces but held by the Japanese. All the Squadron officers were killed but Sergeant Major Craddock continued the attack to capture the position; he received the DCM. The 3rd Carabiniers provided the nucleus of the war-constituted 25th Dragoons and in 1947 were the last Regular Cavalry to leave India. Waterloo and Nunshigum are commemorated annually.

In 1894 Queen Victoria appointed Tsar Nicholas II Colonel-in-Chief of The Royal Scots Greys. He relinquished the appointment a year before his assassination in 1917. In 1895 The Tsar had received the Commanding Officer and three regimental representatives in St Petersburg, and his final homecoming and internment in 1998 was attended by a similar delegation. Although the Carabiniers were not similarly honoured, HM The Queen agreed to be Colonel-in-Chief of The Greys in 1953 and of The Royal Scots Dragoon Guards in 1971. Her Majesty's predecessors were HRH Prince Arthur of Connaught and HM King George VI.

1997 marked the fiftieth anniversary of the formation of the Greys Pipes and Drums. With the Military Band they achieved international fame through their rendering of 'Amazing Grace' which won several Gold discs. The Band of the Dragoon Guards now performs with the Pipes and Drums on ceremonial occasions. The pipers wear the Royal Stewart tartan, a privilege granted by King George VI; their feather bonnets have the distinctive yellow vandyke band and a white feather plume and the plaid brooch bears the White Horse of Hanover. The drummers wear scarlet tunics, blue overalls with yellow stripes and a white plume on their black bearskin – the traditional full-dress uniform of the Regiment. The bass drummer wears the unique white bearskin with a red plume over, also worn by the rider of the black Drum Horse, a gift from Her Majesty.

The Regiment maintains strong affiliations, forged during the Boer War with The Natal Carabineers and The 12th/16th Hunter River Lancers of Australia; later with The Windsor Regiment of Canada and The New Zealand Scottish. Similar ties exist with HMS Glasgow, The Scottish Yeomanry and several Cadet detachments. The Regiment recruits primarily from Scotland, although soldiers and officers from across the United Kingdom serve in The Royal Scots Dragoon Guards.

Before converting to an Armoured Regiment, squadrons and troops had deployed to Northern Ireland, Belize and the UN in Cyprus. The norm of postings between Germany and the UK was interrupted by the Gulf War; having deployed to Saudi Arabia with 1 Armoured Division in October 1990, this short conflict and decisive victory, achieved on 28 February, brought the battle honour 'Gulf 1991'. A short tour with the NATO Stabilisation Force in Bosnia followed in 1997. The Royal Scots Dragoon Guards, now under command of an Armoured Brigade, is part of The Royal Armoured Corps.

The long and frustrating wait for Challenger II finally ended in 1998. The Regiment enters the 21st Century with the world's best tank and an establishment of four sabre squadrons, to continue The Royal Scots Dragoon Guards (Carabiniers and Greys) tradition of being Second to None.

Above and Right, top: 'SCOTLAND FOR EVER!'
The charge of the 2nd Royal North British Dragoons (Scots Greys) took place at Waterloo when Lord Uxbridge, commander of the cavalry, ordered a charge to relieve the hard-pressed infantry at La Haye Sainte. A witness recalled that in front of them were the Highland Brigade who were ordered to wheel back, and the cavalry rushed through them: 'at the same time they huzzaed us, calling 'Scotland for ever!'

The French infantry could not withstand the charge, as they slashed about them with their long swords, and 6′ 4″ Sergeant Ewart captured the Eagle of the French 45th Regiment, the 'Invincibles'. But so carried away were the officers and men with their success that they were deaf to the trumpeter sounding the recall and galloped on, up the opposite side of the valley, under a hail of fire towards the French guns, annihilating the crews and everyone else in their path – until a counterattack by the French cavalry, as they attempted to return on their now blown horses, led to their being cut to pieces, reduced to little more than a squadron in number, only one man in three regaining his own lines.　　　　　LADY BUTLER

Gulf War – the moment of Victory, 28 February 1991, astride the Kuwait-Basra highway.

THE ROYAL DRAGOON GUARDS

The Royal Dragoon Guards formed on 1 August 1992 as a result of the amalgamation of the 4th/7th Royal Dragoon Guards and the 5th Inniskilling Dragoon Guards. As both these were in their turn the result of earlier amalgamations in the 1920s, The Royal Dragoon Guards now carries with it the traditions and history of four of the finest Regiments of the British Cavalry; the 4th Royal Irish Dragoon Guards, the 5th Dragoon Guards, the 6th Inniskilling Dragoons and the 7th Dragoon Guards. All four were raised between 1685 and 1689, during the protracted contest between James II and William of Orange for the English throne.

Both the 4th and 5th Dragoon Guards were formed in 1685 from Troops of Horse raised by James to defend London from William's expected invasion. The Regiments were originally known as Arran's Horse and Shrewsbury's Horse, taking the names from their Commanding Officers, as was the custom in those times. In the event, these Regiments, together with the rest of James's Army, refused to support him and he fled to France, abandoning the throne to William of Orange. The next year, however, still claiming the throne, he landed in Ireland. Only Carrickfergus, Londonderry and Enniskillen held out against him. The town of Enniskillen raised three Regiments from Protestants who had taken refuge there. One of these was Conyngham's Dragoons, which became the 6th Inniskilling Dragoons. On 11th June 1690, King William himself landed at Carrickfergus with a Protestant Army, which included both the 4th and 5th Dragoon Guards, and on the 1st July that year, all three Regiments earned their first battle honour, fighting side by side at the Battle of the Boyne. James was defeated and returned to France.

Back in England in 1688, Lord Devonshire raised six Troops of Horse to mark his support for the new Protestant King. Devonshire Horse, as they are known, became the 7th (Princess Royal's) Dragoon Guards. Within a few years they were to find themselves, together with the 5th Dragoon Guards, embarked for Holland and Marlborough's famous campaigns; both Regiments earning honours side by side at Blenheim, Malplaquet, Ramillies and Ouden-arde, as well as the celebrated cavalry action at Elixem in 1705 where the 5th Dragoon Guards captured four Standards from the Bavarian Horse Grenadiers.

In 1720, King George I conferred the Colonelcy of the 7th Dragoon Guards on Colonel John Ligonier. His influence was profound, and during his twenty nine year tenure, the Regiment was to reach a peak of discipline and training. It was at this time they acquired the nickname 'The Black Horse', and together with the 6th Inniskilling Dragoons, took part in the 1742 campaign in the War of the Austrian Succession, gaining further honours; Dettingen and Fontenoy. At Dettingen, Cornet Richardson of the 7th received thirty seven wounds whilst defending the Regimental Standard. This Standard, the oldest surviving in the Army, is held by this Museum. Little more than ten years later, the 6th and the 7th again found themselves marching side by side, this time through Paderborn to the Battle of Warburg, where both Regiments took part in the famous Cavalry Charge which won the day over the French for the Allied Forces under the Marquis of Granby.

All the while our two senior Regiments the 4th and the 5th, were languishing in Ireland, clocking up a total of some one hundred and eighty years joint service in that country. However, their moment was shortly to come. Both played a major role in Wellington's Peninsular campaign and gained honours including Salamanca, where the 5th Dragoon Guards captured the Staff of the Drum Major of the French 66th Infantry Regiment. This Staff is still carried today on parades by the Senior Regimental WO2. Colonel Sir William Pon-sonby, who commanded the Regiment at Salamanca, was later killed whilst leading the Union Brigade charge at Waterloo. The Inniskillings, who took part in this charge, were so praised by the Duke of Wellington that a statue of an Inniskilling Dragoon was erected on the Wellington Memorial in Hyde Park.

In 1854, the 4th, 5th and the 6th, who had last fought together at the Boyne, rode together again in the charge of the Heavy Brigade at Balaclava. In this action, eight hundred men, commanded by Major General J York-Scarlett, himself a past Commanding Officer of the 5th Dragoon Guards, utterly routed nearly three thousand five hundred of the Tsar's finest Cavalry, with minimal loss to themselves, and so demoralised the Russian horseman that they did not dare to follow up the subsequent disaster to the Light Brigade later that same day.

After the Crimean War came several years service at home and in India for all our parent Regiments. The peace time routine was broken briefly for the 4th and the 7th when in 1882, they took part in the short, but spectacularly successful campaign to defeat the forces of Arabi Pasha in Egypt. The campaign culminated in the battle of Tel El Kebir when an Egyptian Force of thirty eight thousand men and sixty guns was defeated with the loss of only fifty seven all ranks killed; the 4th and 7th Dragoon Guards escaping without a single casualty.

Such one sided success was not to be repeated, however, during the Boer War of 1899–1902, The 5th Dragoon Guards formed part of the force besieged at Ladysmith, whilst the 6th Inniskillings and the 7th 'Black Horse' earned

their spurs in innumerable skirmishes and many long patrols over the Veldt. Two Officers serving at that time were later to achieve world wide fame. Lieutenant Colonel Robert Baden-Powell, who commanded the 5th Dragoon Guards, was to put his South African experience to good use as the founder of the Boy Scout Movement, while Lieutenant L E G Oates, of the 6th Inniskilling Dragoons, became a legend of self sacrifice when, as a member of Scott's ill fated Antarctic Expedition of 1912, he chose to sacrifice himself rather than impede the progress of his comrades.

Both the 4th and the 5th Dragoon Guards saw action from the outset of the First World War. Indeed history allows C Squadron, the 4th Dragoon Guards the honour of the first action by the British Army in the War, with Corporal Thomas firing the first shot and Captain Hornby the first Officer to draw blood with his sword. Only a few days later the Commanding Officer of the 5th Dragoon Guards, Lieutenant Colonel G K Ansell, was killed in action at Nery. By October of that year both the Inniskillings and the 7th had arrived in France from India. All four Regiments spent the greater part of the next four years acting in the dismounted role, but the last weeks of the War found both the 5th Dragoon Guards and the 7th Dragoon Guards in action again on horseback; the 5th capturing or killing over seven hundred German troops when they attacked a troop train at Harbonniers, and the 7th claiming the last cavalry action of the War when they captured the town of Lessines at 10.55am on the 11th November 1918.

In 1922, the large reductions in the strength of the Army brought about widespread amalgamation of cavalry regiments. The 4th Royal Irish were combined with the 7th (Princess Royal's) Dragoon Guards to form the 4th/7th Royal Dragoon Guards, while the 5th and the 6th amalgamated to form, initially the 5th/6th Dragoons, but in 1927 this was changed to the 5th Inniskilling Dragoon Guards. 1938 brought about mechanisation for both Regiments, with both initially equipped with the 4½ ton two-man MK2 Light Tank.

Only one year after mechanisation came mobilisation and the start of World War 2. The two Regiments were the first armoured units to be deployed to France in support of the British Expeditionary Force, fighting side-by-side in the desperate but gallant withdrawal to Dunkirk. Both Regiments spent the next four years training and re-equipping with heavier tanks in preparation for the Normandy landings, and in 1940 a cadre of men from both Regiments was formed which was to be the nucleus of a newly raised Cavalry Regiment, the 22nd Dragoons. The 22nd Dragoons were disbanded after the war. On D-Day, the 4th/7th, equipped with specially waterproofed tanks, were the first British armour ashore in Normandy, the Skins following a few weeks later. The 4th/7th, as part of the Eighth Armoured Brigade, were the first tanks to cross the River Seine and led the rescue column to Arnhem. The Skins for their part were in almost continuous action from Normandy to the end of the War, taking part in the successful action to capture S-Hertogenbosch and the breakout from the Rhine bridgehead.

After the war, the 4th/7th were dispatched to Palestine to help in the peace keeping operations there. The Skins completed tours in Korea and the Suez Canal. Since the mid 1950s, both Regiments have served in the Middle East, Aden, England, Germany, Northern Ireland and Cyprus. The Royal Dragoon Guards, now equipped with Challenger, are stationed at Tidworth as part of 1st Mechanised Brigade, continuing a tradition of service that now runs over three hundred years.

4th Dragoon, 1914 *Right*: 7th Dragoon, 1845.

THE QUEEN'S ROYAL HUSSARS
(The Queen's Own and Royal Irish)

As the senior light Cavalry Regiment in the British Army, *The Queen's Royal Hussars* has a proud history and traditions dating back over 300 years. The amalgamation of *The Queen's Own Hussars* and the *Queen's Royal Irish Hussars* in 1993 has seen the strengths and abilities from both, forged together in the new Regiment.

The Queen's Own Hussars and the Queen's Royal Irish Hussars both sprang from the previous amalgamations of the four senior Light Cavalry Regiments; the 3rd, 4th, 7th & 8th Hussars. Their combined histories give the Regiment a magnificent tradition and powerful inspiration for those serving in our ranks today. Of the *172 Battle Honours* bestowed on those Regiments there is only room for 44 on the Guidon, a Cavalry Regiment's Colours; these honours spread across all the major Campaigns in which the British Army has fought over the past three centuries.

At the Battle of Dettingen in 1743, the last time a British King led his Army into battle, Trooper Thomas Brown of The 3rd The King's Own Hussars was the last man ever to be knighted in the field for bravery. He courageously recovered one of the Regiment's standards from the French Cavalry. An engraving of the time describes the sheer bravery of this Trooper: 'He had two horses killed under him, two fingers of ye bridle hand chopt off and after retaking the Standard from ye Gen D'Arms, whom he killed, he made his way through a line of the enemy exposed to fire and sword, in the execution of which he received 8 cuts in ye face head and neck, 2 balls lodged in his back, 3 went through his hat, and in this hack'd condition he rejoined his Regiment who gave him three Huzzas on his arrival' The 3rd, 4th & 7th Hussars all took part in the Duke of Wellington's Peninsula Campaign in the early 19th century and at the *Battle of Waterloo in 1815*, the 7th Hussars routed the French Imperial Guard. During the *Battle of Balaklava in 1854*, the 4th and 8th Hussars took part in what is now known to be the most famous of all Cavalry actions, the Charge of the Light Brigade. Here Private Samuel Parkes won a Victoria Cross for his courageous defence of the Trumpet Major from a hoard of Russian Cossacks. Both Dettingen and Balaklava are commemorated each year by the Regiment.

Winston Churchill joined the 4th Hussars in 1895 and has been justly called 'The greatest Hussar of all times'. He became the Colonel of the Regiment during World War 2 and remained so until his death in 1965. During the Regiment's distinguished history it has gained many unique privileges and traditions. After the Jacobite rebellion in 1745, the King absolved the Regiment from drinking the loyal toast saying that its loyalty was beyond question, a tradition which remains today. At the *Battle of Alamanara in 1710*, the 8th Hussars, or Dragoons as they were styled then, pursued the Spanish Cavalry and, equipping themselves with the crossbelts of the enemy, cut down the Spaniards' with their own swords. For many years after that day, the Regiment had the nickname 'St George's Crossbelts', and this is now reflected in the title of the Regimental journal, 'The Crossbelts'. In total, members of the former Regiments have been awarded 8 Victoria Crosses and hundreds of bravery and gallantry awards over the past 300 years. This is testimony to the calibre of soldier who has graced the ranks of our Regiments past and present, and makes us all proud to be a part of 'The Queen's Royal Hussars'.

This century the Regiments have been involved in all major campaigns. During the Great War, over 45 Battle Honours were awarded, and at Villiers-Faucon D Sqn of the 8th King's Royal Irish Hussars mounted the Regiment's last heroic Cavalry charge. By the Second World War all Cavalry Regiments had converted to armoured vehicles and action was seen in many countries. In North Africa the 3rd, 4th and 7th Hussars were all members of the famous 7th Armoured Division; the 'Desert Rats', and took part in heroic battles; *El Alamein* and the bitter struggle of *Sidi Rezegh* where the 7th Hussars halted the advance of 200 German Tanks. In 1950 the 8th Hussars were deployed to Korea where they were the first Armoured Regiment to use the new Centurion Main Battle Tank in combat. After the first amalgamations in 1958 the Regiment continued to serve in a variety of conflicts throughout the World. From Aden and Malaya in the 1960s to Cyprus and Northern Ireland in the 1970s. More recently, 'The Gulf 1991' and 'Wadi Al Batin' have been awarded as battle honours for the Regiment's part in leading the British forces advance onto Iraqi soil, in *Operation Desert Storm*. In January 1996, two armoured squadrons and Headquarter Squadron deployed to Bosnia as part of the British contingent of the Nato led Peace Implementation Force. For the outstanding contribution made under the spotlight of the world's media, the Regiment was granted the Canadian Forces Commendation, awarded for the first time to any unit since the Korean war. Setting the final seal on the latest amalgamation, and the final chapter in the Regiment's History to the end of the twentieth century, on June 13th 1997, our Colonel-in-Chief, Her Majesty Queen Elizabeth The Queen Mother, presented the Regiment with its new Guidon.

Shortly after returning from an operational tour in Northern Ireland, The Queen's Royal Hussars moved to Sennelager in Germany in August 1998 from Catterick in Northern Yorkshire, and received the new Challenger 2 Tank.

The Regiment's links for some 30 years with Birmingham were confirmed by granting of the Freedom of the City to The Queen's Own Hussars in May 1985, and reaffirmed on amalgamation in 1993. The West Midlands is the Regiment's primary recruiting area and the home of many of its members and ex-members. The Regiment also has close links with the Polish community through the Polish Ex Combatants' Association and has sporting ties with the West Midlands Police. Every year our historic link is celebrated by holding a reunion dinner on the evening before the Remembrance Sunday parade in the City Centre.

'MENTE ET MANU'

The varied life of the Regiment – October 1997 to March 1998, Northern Ireland.

Right, top: On 13 June 1997, The Colonel-in-Chief Her Majesty Queen Elizabeth The Queen Mother presented the new Regimental Guidon at Catterick, N. Yorkshire.

Right, Bottom: January to July 1996, Bosnia as part of NATO's IFOR, in a particularly devastated area in temperatures of – 28c.

PERKINS ENGINES COMPANY LTD

THE 9TH/12TH ROYAL LANCERS
(Prince of Wales's)

The 9th/12th Royal Lancers (Prince of Wales's) was formed at Tidworth in 1960 by the amalgamation of the 9th Queen's Royal Lancers and the 12th Royal Lancers (Prince of Wales's). Both Regiments first came into existence in the July of 1715 as a result of the revolt by the supporters of the Stuarts against the rule of King George I. The 9th first saw action in the rebel's defeat at Preston in November 1715, whilst the 12th escorted state prisoners to London.

In the following two hundred years the Regiments won battle honours in Italy (1793), Egypt (1801), the Peninsular Wars, the Buenos Aires campaign (1806), France, the Netherlands, India (1842–1857), the Afghan campaign (1879–1880), South Africa (1899–1902) and in both World Wars. In 1768 King George III conferred upon the 12th the honour of bearing the title 'The Twelfth or Prince of Wales's Regiment of Light Dragoons'. Whilst in 1783 the 9th became a light cavalry regiment becoming the 'The 9th Light Dragoons'. From 1789 to 1791 Lieutenant the Honourable Arthur Wellesley, later the Duke of Wellington, served in the 12th Lancers. It was not until 1793, on the declaration of war against France, when the 12th went on active service for the first time. They were sent to the Mediterranean, where some of them were present at the taking of Bastia in Corsica. The remainder sailed to Italy where they landed at Civita Vecchia in the Papal States. The good conduct of the 12th so impressed Pope Pius VI, that he received some of the officers at the Vatican and presented them with gold medals. He also gave the Regimental Hymns. In 1802 the 12th on returning from Egypt were honoured with the Royal Authority to bear, on its Guidons and Appointments, the Sphinx and 'Egypt', the 12th's first battle honour.

Both regiments underwent a major role change in the light of the success of the lancer regiments of Napoleon's Army. Lances proved dramatically effective in the pursuit of dispersed infantry. Therefore in 1816 an order was published, which directed the 9th and 12th Light Dragoons to be armed with the lance. After the Napoleonic wars both regiments achieved Royal recognition for their services. In 1817 the 12th became a royal regiment: the 12th or Prince of Wales's Royal Regiment of Lancers'. Whilst the on 23rd July 1830 the King directed that the 9th should assume the title of the '9th Queen's Royal Lancers'. The monogram of his Royal Consort, Queen Adelaide, still adorns the 9/12th Lancers' insignia today.

The 9th and 12th soon returned to active service, this time in India. During Indian Mutiny in 1857 the 9th won their title 'The Delhi Spearmen' bestowed upon them by the defeated mutineers. The Regiment was awarded twelve Victoria Crosses in this campaign. *The 'Last Patrol' painted by Beadle in 1905* represents the period of the South African campaign. Both regiments served there and took part in the Relief of Kimberley, and in the operations that led to Cronje's surrender. In the Great War 1914–18 both Regiments served on the Western Front. Today the Regiment celebrates Mons/Moy Day annually, which commemorates the last occasions, on which the two Regiments charged with the lance. On 28th August 1914 'C' Squadron of the 12th made a successful charge against the 2nd (Queen Victoria's Own) Prussian Dragoons. Whilst on the 7th September Lieutenant Colonel David Campbell charged at the head of two troops of B Squadron of the 1st Guard Dragoons. This was the only lance versus lance action of the Great War and is depicted by the *'Charge of the 9th Lancers' painted by Caton Woodville in 1931.*

Between the wars both Regiments faced a major cultural change with the advent of armoured warfare and the demise of the horse, as a fighting platform. In 1928 while serving in Egypt the 12th converted to armoured cars, whilst the 9th became a light tank regiment in 1936. Subsequently, on 10 May 1940, as an armoured regiment, the 12th was the first regiment to cross the Belgian Frontier and covered the withdrawal of the British Expeditionary Force. In his despatches Lord Gort wrote, 'Without the Twelfth Lancers only a small part of the Army would have reached Dunkirk'. Both Regiments served with the 8th Army throughout the North African and Italian campaigns. The 9th played a leading part in the Battle of Alamein and the 12th were the first British troops to link up with the Americans in Tunisia in April 1943. Both Regiments were employed as infantry during the winter of 1944 and fought the length of Italy during the final stages of the war. In the post-war period both served in Palestine, Malaya, Germany, Cyprus, Northern Ireland and Aden.

On the 11th September 1960, the 9th and 12th marched, for the last time as independent regiments, to the Garrison Church at Tidworth. As a plaque records in the church 'Here on 11th September, 1960, 9th/12th Royal Lancers (Prince of Wales's) was formed by 9th Queen's Royal Lancers and 12th Royal Lancers (Prince of Wales's) coming together before God. It is not the beginning but the continuing of the same until it be thoroughly finished which yieldeth the true glory'. Shortly after its formation, the 9th/12th Royal Lancers moved to Northern Ireland where both its parents had started their careers almost two hundred and fifty years before.

Over the next 38 years the Regiment moved periodically between bases in the UK and Germany, from where it has sent troops, squadrons and on occasions the Regimental Headquarters, to numerous areas of conflict in many parts of the world. The Regiment has served in Cyprus (between 1987 and 1991), on Operation GRANBY during the Gulf War, Bosnia (the first UN troops 'up-country' in 1992, the last in 1995 and again in 1998 but this time as NATO troops), Belize and Northern Ireland. Moreover, individual members of the Regiment have served in many far-flung places such as Africa and even as far away as New Zealand.

Another major role change took place, this time in 1976 when the Regiment retrained to the reconnaissance role. Their primary role is to provide accurate and timely information on the terrain and enemy; the 'eyes and ears' of a division or corps. This is achieved either on foot or mounted in light weight (approximately 8–10 tonnes), tracked vehicles called Combat Vehicle Reconnaissance (Tracked) (CVR(T)). The Regiment is organized into five squadrons. The largest, Headquarters Squadron, deals with logistics, which provides the four 'sabre' squadrons with essential logistical and administrative support both in camp and in the field. A 'sabre' squadron is made up of several constituent parts. The headquarters is based on two command vehicles (called Sultans). It has 3 Sabre troops of four vehicles (Scimitars), each armed with a 30mm cannon. It has four anti-tank guided missile launchers (Strikers) and four armoured personnel carriers (Spartans, which carry the squadron's own assault pioneers). It also has an armoured ambulance (a Samaritan) and a repair and recovery section, equipped with Samsons. The Regiment is about 500 strong, with men and women attached from the Royal Electrical and Mechanical Engineers, Royal Logistics Corps (RLC) and Adjutant General's Corps (AGC), all of whom play an integral and vital part in the successful working of the Regiment.

The Regiment's home headquarters are in Leicester and it recruits from Leicestershire, Derbyshire, Northamptonshire, Cambridgeshire, Bedfordshire, Hertfordshire, London and Essex. At present the Regiment is based in Swanton Morley in Norfolk, as a Formation Reconnaissance Regiment, providing the county with its first regular Army unit for many years.

Halt! The 12th Lancers.   ERNEST CROFTS

'The Empty Saddle', South African campaign.

Top: The Charge of The 9th Lancers, 7 September 1914 – the only Lance versus Lance action of the Great War.

CATON WOODVILLE

THE KING'S ROYAL HUSSARS

The King's Royal Hussars was formed by the amalgamation of The Royal Hussars (Prince of Wales's Own) and the 14th/20th King's Hussars on 4 December 1992. The Regiment is a Type 50-Armoured regiment equipped with the Challenger Main Battle Tank. It is stationed at York Barracks, Munster, Germany as part of the 4th Armoured Brigade. Since its formation the Regiment has exercised in Canada at the British Army Training Unit Suffield and in Poland. It completed a six-month operational tour in Northern Ireland in 1994 and went to Bosnia in June 1997 as part of the Stabilisation Force.

The Regiment recruits primarily from the counties of Buckinghamshire, Berkshire, Gloucestershire, Hampshire, Oxfordshire, Wiltshire, the Isle of Wight, the Channel Islands, Lancashire, Greater Manchester and Cumbria.

The Royal Hussars (PWO) was formed on 25 October 1969 by the amalgamation of the 10th Royal Hussars (Prince of Wales's Own) and the 11th Hussars (Prince Albert's Own).

The 10th was raised as Gore's Dragoons at the time of the First Jacobite Rebellion in 1715. They subsequently saw service in the Second Jacobite Rebellion in 1745 and then during the Seven Years War in Germany. In 1783 the Regiment changed its title to the 10th Light Dragoons (Prince of Wales's Own) by command of King George III who appointed his son, the then Prince of Wales, as Colonel. In 1806 the Prince of Wales clothed and equipped the Regiment as Hussars – thus making them the first Hussar regiment in the British Army. In 1808 the Regiment landed at Corunna and distinguished itself in the ensuing campaign of the Peninsular War. In 1815 it was Captain Grey's patrol that brought news of the Prussian retreat at Wavre, thus influencing the Duke of Wellington to fight at Waterloo. Throughout the rest of the 19th Century the Regiment saw service in the Crimea, Sudan, Afghanistan and in the South African War. During the First World War, the Regiment fought in France and Belgium, and in the Second World War served in North Africa and up through Italy. Thereafter the Regiment served in England, Jordan, the Arabian Peninsular and Germany.

The 11th was raised in 1715 as Honywood's Dragoons, and also saw service in both the First and Second Jacobite Rebellions. As with the 10th, they next saw action during the Seven Years War. Under the Duke of Wellington, the Regiment saw action in the Peninsular War, traditionally earning the name 'Cherrypickers' for an action in an orchard. Later at Waterloo they captured the last French guns in action.

In 1840, the Regiment escorted Prince Albert of Saxe-Coburg from Dover to Canterbury before his marriage to Queen Victoria. Impressed by their smartness, Prince Albert requested that the Regiment should henceforth be called the 11th Prince Albert's Own Hussars, and should wear his crimson livery trousers, which survive to this day. During the Crimean War, the Regiment played a prominent part at Balaklava in the Charge of the Light

Brigade. From 1856, the Regiment served in England, Ireland, India, Abyssinia and South Africa. For the duration of the First World War, the Regiment fought dismounted in Flanders.

In 1928 the Regiment became the first Cavalry Regiment to be mechanised. During the Second World War they saw distinguished service in the Desert Campaign and in NorthWest Europe. Thereafter the Regiment served in Malaya, Northern Ireland, Aden, Kuwait and Germany.

Following formation in 1969 The Royal Hussars (PWO) saw service in Cyprus, Hong Kong, Belize, BAOR, Canada and Northern Ireland. In 1983 they became the first regiment to receive the Challenger Main Battle Tank. In early 1990, following a short period at Tidworth, D Squadron was detached to Cyprus while the remainder of the Regiment moved to Munster, Germany, where it remained until amalgamation in 1992.

The 14th/20th King's Hussars were formed on 1 October 1922 by the amalgamation of the 14th (King's) Hussars and 20th Hussars.

The 14th was raised as Dormer's Dragoons in 1715 to combat the First Jacobite Rebellion. Following the Second Jacobite Rebellion in 1745, the Regiment was subsequently employed on internal security duties in Ireland for the greater part of the 18th century. Perhaps the period of greatest achievement for the 14th was the 6-year Peninsular War in Portugal and Spain. The 14th gained a reputation second to none as Light Cavalry, and were particularly highly thought of by the Duke of Wellington who did not always have kind things to say about the British Cavalry. The Officers Mess still has a silver chamber pot that a patrol of the 14th removed from the carriage of Napoleon's brother (Joseph, King of Spain) after Vittoria in 1813. The 14th played a major role in the Sikh Wars 1846–49 and in the invasion of Persia in 1857, following which the Regiment returned to India and operated with conspicuous success against rebels in the Indian Mutiny. Following the South African War, where the Regiment was heavily involved, the 14th served in Mesopotamia and Persia from 1915–19.

The 20th, originally raised in Inniskilling in 1759, served only in wartime until 1862, and being a junior regiment was subjected to a number of disbandments after each successive conflict. In 1861 it was re-raised from European Cavalry in the service of the East India Company and saw action in Sudan and South Africa. The 20th were also actively involved in the First World War, seeing the majority of their service in France and Flanders. They then took part in operations against Turkish Nationalists in Ismid in 1920 where they carried out the last regimental cavalry charge in British military history.

After formation in 1922 and mechanisation in 1938, the 14th/20th King's Hussars found itself in India at the outbreak of the Second World War. It formed the spearhead for the invasion of Persia in 1941, and remained in the Middle Eastern theatre until the end of 1944 when it joined the British 8th

PAUL C. R. WATES

Army in Italy. On 16 April 1945 the Regiment, with the Gurkhas, took by assault the strongly fortified town of Medicina. Since the Second World War the Regiment has carried out every conceivable role including active operations in Cyprus, Northern Ireland and the Middle East. In 1988, following a short period at Catterick, a squadron (B followed by C) was detached to Berlin while the remainder of the Regiment moved to Munster where it remained until amalgamation in 1992. During the Gulf War 1990–91 the Regiment equipped with Challenger Main Battle Tanks, played a leading part in the land offensive to force the Iraqi Army out of Kuwait.

The Regiment has 2 museums and they are located as follows:

The King's Royal Hussars Museum
Peninsula Barracks
Winchester
Hants
SO23 8TS

14TH/20TH King's Hussars
Museum of Lancashire
Stanley Street
Preston, Lancashire
PR1 4YP

Left and Above: The Kosovo crisis – The Regiment's Challenger Tanks arrive and deploy in Macedonia, March 1999.

Top: An earlier more peaceful visit to Bosnia. Members of the Regiment using horses in the difficult terrain, befriend the locals – including the horse on the left. September 1997.

THE LIGHT DRAGOONS

Formerly the 13th/18th Royal Hussars (Queen Mary's Own) and 15th/19th The King's Royal Hussars.

'It is right to have some cavalry to support and assist infantry, but not to look upon them as the main force of an army, for they are highly necessary to reconnoitre, to scour roads . . . and to lay waste an enemy's country, and to cut off their convoys; but in the field battles which commonly decide the fate of nations, they are fitter to pursue an enemy that is routed and flying, than anything else'.

MACHIAVELLI, *The Art of War*

When the Northern Light Horse, formed from the bands of cattle reivers and drovers of the Scottish borders, swept up a hillside in France in 1544 in a demonstration of their speed and manoeuvrability, Charles V, the Holy Roman Emperor, was said to have cried out with honest delight. Three hundred years later another foreign observer, the French General Bosquet, said of the Light Brigade's advance towards the Russian guns at Balaklava, *'C'est magnifique'*. Light cavalry have always excited admiration, even if their exploits have sometimes justified Bosquet's qualification, *'mais ce n'est pas la guerre'*.

The word 'dragoon' derives from the French *dragon*, a short musket, or carbine, which suggested a fire-spouting dragon. It was carried in the middle of the sixteenth century by Marshal de Brissac's mounted foot, who seem to have been the first to be called dragoons. Dragoons were really infantry. Their horses were meant to carry them from place to place: dragoons were not supposed to fight from their horses, but to dismount and use musket and bayonet. The 13th Dragoons were raised in 1715 to fight in the first Jacobite rebellion.

The Army at this time had no mounted light troops. The French had had their hussars since the seventeenth century, and it was becoming obvious that this deficiency needed remedying. In 1756, at the outbreak of the Seven Years' War with France, and under threat of invasion, a light troop was added to eleven regiments of dragoons. Each man in the troop wore a jockey's cap and boots and was expected to carry out his task mounted, unlike the rest of the regiment. Three years later, as the war intensified, six whole regiments of light dragoons were raised, of which the first was the Fifteenth, or 'Eliott's Light Horse' after their colonel, George Augustus Eliott. In 1760 Eliott's Light Horse were sent out to Germany, and in July at Emsdorf, near Kassel, this new regiment astonished the veterans by charging three times against formed French infantry, routing them completely. At a stroke the 15th Light Dragoons had restored the cavalry's reputation, lost almost irretrievably at Minden the previous year when an incompetent commander had sat idly by while the infantry did the fighting. The brilliant affair at Emsdorf confirmed the value of light dragoons, and was the first time an action was recognized as a battle honour.

Meanwhile in Ireland, another regiment of light dragoons was being raised at Moore Abbey, Kildare – seat of Charles Moore, Sixth Earl of Drogheda. They were numbered 'Nineteen' and known as Drogheda's Light Horse, but in 1762 they were renumbered 'Eighteen'. Increasingly, too, light dragoons were referred to as 'hussars', reflecting their scouting and raiding role. The word *hussar* itself is sometimes rather fancifully believed to derive from the Hungarian *husz*, 'twenty', because at one time in Hungary one cavalry soldier used to be levied from every twenty families. However, the word probably entered the Hungarian language from the Italian *corsaro* – a pirate or freebooter. 'Properly speaking,' maintained one senior French officer, 'hussars are little more than bandits on horseback'.

After Emsdorf, light dragoons became very much the mode with the War Office. Regiments were raised and then disbanded shortly afterwards when the immediate need was past. In 1779 the number 'Nineteen' was again seen in the line: the 19th Light Dragoons were raised, together with four other light dragoon regiments, largely because the revolutionary war in America was going badly for Britain. However, they were disbanded four years later when Britain recognized American independence and concluded a peace. The 23rd Light Dragoons remained after this 1783 contraction because they had been raised specifically for service with the Honourable East India Company and had arrived in Madras only the previous year. In 1786 the War Office renumbered this regiment 'Nineteen'. So by this year, all the regiments of the present-day Light Dragoons were wearing the blue jackets and fur-fringed caps of the light cavalry because, in 1783, the Thirteenth were converted from heavy to light dragoons.

Throughout the latter part of the eighteenth century the four regiments saw their share of service in some of the most punishing of climes – notably India and the West Indies – and were frequently in action. The Nineteenth gained a unique cavalry battle honour in India – at *Assaya* in the Mahratta Wars, the battle of which the Duke of Wellington, commanding the East India Company's forces, always said he was most proud. The Fifteenth and the Eight-

eenth distinguished themselves in the Duke of York's infamous campaigns in the Low Countries in the 1790s. But it was during the war with Bonaparte in the Iberian Peninsula, from 1808 to 1814 (and afterwards at Waterloo), that the regiments really came of age. After the Peninsula, light cavalry was confirmed as an indispensable arm, principally for reconnaissance. However, Parliament was seeking economies, and when this 'never ending war' was over, the Eighteenth and the Nineteenth were disbanded – only to be re-raised, forty years later, at the height of Victorian imperial expansion.

The nineteenth century saw the regiments travelling the globe – India, Canada, South Africa, Egypt and the Sudan. One of them, the Thirteenth, had to endure the Crimean War, and was in the front rank of the Light Brigade at Balaklava in 1854 when Lord Cardigan led the futile charge at the Russian guns. They lost a great many men and horses but gained immortality as one of the regiments of 'the noble six hundred' in Tennyson's celebrated poem *The Charge of the Light Brigade*.

The century ended with all four regiments (by now officially retitled *Hussars*) in South Africa in conflict with the Boer settlers. The Second Boer War, from 1899 to 1902, came as a profound shock to the Army, where its organization and tactics were found wanting. In the decade that followed, however, huge reforms were made: horsemastership improved, as did shooting and field training generally. By the time that the Great War broke out, in August 1914, the Army was probably in the highest state of efficiency that it had ever been. Three of the regiments were in action at once with the British Expeditionary Force (BEF) in Belgium and France, and were soon joined there by the 13th Hussars. Arguably, it was the BEF that tipped the balance and slowed the German advance – the much vaunted Schlieffen Plan – so that the Anglo-French counter-attack at the Marne was able to prevent France's being over-run. For the rest of the war the regiments endured life on the Western Front with continual losses, sometimes acting as infantry in the trenches. In 1916 the Thirteenth went to Mesopotamia with the Indian Cavalry Corps to take part in the campaign to eject the Turks, and saw some hard fighting both on foot and on horseback. Finally, in 1918, the long ordeal of the 15th, 18th and 19th Hussars ended when they joined the great counter-offensive that finally knocked Germany out of the war.

It was perhaps not surprising that after the war (just as after Waterloo) the government should seek economies. Disbandments and amalgamations took place throughout the Army, and the cavalry was reduced by a third, the later-raised regiments being amalgamated. So it was that the 13th and the 18th were coupled, and the 15th and the 19th. In the inter-war years they served in the Middle East and India, still with their horses, until, in 1938, the process of mechanization caught them up. When the Second World War broke out the following year, the two regiments found themselves in the same role as in 1914 – reconnaissance troops for the BEF. This time, however, they were mounted in fast, light tanks. But unlike 1914, the Anglo-French forces were unable to halt the German *'Blitzkrieg'*, and the BEF was evacuated via Dunkirk. For the next four years the regiments trained for the liberation of Europe, and were latterly equipped with the remarkable swimming variant of the tank – the 'DD' (duplex drive). The 13th/18th were among the first troops to hit the Normandy beaches, their DDs having swum nearly three miles in the choppy waters of the Channel after launching from their landing crafts.

In the 1950s and 60s both regiments, their ranks filled largely by National Servicemen, fought the Communist insurgency in Malaya. Then it was Northern Ireland, and its almost insatiable demand for troops to patrol, guard and observe. And throughout this time, NATO maintained its deterrent presence in Western Germany. Germany was, indeed, both regiments' real home: by the end of the 'Cold War', when the Berlin Wall came down and Germany was unified, the 13th/18th and the 15th/19th Hussars had, between them, since the end of the war, spent over half a century on the north German plain.

At the end of the Cold War – as at the end of the Napoleonic Wars and the end of the Great War – there were expectations of a 'peace dividend'. And it soon became clear that the dividend was not going to be paid to the Army. Consequently there was a further round of amalgamations, the Royal Armoured Corps reducing by about 40%. Shotgun marriages were hastily arranged throughout the Army, but the 13th/18th Royal Hussars (Queen Mary's Own)

PROCTER & GAMBLE

Elliots Light Horse *Top*: D-Day, 6 June 1944, 13th/18th lead the assault on Queen Beach, Normandy.

and 15th/19th The King's Royal Hussars proposed to each other, both regiments having recruiting areas in the north of England (South Yorkshire and Humberside, and East Yorkshire, Cleveland, Durham and Northumberland respectively). The 'wedding' took place in Hohne, Germany, on 1st December 1992, and has been remarkably happy. One of the reasons, perhaps, is that the 'honeymoon' – a very extended one – has been spent in Bosnia. Indeed, the regiment has had a virtually continuous presence in that unhappy country almost from the first deployment of British troops there. There is nothing like active service to put things into proper perspective.

Why the name *Light Dragoons* for the new regiment? The historical roots are obvious, but it was also a conscious effort not to try to condense old titles – for this was, indeed, to be a new regiment, not merely the remnants of the two older ones. But the Light Dragoons, although they have already established themselves independently as an armoured reconnaissance regiment of great professionalism, still derive enormous pride and inspiration from their forebears' history – the *dash, panache, elan* of light cavalry. 'There was much smartness in these light dragoons,' wrote the British Army's greatest historian, Sir John Fortescue, of the first light cavalrymen. There still is.

THE QUEEN'S ROYAL LANCERS

16th The Queen's Lancers

The Regiment was raised in 1759 as the 16th Light Dragoons by Lieutenant Colonel Burgoyne.

The 16th Light Dragoons received their baptism of fire in 1761 against the French at Bellisle, an island off the North West coast of France. Between 1761 and 1815 the Regiment fought in all major wars; The American War of Independence 1766, the War of the French Revolution 1793, the Peninsular War 1809 – 1814 (in which no less than six battle honours were gained) and the Battle of Waterloo.

In 1816, as a result of experiences in the Napoleonic wars, the 16th were armed and equipped as a Lancer Regiment. In 1822 they went to India and were the first Regiment to use the Lance in action, at the capture of Bhurtpore. In 1833 the Regiment's uniform was changed from blue to red hence the nickname 'The Scarlet Lancers'. The 16th stayed in India until 1846, taking part in the Battle of Aliwal on 28th January 1846. In this battle the Regiment took a very active part, suffered heavy casualties, and performed many acts of gallantry. The Battle of Aliwal has been commemorated ever since and this is the reason why the Regiment's Lance Pennons are crimped to this day (after the Battle they appeared to be crimped from being so thickly encrusted with blood).

After further service in England and India the 16th went to the South African war in 1900 and served throughout the campaign returning to England in 1904.

In 1905, His Majesty King Alfonso of Spain was appointed Colonel-in-Chief of the Regiment. By 1909 the Regiment had been awarded 18 Battle Honours, the largest number of any Cavalry Regiment in the Army.

In the First World War the Regiment served continuously in France and Flanders in the 3rd Cavalry Brigade which was at first commanded by Brigadier (later General) H de la Gough, himself a 16th Lancer. It is of note that Field Marshal Robertson, who enlisted in the 16th Lancers as a trooper, was CIGS.

17th Lancers

The history of this Regiment begins in the year 1759 with the War against the French in Canada. The English force was under the overall command of General Wolfe, one of whose commanding officers was a Lieutenant Colonel Hale of the 47th of Foot.

The conclusive action in this campaign was the storming of the heights of Quebec. General Wolfe was mortally wounded during this battle, but before he died he gave Colonel Hale the task of carrying the news of his victory back to the King, as reward for the outstanding part that the officer had played in the action.

When he arrived in England, he was 'well received by the King', who, as a mark of his gratitude, commissioned Colonel Hale to raise a regiment of Cavalry. Thus, on 7th November 1759 the 17th Light Dragoons were born. As a lasting mark of respect for General Wolfe, and in memory of his victory at Quebec, Colonel Hale chose a Death's Head emblazoned with the words 'or Glory' as the new Regiment's principal distinction. The Regiment, recruiting primarily in Hertfordshire, was soon up to strength of 678 rank and file.

The Regiment served in Ireland from 1765, and it was from there that they embarked as the first Cavalry Regiment to be deployed to the American War of Independence. After eight years of fighting, in which the 17th distinguished themselves in this their first campaign, they returned once again to Ireland.

On 25 October 1854, the Regiment formed part of the ill fated Charge of the Light Brigade. The 17th Lancers under Captain William Morris were on the left flank of the charge, the Russian guns were overrun at the cost of 107 dead and wounded from the original 145 that charged. The Regiment earned three VCs in that action.

In 1856 the Regiment deployed to India to help put down the mutiny led by Tantia Topi; in 1879, the 17th Lancers destroyed the Zulu Impis at the battle of Ulundi, who as a result never took to the field again.

From 1900 to 1902 the Regiment fought in the Boer War. The most famous fight was C Squadron's stand at Moderfontien Farm against a force led by J C Smuts. The Lancers were wiped out almost to a man but distinguished themselves by their fortitude and discipline.

Throughout the First World War the Regiment lived close behind the front lines and were employed either dismounted or in trenches or digging new defensive lines and always training for the long awaited breakthrough. In March and April 1918 the 17th formed part of the 5th Army, and at long last, some opportunities arose for mounted cavalry actions.

In June 1922 the 17th Lancers were amalgamated with the 21st Lancers to form the 17th/21st Lancers.

5th Royal Irish Lancers

The Regiment was raised in 1689 as Wynne's Regiment of Enniskilling Dragoons and first saw action in Ireland the next year at the Battle of the Boyne. In 1694 the Regiment took part in the Flanders campaign, but saw little action and returned to Ireland in 1698. In 1704 the title was changed to The Royal Dragoons of Ireland. The same year saw the Regiment back in Europe with Marlborough's Army for the war of the Spanish Succession, taking part in all four major battles; Blenheim 1704, Ramillies 1706, Oudenarde 1708 and Malpaquet 1709, all of which were awarded as Battle Honours. From 1715 to 1798 the Regiment was stationed continuously in Ireland where it was disbanded in 1799. In 1858 the Regiment was re-raised as the 5th Royal Irish Lancers.

The 5th saw service in England, Egypt and India before going to South Africa in 1898. They took part in the South African War, particularly distinguishing themselves at the Battle of Elandslaagte in 1899.

21st Lancers

The 21st 'Light Dragoons' were first raised in 1760. The Regiment was subsequently disbanded and raised for different campaigns, with their history really starting with the Indian Mutiny in 1858, and leading to their greatest hour in the Sudan.

The first encounter with the Dervish masses occurred at Omdurman in September 1898 where the famous charge of the 21st Lancers took place. Three VCs were won that day by the Regiment and the Dervishes were defeated soon after.

As a result of this action the Regiment was awarded the title of 'Empress of India's' by Queen Victoria and was allowed to return to their French grey facings which had unpopularly been replaced by scarlet ones.

In 1921, having returned to England from France, the Regiment was reduced to one squadron and then in June 1922 amalgamated with two squadrons of the 17th Lancers to form the 17th/21st Lancers.

16th/5th The Queen's Royal Lancers

In 1922 the amalgamation of the 16th and 5th Lancers was announced. The 5th were to form one squadron of the 16th/5th Lancers, as the Regiment was to be called. The newly-formed Regiment served in Egypt, India, England and Scotland between the two World Wars, being in India at the outbreak of the Second World War in 1939. The Regiment returned to England late in that year to be mechanised. They were Brigaded with the 17th/21st Lancers and the Lothian and Border Horse; the three Regiments remained together throughout the war.

In the autumn of 1942 the Regiment went to North Africa and took part in the Tunisian campaign with the 6th Armoured Divison. The 16th/5th took part in both battles for Cassino and during the winter of 1944/45 fought as infantry in the Apennines, in Northern Italy. They took part in the final battle of the Po Valley and advanced further west than any other Regiment of the 8th Army, linking up with the Americans and South Africans of the 5th Army.

In June 1947 Her Royal Highness Princess Elizabeth was appointed Colonel-in-Chief of the 16th/5th Lancers.

It was in 1954 that the Regiment was designated 16th/5th The Queen's Royal Lancers. In the same year the old collar badge was replaced by the combined badge – known as The Queen's Badge.

Since the last war the Regiment has served in Egypt, Germany, Aden, Bahrain, Hong Kong, Cyprus, Northern Ireland, Denmark, Italy, Turkey and the Gulf. During the Gulf War the Regiment was the 1st Armoured Division's Medium Reconnaissance Regiment, and as a result led the Division into both Iraq and Kuwait.

17th/21st Lancers

In 1938 the Regiment became mechanised whilst stationed in India. At the outbreak of war it returned to England. The next two years were spent training in the armoured role. In October 1942 the Regiment deployed with Valentine tanks to North Africa as part of the 6th Armoured Divison, where it was brigaded with the 16th/5th Lancers.

At Fondouk, the Regiment was ordered to clear the pass 'at all costs'. This mission was successfully achieved. The strength of the German position, however, meant the loss of 80% of the Regiment's tanks and many lives.

At the 'Cap Bon' peninsula, the Germans were trying a Dunkirk style withdrawal of their remaining forces. The 17th/21st Lancers successfuly outflanked the position which finally broke the remaining defences.

 TI GROUP plc

Top: 'The Scarlet Lancers', the 16th charge at the Battle of Aliwal, January 1846.

Bottom: Challenger Tanks of the Regiment exercise in Canada.

In the spring of 1945 the Regiment was equipped with new Sherman tanks and played an important part in the Italian campaign eventually leading to the capture of San Agostino.

Between the end of the war and 1948 the Regiment was used as an occupying and peace keeping force in Austria, Greece, and, finally, Palestine, where it again saw active service.

During the last thirty years the Regiment has served in Hong Kong, Aden, Borneo, Cyprus, Northern Ireland and England, with tours spread over several locations in Germany and other parts of Europe. During the Gulf war troops from the Regiment were attached to the Royal Scots Dragoon Guards and the Queen's Royal Irish Hussars.

The Queen's Royal Lancers

Following amalgamation in 1993, the new Regiment established themselves in barracks in Germany, before commencing an extensive programme of exercises and training.

The final parade of the Regimental Band of The Queen's Royal Lancers took place on 11th July 1994 at Osnabrück.

From December 1994 to June 1995 the Regiment deployed to Cyprus along the central 30 kilometres of the United Nations buffer zone, which included the divided city of Nicosia. The task was a delicate one which called for a detailed knowledge of the two cease fire lines and the cease fire agreements combined with diplomacy, skilled and persuasive negotiation, patience, robustness, determination and a good sense of humour.

Other areas of training and operations included Canada, Poland, Bosnia and live firing on the US Army ranges in southern Germany.

The Regiment maintains a high standard of readiness and has received the latest main battle tank Challenger II.

THE ROYAL TANK REGIMENT

The story of the Royal Tank Regiment is one of struggle, triumph and achievement. Its origins are a mere three-quarters of a century old, back in the days when the soldiers on the Western Front were faced with the full horrors of static trench warfare, in which the artillery shell and the machine gun bullet inflicted horrendous casualties. Warfare had ground to a bloody halt whilst both sides searched desperately for a weapon system that would break the deadlock. The British were the first to achieve this technological breakthrough. The tank, with its vital characteristics of firepower, protection and mobility, was born and mechanised forces slowly began to emerge as a dominant factor in battle. Tanks would go on to reaffirm their position as the decisive weapon of the all arms team in all the major operational theatres during the Second World War and in nearly every major conflict thereafter, up to and including the recent Gulf War.

The present Royal Tank Regiment, composed of two regular regiments, the First and the Second, is the direct heir of the original armoured pioneers, who in 1914, manned the first armoured cars in the Naval Brigade and RNAS squadrom, which augmented the British Expeditionary Force in the defence of Antwerp, when their wheeled lightly armoured vehicles brought a new dimension to ground combat. However, with the onset of trench warfare, the Western Front ground to a halt and the armoured cars were withdrawn to be used thereafter in the Middle East. They would emerge again towards the end of the war when, for example, the 17th (Armoured Car) Battalion of the Tank Corps led the triumphant march across the Rhine.

Meanwhile, the first tanks had been produced in 1915. They were to be manned by the volunteers of the Tank Detachment, based upon the Armoured Car Section of the Motor Machine Gun Service, based at Siberia Camp near Bisley. Six companies of volunteers would be raised for what was described as being an '... exceedingly dangerous and hazardous duty of a secret nature.' Now called 'The Heavy Section', they first saw action at Flers on the Somme, on 15 September 1916. It was about this action that the British press printed the famous headline: 'A tank is walking up the High Street of Flers with the British Army cheering behind.' The tank was D17 (Dinnaken) and belonged to 'E' Company, later to become the 5th Royal Tank Regiment.

The six Heavy Branch companies were expanded to form tank battalions, then renamed the Tank Corps in 1917. During these early days they were used only in small numbers, often on exceptionally difficult terrain and did not realise their true potential. Then at dawn on 20th November 1917, just south of Cambrai, 476 heavy tanks of the Tank Corps, led by Brigadier Hugh Elles, advanced against the German positions penetrating the Hindeburg Line and achieving the most rapid advance of the war. So successful was this action initially, that the church bells were rung throughout Great Britain and 'Cambrai Day' became the Regiment's yearly day of celebration.

From then on the Tank Corps went from strength to strength, so that by December 1918, there were 26 Battalions, eighteen of which were serving in France, whilst a detachment of the Corps had served with Allenby at Gaza in Palestine in 1917. One leading German historian was so impressed by the power of the new weapon that he wrote that Germany had been beaten: '... not by the genius of Marshal Foch, but by "General Tank."' Just after the end of the war, the tank again showed its power, when a *single* British-manned tank, one of three small tank detachments sent to Russia to support the White Russians against the Bolsheviks, captured the *entire* 40,000 strong garrison of Tsaritsin – later called Stalingrad, a feat which an entire German tank army could not achieve in the Second World War!

Postwar saw cuts in all sectors of the Army and the re-emergence of the 'anti-mechanisation' lobby, which almost led to the abolition of the Tank Corps, so that by 1920, it had been reduced to a Depot and four battalions. Nevertheless, its future was secured by the granting of the prefix 'Royal' in 1923, by HM King George V, our Colonel-in-Chief since 1918. In addition the Royal Tank Corps (RTC) provided some twelve armoured car – later light tank – companies in Ireland, Iraq, Persia, Palestine, China, Egypt and India between the wars. From 1928, as mechanisation inevitably increased, the RTC began training the cavalry to man the armoured fighting vehicles (AFV), which had up to then been their entire responsibility.

When the Royal Armoured Corps was formed in April 1939 by 'merging' the Cavalry of the Line with the Tanks, the RTC changed its title to: 'Royal Tank Regiment (RTR)' and from then on was committed to a massive expansion. Between 1935–1938 it had expanded to form eight regular and six TA battalions, now the TA element was doubled and more wartime battalions formed, so that by the end of World War II there were 24 RTR Regiments, which had seen active service all over the world in *every* theatre of operations. The armoured battle group, led by the tank, was undoubtedly now the prime battle-winner and the RTR had played a major role in its success.

Postwar, the reductions inevitably again came thick and fast. The regular regiments were reduced to eight, then to four and now to two, whilst the TA regiments were axed completely. Nevertheless, the Regiment has seen active service in Aden, Borneo, Malaya, Egypt, Cyprus, Korea, Northern Ireland and the Gulf, mainly in the armoured reconnaissance role (and the dismounted role in Northern Ireland), whilst other RTR units have been stationed in Germany, Lybia, Hong Kong and Great Britain.

The Royal Tank Regiment now faces the future with pride and determination, living up to its motto 'FEAR NAUGHT', having been the first regiment of the British Army to embrace the challenging new role of NBC reconnaissance, whilst retaining its tank roots by manning the latest British main battle tank – Challenger 2.

Former Tank Regiment Chelsea Pensioner beside his World War II tank.

Top: Her Majesty The Queen Reviews The Royal Tank Regiment Association from a World War I armoured car, Bovington 1992.

Left: Challenger II, equipment for the year 2000, night firing at Lulworth.

THE ROYAL REGIMENT OF ARTILLERY

Ever since guns began to be made in Europe in the 13th Century, there have been gunners to man them. Used as siege pieces, guns gradually replaced machines like catapults, but they first appeared on the battlefield at Crécy in 1346. In 1486, a Chief Gunner and twelve gunners were appointed as part of what became the Board of Ordnance, and were paid by the Crown. These were the direct ancestors of the Gunners of today in an unbroken line of over 500 years of service to the nation.

Master Gunners were appointed to fortresses where their duties included the care of ordnance and the training of gunners. The latter were often civilians who received instruction and a retaining fee, and were called for service when needed. 'Trains of artillery' were formed for campaigns, with guns and the men to man them.

After the war, Trains were disbanded and forces reduced to a minimum. This was economical, but militarily unsound: when the Jacobites rebelled in 1715, the rebellion was over before the Train was ready. This prompted the Duke of Marlborough to organise a permanent force of artillery and, on 26th May 1716, two Companies of Artillery were created by Royal Warrant. These formed in Woolwich, where most of the personnel were already serving as Gunners under the Board of Ordnance, working in the embryo Royal Arsenal. The early foot companies had no guns allotted, nor were drivers or horses included in the establishment. If stationed in a garrison, a company manned the guns of the defences. On a campaign, it drew field equipment, with horses and civilian drivers hired for the expedition.

The Regiment expanded rapidly during the 18th Century, serving in every campaign and every British garrison world-wide. By 1757, the Royal Artillery had twenty-four companies, grouped for administration into two battalions each of twelve companies: no operational command was involved.

In 1762, the Royal Artillery Band was formed, although Trains of artillery had their 'drum and fife' as early as 1557; it remains Britain's oldest formed orchestra.

The Royal Horse Artillery was founded in 1793 to provide greater mobility in the field, and soon became associated with the role of supporting cavalry. Also in 1793, the civilian drivers and hired horses for field artillery were replaced by a Corps of Captains Commissaries. This was disbanded in 1801 and replaced by a similar corps which became the Corps of Artillery Drivers in 1806.

The War against Napoleon provided countless examples of the value of guns on the battlefield, where they remained the only weapon capable of attacking the enemy at ranges greater than about 100 yards. Pouring shot and cased shot into the attacking columns at Waterloo, the guns were fought to the muzzle.

Smooth-bore guns were still in universal use at this time, most field guns being made of bronze while larger guns tended to be of cast iron. Their effective range was usually as far as the gunner could see to aim his gun at direct fire. Lieutenant Henry Shrapnel's famous shell gained a fearsome reputation and Congreve's rocket system came into use.

In 1833, King William IV marked the Regiment's contribution on every battlefield by granting a single battle honour to replace all others – the motto *UBIQUE* (*Everywhere*), with an accompanying motto *QUO FAS ET GLORIA DUCUNT* (*Whither Right and Glory Lead*). Although the leading gun would no longer carry a standard, the Regiment continued to salute the guns, treating them as its 'colours,' as it still does today.

After a long period of peace in Europe, the Crimean War once again demanded guns in great numbers, especially for the siege batteries. Following the War, in 1855, the Board of Ordnance was abolished and the Royal Artillery became part of the Army under the War Office: hitherto, it had been controlled by the Master General of the Ordnance.

Throughout the 19th Century, artillery continued to play a major part of actions all around the Empire, but always deployed close up to the front line, where the gunners could see their targets. However, by the time of the South African War at the end of the century, advances in infantry firepower made the front line unsafe to deploy vital assets like guns, and they moved back to engage targets at indirect fire.

The move to indirect fire made use of many new technologies. Guns became more powerful, firing more efficient munitions at higher rates, to longer ranges and with increased accuracy. With more space available to deploy behind the front line, more guns were brought into play. The Great War of 1914–18 proved to be an artillery war. The number of gunners increased dramatically, serving 6,655 guns by November 1918, with anti-aircraft (AA) guns joining in against the new threat from the air. Huge amounts of ammunition were fired, over 100 million rounds from the 18-pounder field guns alone.

The inter-War years provided active service on the fringes of the Empire, especially for the mountain batteries on the North West Frontier of India, but the 1930s saw the Regiment once again arming for war. Full mechanisation replaced the draught horses which had served the Regiment for so long, an era now represented only by The King's Troop RHA.

During the Second World War, the Regiment again provided firepower in every theatre, on land, at sea in the Maritime Artillery, and in the air with Air Observation Posts. Manning huge numbers of AA guns both in the field and in the home base, Gunners played a major role in the Battle of Britain and, later, against the flying bombs. Many of the AA Regiments were formed from Territorial Army units and most of the Light AA gunners began the war as infantrymen. Women of the ATS also took part, not only on searchlights and fire control instruments, but also serving in gun detachments during some of the most intense raids, fully meriting their gun badges.

At its peak, in June 1943, the Regiment consisted of almost 700,000 officers and men, some 26% of the Army. Providing constant readiness to engage the enemy by day or night, in fair weather or foul, the Regiment lived up to its proud traditions. Field Marshal Montgomery wrote,

'. . . . *The contribution of the artillery to final victory in the German war has been immense. This will always be so; the harder the fighting and the longer the war, the more the infantry, and in fact all the arms, lean on the Gunners. . . .*'

In the years since 1945, Gunners have been kept fully employed, whether manning their own equipment in combat or working as infantry to assist in the peace-keeping roles at home and abroad. The places and actions are too many to list, but the world 'UBIQUE' says it all.

Despite the reduction of the Army in the post-war years, the Regiment has been armed with some of the most potent, long-range guns and missiles it has ever manned, including nuclear weapons until the Cold War ended. Today it uses the widest span of technology of all the Arms, with virtually no branch of military science unexplored.

The Regiment's history is the foundation stone on which it rests. Most of its batteries bear Honour titles marking special service in particular campaigns. For over 280 years of unbroken service since 1716, and reaching back a further 400 years to the first guns, artillerymen have provided the Army with the firepower it has needed in defence and attack. Sixty-two Victoria Crosses and countless other decorations attest to the manner in which that firepower has been provided.

Right, top: 'Saving the guns at Le Cateau' – the action on 27 August 1914 when 37 Battery RFA was almost overwhelmed and had to mount the rescue of guns whose detachments had been slaughtered: 3 VCs, a DSO and a DCM were awarded.   TERENCE CUNEO

Right, bottom: The action at the Belgian village of Hondeghem on 27 May 1940, when K Battery Royal Horse Artillery held up an immensely superior force, buying time for others to withdraw,   DAVID SHEPHERD

THE CORPS OF ROYAL ENGINEERS (RE)

The Corps of Royal Engineers, known as the Sappers (derived from the trenches, or 'saps', dug by military engineers whilst assaulting enemy fortifications), can claim direct descent from the military engineers brought over by William the Conqueror in 1066. Sappers have taken an active part in all the British Army's campaigns hence the motto 'Ubique' (Everywhere) granted by King William IV in 1832 in lieu of individual battle honours. The Corps has 52 holders of the Victoria Cross, testament to its philosophy of 'first in, last out'.

The status of military engineers was formalised by the Board of Ordnance in 1518. In 1716 George I authorised the separate formation of the Royal Regiment of Artillery and the Corps of Engineers. In 1785 it was decided to raise the Royal Military Artificers, later designated the Royal Sappers and Miners. After the Crimean War in 1856, the officer and soldier elements joined to form the Corps of Royal Engineers.

The Corps' contribution to pioneering technology and innovation has been formidable. It was responsible for introducing telegraphy in the Crimean War, photography in the Abyssinian Campaign of 1867, and submarine mining (eventually handed to the Royal Navy in 1905). Sappers developed the torpedo, operational diving, and military aviation. The Corps began operating balloons at the time of the American Civil War and subsequently graduated to powered flight. The Air Battalion Royal Engineers evolved into today's Royal Air Force. Amongst many other roles, the Corps was responsible for wireless communications during the First World War before the task was given to the Royal Corps of Signals. Other Corps that trace their origins to the Sappers include the Royal Electrical and Mechanical Engineers and the Royal Corps of Transport (now part of the Royal Logistic Corps). The development of the tank was spearheaded by Sappers; it was a Sapper, Brigadier Hugh Elles, who commanded the Tank Corps at the battle of Cambrai in 1917.

Today's Corps of Royal Engineers totals some 9,000 all ranks. The significant elements comprise.

* 10 regular engineer regiments (including an EOD regiment and a parachute squadron) and an independent commando squadron.
* 9 TA engineer regiments and 3 independent squadrons.
* The Royal School of Military Engineering (including 2 training regiments).
* Military Survey.
* Military Engineering Services.

The current role of the Royal Engineers is to help the three Services to fight, to move and to survive on the battlefield. Sappers are combat soldiers first, military engineers second and artisan tradesmen third. The Corps' principal role can be further sub-divided into war-fighting, nation-building and specialist support; many of the required skills are common to these three elements.

War-fighting tasks comprise: mobility, counter-mobility and survivability. The skills required to perform all three were tested during the Falklands War in 1982 and the Gulf War in 1991.

* It is the Corps' job to enable our forces to manoeuvre around the battlefield. Sapper units conduct bridging operations with tank mounted, amphibious, vehicle launched and equipment bridges. Sappers clear enemy minefields by hand breaching, with explosives and with vehicles fitted with mine ploughs and other mechanical devices.
* Counter-mobility describes efforts to hinder the enemy's battlefield movements. The Corps uses explosive demolitions to create obstacles and deny routes by destroying bridges and cratering roads. The Sappers lay minefields, both by hand and mechanically. The Corps uses earth moving plant to create battlefield fortifications.
* Survivability tasks incorporate those elements needed to live on the battlefield. They include the preparation of protective trench systems with plant machinery. Sappers supply water and construct camps away from the immediate area of the battlefield.

Nation building or Post-Conflict Restoration tasks include construction works, and general support to United Nations-style operations.

* Construction projects are conducted world-wide by the Corps. Recently, tasks have been conducted in: Canada (facilities and buildings for military bases); Nepal (re-construction of 3 bridges destroyed by floods); and Angola (refurbishment of a barracks).
* Support to UN-style operations are typified by the Corps' involvement in the Former Republic of Yugoslavia. Sappers carry out route clearance and bridge construction. They have helped local people to dispose of unexploded ordnance; in the Summer of 1996, Sappers helped clear 53 of the 153 minefields around the town of Vitez. Royal Engineer units have provided water supply facilities and have constructed more than 40 bridges along humanitarian aid supply routes. The Corps has deployed mine advisory teams to assist clearance operations in Afghanistan and Cambodia.

There are a number of specialist functions which impact across the spectrum of Sapper roles:

* The Corps maintains its historical links with the RAF through specialist air support to the Harrier force and to airfields. Tasks include airfield damage repair and the provision of essential services and operating surfaces.
* The Sappers have been responsible for disposing of enemy air-dropped weapons since the Blitz in 1940. The Corps is currently responsible for Explosive Ordnance Disposal on the battlefield and for routine battlefield area clearance in peace. It also maintains expertise in the search for terrorist munitions and associated material.
* Military Survey provides the Government's Military Mapping Agency and is tasked with the provision of geographic information required by the defence community. Tasks include generating mapping, digital geographic data and terrain analysis.
* Military Engineering Services provide professional and technical engineering expertise. The Military Works Force is the largest of the specialist units and provides a military design consultancy covering Civil, Mechanical and Electrical disciplines. Its world-wide role has recently taken its members as far afield as Angola, Bosnia and Rwanda.
* The Corps is responsible for all aspects of Army diving. Most engineer units have diving teams which carry out tasks that include river reconnaissance, underwater construction and demolition work.

The expanding range of technical skills demanded of tomorrow's Sapper require a pioneering spirit, ingenuity and versatility. This ethos is echoed in the Corps' history to date and will enable the Corps of Royal Engineers to fulfil its many roles through the whole spectrum of conflict well into the next millennium.

Providing water supplies in Rwanda, 1994

Right Top: Bridging an Iraqi defensive obstacle of burning oil wells in the desert, Gulf War 1992.

Right Bottom: Steam traction engines ford a river, South Africa 1900.

GIBB LTD

THE ROYAL CORPS OF SIGNALS

From earliest times, some form of signalling has been used by armies in the field. The Greeks had the Torch Telegraph and the Water Telegraph, and the Roman Army used coloured smoke as a means of communication. In England, during the 16th century, beacons were used and in 1796 the Admiralty adopted a shutter-type machine, known as the 'Murray Lettering Telegraph'. Morse Code and electric telegraph were used for the first time in the Crimean War (1835–1837) and following the Abyssinian War of 1867, a Signal Wing was formed by the Royal Engineers at Chatham.

In 1884, the Telegraph Battalion Royal Engineers was formed and took part in the Nile Campaign, later playing a prominent role in the Ashanti Campaign of 1895–1896. It was during this campaign that men of the telegraph Battalion hacked a path for an overhead line from the Cape coast to Prahsu, covering 72 miles through jungle, staggered out of the jungle and confronted King Prempeh and accepted the surrender of his Army. King Prempeh's throne is now displayed in the ROYAL SIGNALS Museum at Blandford.

Signalling remained the responsibility of the Telegraph Battalion during the Boer War and until 1908, when the Royal Engineer Signals Service was formed and provided communications during World War One. At this time, the Despatch Rider came into prominence and wireless 'sets' were introduced into service. Wireless communications were provided in France and Flanders and also in the campaigns in Salonika, Palestine and Mesopotamia.

The first official agreement to form a separate Signal Corps was made in 1918 before the end of World War One, but due to various policy delays the formation of the 'Corps' was delayed until 1920. A Royal Warrant was signed by the Secretary of State for War, the Rt. Hon Winston S. Churchill, who gave the Sovereign's approval for the formation of a 'Corps of Signals' on 28th June 1920. Six weeks later, His Majesty the King conferred the title 'Royal Corps'.

During the 1920s and 1930s, the Corps increased its strength and had personnel serving in overseas stations such as Shanghai, Hong Kong, Singapore, Ceylon, Egypt, Jamaica and many other 'out-posts of the Empire'. The largest portion of the Corps overseas, one third, was concentrated in India.

Throughout World War Two, members of the Corps served in every theatre of war and, at the end, it had a serving strength of 8,518 officers and 142,472 soldiers: 4,362 members of ROYAL SIGNALS gave their lives. In the post-war period, the Corps has played a full and active part in numerous campaigns, being involved in: Palestine (1945–1948); the long campaign in Malaya (1949–1960); the Korean War (1950–1953); the various operations in Cyprus, Borneo, Aden, Arabian Peninsula, Kenya and Belize. Throughout this time, until the ending of the Cold War, the main body of the Corps was deployed with the British Army of the Rhine confronting the former Communist Bloc forces, providing the British Forces contribution to NATO with its communications infrastructure.

It is the task of Royal Signals to faciliate the accurate generation of vital information and to provide for its speedy, precise and secure passage around the battlefield in order to assist commanders to win the information battle. By so doing, the Royal Signals act as a 'force multiplier' which permits commanders to get the very best from the complex mix of tanks, guns, infantry, engineers and logistic support which makes up a balanced fighting force.

The communications which the Royal Signals provide the British Army vary from hand held radios, to imposing satellite dishes which carry vast amounts of information on intercontinental links. Between these extremes, more powerful radios are fitted in armoured vehicles, whilst smaller satellite terminals, for example, are deployed with parachute and other special forces. Where large amounts of information have to be transferred simultaneously around the battlefield, extensive area systems are used. These provide high quality and accurate information transfer between users in the form of secure voice, telegraph, facsimile and data. The service is similar to that provided by national commercial systems, with the important difference that it must be mobile and be able to operate under enemy attack 24 hours a day.

The men and women of the Royal Signals must be able to keep abreast of the ever growing and fast changing developments in modern technology. They are deployed in small detachments or in larger formations; from the forward edge of any operation or battlefield, back to the highest level of command. Their units interoperate with the Royal Navy and Royal Air Force and, in the United Kingdom, with civilian and Government agencies.

The Royal Signals presently constitutes approximately ten per cent of the Army's strength, recruiting from all over the United Kingdom. It's Territorial Army units play a vital role, providing a large proportion of its manpower. The heart of the Corps, once in Catterick, North Yorkshire is now based in Blandford, Dorset and Regimental Headquarters supports an extensive country wide Association which fosters social activities and the welfare of retired members of the Corps.

Most recently, members of the Corps have spearheaded operations, including: the Falkland Island campaign; the peace-keeping force in the Lebanon; supervising the peaceful transition of Namibia to independence; and 3,000 members of the Corps joined Operation Granby in the Persian Gulf. Since then, members of the Corps have been deployed to Kurdistan, to the states of Bosnia and Croatia, the Western Sahara, Cambodia, Rwanda and Angola.

Today's Corps, built on a fine tradition, now moves into the developing Information Warfare era of the future. It strives to live up to its motto, 'Certa Cito', which freely translated means 'Swift and Sure'. The motto of the Royal Signals could equally be 'First In – Last Out'.

The Royal Corps of
Signals Gulf War, 1991

HALL & WOODHOUSE LTD – BREWERS OF BADGER ALES

Top: Last transmission, Imjin, Korea 25 April 1951. Colonel Carne VC commanding the Glosters orders his signallers to destroy their equipment and codes.

Bottom: Corporal Thomas Waters of 5th Parachute Brigade Signal Section won the Military Medal for laying the field line under heavy enemy fire across the Caen Canal Bridge on D Day 1944.

THE GRENADIER GUARDS

In 1656 King Charles II was in exile and England lay under the military dictatorship of Cromwell, the Lord Protector. In May of that year the King formed his Royal Regiment of Guards at Bruges, under the Colonelcy of Lord Wentworth. After the Restoration in 1660 a second Royal Regiment of Guards was formed in England under the Colonelcy of Colonel John Russell. In 1665, following Lord Wentworth's death, both Regiments were incorporated into a single Regiment with twenty-four Companies, whose royal badges or devices, given by King Charles II, are still emblazoned on its Colours.

The Regiment, later termed 'The First Regiment of Foot Guards', and now called 'The First or Grenadier Regiment of Foot Guards', has fought in almost every major campaign of the British army from that time until our own. Under the last two Stuart Kings it fought against the Moors at Tangiers, and in America, and even took part as Marines in the naval wars against the Dutch. In the Wars of the Spanish Succession, the 1st Guards served under Marlborough who had joined the King's Company of the Regiment as an Ensign in 1667, who was Colonel of the Regiment, and who, with his brilliant victories of Blenheim (1704), Ramillies (1706), Oudenarde (1708) and Malplaquet (1709), established his reputation as one of the greatest soldiers of all time. Later they fought at Dettingen and at Fontenoy, where the superb steadiness of their advance under a murderous cannonade won the admiration of both armies. Rigid attention to detail, flawless perfection of uniform and equipment, and a discipline of steel were the hard school in which the tempered metal of the Regiment was made in the service of the State. Yet running through the tradition of discipline, of harsh punishments, of undeviating rule, ran a vein of poetry, of humour, of loyalty to comrade, of sense of belonging to something greater than any individual, something undying and profound. And the letters and diaries of men of the Regiment of those days bear witness to it.

In the autumn and winter of 1808 they took part in Sir John Moore's classic march and counter-march against Napoleon in Northern Spain. Subsequently they fought at Corunna and when Sir John Moore fell mortally wounded in the hour of victory it was men of the 1st Foot Guards who bore him, dying, from the field. Remaining in Spain they took part in the desperate engagements of the Peninsular War under Arthur Wellesley, first Duke of Wellington, who also later became Colonel of the Regiment.

When Napoleon escaped from Elba and re-entered Paris, the Regiment returned to the Low Countries. In the middle of June 1815 the Emperor struck at the British and Prussian forces north of the Meuse. After a fierce encounter at Quatre Bras on June 16th 1815, in which the 3rd Battalion suffered heavy casualties, Wellington's Army withdrew to Waterloo, and on Sunday June 18th, was fought the battle in which the Regiment gained its present title and undying fame. During the morning the light companies of the Guards defended the farm of Hougoumont, the light companies of the 1st Guards being withdrawn later to join their battalions – the 2nd and 3rd Battalions. At evening these two battalions, together forming the 1st Brigade, were in position behind the ridge which gave shelter to the Army. At this point Napoleon directed his final assault with fresh troops – the Imperial Guard, which had hitherto been maintained in reserve. That assault was utterly defeated, and, in honour of their defeat of the Grenadiers of the French Imperial Guard, the 1st Guards were made a Regiment of Grenadiers, and given the title of 'First or Grenadier Regiment of Foot Guards' which they bear to this day.

During the Crimean War, the 3rd Battalion took part in the Battle of Alma and then as part of the grim siege of Sebastopol, the Battle of Inkerman. The defence of the Sandbag Battery on 5 November 1854, in the fog and against overwhelming odds is one of the epics of British military history. On that day the Brigade of Guards, of which the 3rd Battalion of the Grenadier Guards formed part, lost half its officers and men but not a single prisoner or an inch of ground.

The Grenadier Guards fought at Tel-el-Kebir and in the Boer War, proving the worth of discipline and esprit de corps in the era of khaki. In the first Great War 1914–18, they fought in nearly all the principle battles of the Western Front. At First Ypres all but 4 officers and 200 men of the 1st Battalion and 4 officers and 140 men of the 2nd fell in action.

During this war a 4th Battalion was formed for the first time and covered itself with glory in the critical fighting in the spring of 1918. The Marne, the Aisne, Ypres, Loos, the Somme, Cambrai, Arras, Hazebrouck and the Hindenburgh Line are inscribed on the Battalion's Colours. 12,000 casualties were suffered by the Regiment.

In 1939 the 1st, 2nd and 3rd Battalions again returned to the Continent, forming part of the British Expeditionary Force under Lord Gort, himself a Grenadier. During the retreat of 1940, the traditional discipline of the Regiment stood the test as it had done at First Ypres, Corunna and Waterloo. At Dunkirk, which the Regiment had garrisoned under Charles II, it took part in the defences of the perimeter, under cover of which the embarkation of the Army was made. In the course of that year the 5th Battalion was re-formed, and in 1941 two further Battalions, the 5th and 6th, were raised.

The Regiment was represented in the Eighth Army's famous advance of Tunisia, taking part in the battle of Mareth, where the 6th Battalion, suffered heavy casualties but won the respect of friend and foe alike. The 3rd and 5th Battalions shared with the 6th Battalion the invasion of North Africa; all three Battalions were engaged in the Italian campaign, the 5th Battalion forming part of the force which landed at Anzio.

Meanwhile, in England the 2nd and 4th Battalions had been converted to armour, and the 2nd Battalion, with the 1st Battalion, which had become a Motor Battalion, served in the Guards Armoured Division under the command of Major General Allan Adair, another Grenadier, and later to become Colonel of the Regiment. The 4th Battalion formed part of the 6th Guards Tank Brigade. These three Battalions fought in the battles of Normandy and across France and Germany. In September 1944 the 1st and 2nd Battalion entered Brussels. On September 20th tanks of the 2nd Battalion and troops of the 1st Battalion crossed the Nijmegen bridge, on their way to Germany and the German surrender.

Since 1945 the Regiment has served in virtually every one of the 'small campaigns' and crises which have marked the last few decades. 1st and 2nd Battalions have undertaken frequent tours in Northern Ireland since the latest troubles flared in 1968. In the Falklands War the Regiment was also represented. In the Gulf War, 493 officers and other ranks of the 1st Battalion were deployed to 17 different Regiments and Headquarters, whilst the Regimental Band were on permanent standby to proceed to the Gulf for deployment as medical orderlies. In addition the Regiment has continued its traditional and privileged task of mounting guard over the Sovereign. The Regiment now consists of the 1st Battalion with the 'Inkerman Company', the left flank Company, retaining the inherited privileges of the 3rd Battalion; and Nijmegen Company, an incremental company within London District, which maintains the Colours and the traditions of the 2nd Battalion.

Behind the ceremony most frequently seen by the public lies a tradition of discipline, comradeship, loyalty and fidelity to one another, to the Country and to the Crown. This is as relevant today as it was in 1656.

Soldiering in 1998. Members of the Queens Company Group on exercise in Jamaica.

Right, top: Lance Corporal Harry Nicholls in the action near the River Escaut, May 1940, in which he was awarded the first Victoria Cross to be gained by any soldier in the Second World War.   D ROWLANDS

Right, bottom: The Light Companies of the First Regiment of Foot Guards (now Grenadier Guards) at the defence of Hougoumont, Waterloo, 19 June 1815.   R SIMKIN

THE COLDSTREAM GUARDS

The Regiment was raised in June 1650 when Oliver Cromwell appointed George Monck to command a New Model Army Regiment. Owing to Monck's former Royalist service, five companies were drafted from Hazlerigg's and Fenwick's staunchly Parliamentary Regiments. Monck's Regiment saw its first action at Dunbar (3rd September 1650), gaining the Dunbar Medal. For three weeks in late 1659 Monck's Regiment stayed in Coldstream, on the Scottish border. Prompted by widespread anarchy, Monck set out on 1 January 1660 to march his Regiment to London. Monck and his Regiment played a significant part in restoring law and order, and supporting the elections that led to the restoration of the Monarchy and the return of King Charles II.

The New Model Army had been almost completely disbanded when Venner led an insurrection in the City of London and Monck's Regiment, almost the only disciplined force available, again restored order. Monck's Regiment was granted the privilege on 14th February 1661, of laying down its arms as a Parliamentary Regiment and taking them up again as the Lord General's Regiment of Foot Guards in the Service of the Crown. The Regiment is thus the oldest Regular British Army Regiment *in continuous succession*. The Regiment has retained some New Model Army distinctions to this day, notably the predominantly white (Parliamentary) colour of the drum hoops; it is likely that the white band on the Coldstream forage cap also reflects this connection. When Monck died in 1670 the Regiment became the Coldstream Guards.

The Regiment has served in every major conflict (and many minor ones) since that time. Detachments served with the Fleet, Monck himself achieving distinction as an Admiral in 1666: men of Monck's Regiment were detached to form the Royal Marines in 1664. Fifty men of the Lord General's Regiment served under Sir Robert Holmes on his expeditions to Guiana and America in 1664 (when he renamed the town he captured New York). Holmes, a Royal Navy Captain held a Coldstream Officer's Commission. Larger contingents served in Tangier (1680) and at the 1695 Siege of Namur during the War of the League of Augsburg. The Regiment garrisoned Gibraltar after its capture in 1704 and fought in the War of the Spanish Succession at the battles of Oudenarde and Malplaquet in the Low Countries in 1708–09. During the Austrian Succession War the Coldstream fought at Dettingen (1743). The Regiment was again in Europe during the Seven Years War, Battalions taking part in the raids on Cherbourg and St Malo (1758). From 1760–62 the 2nd Battalion campaigned in Germany in places later Coldstreamers have known well – Nord-Rhein Westphalia and along the Weser.

During the American Revolutionary War a Composite Footguards Battalion, with Coldstream Companies, was despatched across the Atlantic where they (again) captured New York and fought at Harlem (1776). Two years later the Composite Guards Brigade was ordered to join General Cornwallis in the Carolinas, and Coldstreamers fought at the Catawha River and Guildford Court House in 1781; some of the remnants were forced to surrender at Yorktown in October 1781.

During the French Revolutionary and Napoleonic Wars Coldstreamers served in Flanders, Egypt, at Copenhagen (1807) and in the Peninsula. Despite losses at the Battle of Quatre-Bas, part of the 2nd Battalion Coldstream Guards was deployed on 18th June 1815 to defend Hougoumont Farm, Wellington's vital ground at Waterloo Coldstream Companies, with other Footguards Light Companies, held the Farm throughout the day; by evening almost the whole Battalion had been committed to its defence, and had suffered 50% casualties. Wellington later named one of the defenders – Sergeant Graham – the 'bravest man in the Army': his exploits are celebrated to this day by the Sergeants' Mess. Sergeant Graham was in fact assisted by his brother, four Coldstream Officers and four members of the Third Guards in 'closing the Gate' at Hougoumont at the critical moment of the Battle.

In the 19th Century Coldstreamers served in Canada, the Crimea, and in Egypt (Tel-El-Kebir 1882). In 1885 Coldstreamers saw action with the Guards Camel Regiment in the attempt to relieve General Gordon at Khartoum. Shortly after the formation of the 3rd Battalion in 1897, the 1st and 2nd Battalions sailed for South Africa and fought in several skirmishes and actions including the Modder River.

In 1914 the three Coldstream Battalions deployed to France, saw action at Mons, the Marne, and the Aisne before being committed to the defence of Ypres where the 1st Battalion almost ceased to exist at the Battle of Gheluvelt. The Regiment maintained four Battalions on active service on the Western Front during the War, fighting in many battles including Loos (1915), the Somme (1916) where the 1st 2nd and 3rd Battalions attacked in line together for the only time in their existence, at Passchendaele and Cambrai in 1917, at Arras in 1918 and in the great 1918 Advance.

The 1st and 2nd Battalions served in the BEF in 1939–40 while the 3rd Battalion was in Egypt. From 1941, the Regiment maintained five Service Battalions, with the 1st (Armoured) and 5th Battalions in the Guards Armoured Division, and the 4th (Tank) Battalion in Churchill Tanks: the three Battalions fought across Normandy, the Rhineland, the Netherlands and on to Lubeck. The 2nd and 3rd Battalions served in North Africa and Italy.

Since 1945 the Regiment has served in Palestine, Malaya, Kenya, British Guiana, Aden, Northern Ireland and in the British Army of the Rhine. In 1991 the 1st Battalion served in the Gulf War in 1st (UK) Armoured Division, and in 1993–4 was in the United Nations Protection Force (UNPROFOR) in Bosnia; in 1996 it deployed to South Armagh. The 2nd Battalion was placed in suspended animation in 1993 (as the 3rd Battalion had been in 1959).

The Regiment has been awarded 117 Battle Honours. Thirteen Coldstreamers have been awarded the Victoria Cross, and one the George Cross. In the year 2000 the Regiment, still predominantly recruited from North-East England, celebrates its 350th Anniversary with one Battalion, the independent No 7 Company, a small Regimental Headquarters, the Regimental Band and some 150 Coldstreamers deployed throughout the Army; in size similar to the Regiment George Monck led in 1650.

Wherever or however the Regiment has served, always the same spirit has prevailed, the same discipline, the same courage, the same unconquerable 'Will to Victory' – all these great qualities that, throughout its history, have earned for the Regiment its unchallenged motto – Nulli Secundus – Second to None.

Presentation of New Colours by Her Majesty The Queen on 20 May 1999 at Windsor Castle. On the extreme right is the 27th Colonel of the Regiment, Lieutenant General The Honourable Sir William Rous KCB OBE, who died five days later. His Great Grandfather, John Rous, was badly wounded at Quatre Bras, the Duke of Wellington's pre-cursor battle before Waterloo. SGT IAN LIPTROT

Top: The Closing of the Gates at Hougoumont on 18 June 1815 by Lieutenant Colonel James MacDonnell. Corporal Graham and other officers and men of the 2nd Battalion.

Left: Lieutenant Colonel John Campbell, who rallied his men with his hunting horn, winning the Victoria Cross at Ginchy, Somme, 15 September 1916.

THE SCOTS GUARDS

On 16 March 1642 King Charles I, issued a commission to Archibald, 1st Marquess of Argyle, authorising him to raise a Regiment of 1,500 men for service in Ulster, where the local Irish were in rebellion against the Scottish Colonists. Charles had intended to go himself to take command of these operations and Argyle's regiment was intended as his Royal Guard. However, events in England prevented the King from taking part in this expedition and Argyle sent his Regiment in charge of his Kinsman, Sir Duncan Campbell of Auckinbreck. Both Charles's commissions to Argyle and Argyle's to Auckinbreck are now preserved at Regimental Headquarters.

When King Charles II arrived in Scotland in 1650 following his father's execution, Argyle's Regiment, now returned from Ireland and known as the Irish Companies, became his 'LYFE GUARD OF FOOT' with Lord Lorne, Argyle's son, as its second Colonel. As such the Regiment received its first Colours at Falkland Palace and took part in the disastrous battles of Dunbar and Worcester against the forces of Cromwell and the 'LYFE GUARDS OF FOOT' was scattered.

At the restoration, after raising two Regiments of Foot Guards in England, Charles II turned his attention to Scotland and in October 1660, issued orders for the re-raising of companies of Scottish Foot Guards to garrison the Castles of Edinburgh and Dumbarton. In 1662 these companies were expanded into a full Regiment and the Earl of Linlithgow was appointed as its third Colonel.

In 1686 the Scottish Regiment of FOOT GUARDS was brought onto the Establishment of the English Army for the first time and by a ruling of King William III eight years later, took precedence within the Foot Guards from that date despite its seniority in length of service. In the same year seven companies came south to Hounslow Heath and were brigaded for the first time with the other two Regiments of Foot Guards they became known to the English as the Scotch or Scots Guards and to other Guards Regiments, so legend has it, as 'THE KIDDIES'.

Queen Anne changed the name of the Regiment to the Third Regiment of Foot Guards in 1711 and at the same time laid down the designs for the 16 badges which today form those of the three Battalions and the first 16 companies. In 1831 the Regiment became the Scots Fusilier Guards until 1877, when Queen Victoria restored the original title of the Scots Guards.

The 1st Battalion of the Regiment fought in the Crimean War and in 1857, Lieutenant R J Lindsay and four other members of the Battalion were awarded the Victoria Cross for Gallantry. This was the year the Victoria Cross was instituted and Lieutenant Lindsay therefore became not only the first Scots Guardsman to receive this decoration but also the first in the British Army.

Both 1st and 2nd Battalions of the Regiment fought in the South African War, and in France during the First World War. A 3rd (Reserve) Battalion was raised in August 1914 and served in England until its disbandment in March 1919.

Between the wars Battalions of the Regiment served in China, Egypt and Palestine. The 2nd Battalion went to Palestine in 1936 and then on to Egypt in 1938, and did not return home until 1944.

During the second World War the Regiment had four service Battalions, the 3rd being formed in October 1940 and the 4th in September 1941. The 5th (Ski) Battalion was raised on 6 February 1940 to serve in Finland when that Country was invaded by Russia. However, on 14 March 1940 the Finns capitulated and this short lived Battalion faded out of existence. Battalions of the Regiment fought in British Expeditionary force in Belgium and France in 1939–40, North Africa, Italy and North West Europe. The 3rd Battalion became a Tank Battalion in the Guards Armoured Division and later in 6th Guards Tank Brigade. This Battalion was disbanded in February 1946 and the 4th Battalion October 1943.

Since the Second World War battalions of The Regiment have served in Malaya, Cyprus, Egypt, Germany, Kenya, Malaysia, Borneo, Northern Ireland and Hong Kong. The 1st Battalion was stationed in Edinburgh in 1967 and 1968, the first time part of the Regiment has been stationed in Scotland since 1707.

On the 31st March 1971 the 2nd Battalion was placed in suspended animation and remained so until a change of Government, it was reformed in Edinburgh in January 1972. In the interval F Company served with the 1st Battalion Irish Guards in Hong Kong, S company served independently in British Honduras and later joined 2nd Battalion Grenadier Guards, and the 2nd Battalion Company moved to Edinburgh. On the 21 April 1972 a service or re-dedication was held in St Giles Cathedral and the Battalion became operational on 1st July.

During the 1970s and early 1980s both Battalions of the Regiment completed four four-month operational tours in Northern Ireland and for eighteen months from March 1980 the 1st Battalion was stationed at Aldergrove, near Belfast. In 1979 the Regiment complete with representatives of all branches of the Scots Guards Association, was reviewed on Horse Guards parade by H.R.H. The Duke of Kent, who had succeeded his uncle as 26th Colonel of the Regiment in 1974. The 1st Battalion flew out to Hong Kong for a two year posting in 1981. Regimental Headquarters moved back to Wellington Barracks after eight years in Bloomsbury.

On the 12 May 1982 the 2nd Battalion sailed for the South Atlantic in the Cunard Liner QE2 as part of 5th Infantry Brigade. The Battalion landed at San Carlos, East Falkland on 2nd June. Following a night attack on 14th June they captured Mount Tumbledown. Eight members of the Battalion lost their lives and 41 were wounded. The Battalion returned to England on 10th August 1982.

On 26th October 1983 it was announced that Her Majesty the Queen had approved Battle Honours for the ships and units that had fought in the Falklands. The Regiment was awarded two Battle Honours one being 'Falkland Islands 1982' which would be bourne on the colours and a laurel leaf placed on the Colours on the anniversary of the Battle of Tumbledown Mountain 14 June 1982, the second was Tumbledown Mountain which would not be bourne on the Colours.

The 2nd Battalion moved to Cyprus in January 1984 for a two year tour were it was responsible for the security of the Sovereign Base Areas. The 1st Battalion returned from Hong Kong in 1984 to Pirbright, the Battalion mounting its first public duty in four years.

On the 27th June 1987 the 2nd Battalion received new Colours at Hopetoun House the family seat of the Linlithgows by Her Majesty The Queen. The 1st Battalion moved to Hohne in February 1988 as an Armoured Infantry Battalion.

On the 28th January 1991 the 1st Battalion Scots Guards were deployed to Saudi Arabia (The Gulf War) as Battle casualty replacements in support of 4th and 7th Armoured Brigade, as well as the Battalion being deployed so to was the Regimental Band which was attached to 33 Field Hospital.

Both Battalions were again on parade in Edinburgh at the review of the Regiment by Her Majesty the Queen on their 350th anniversary on the 2nd March 1992, many family members of both Battalions were present and all branches of the Scots Guards Association were represented.

Due to Options for Change the 2nd Battalion was placed into suspended animation on 30th November 1993 and F Company Scots Guards a new Public Duties Incremental Company was formed on the 4th November 1993 at Dreghorn Barracks, with the Company being formed of both 1st and 2nd Battalion personnel. The remainder of 2nd Battalion personnel joined 1SG in the newly re-built Victoria Barracks Windsor.

Since 1972 both Battalions have seen service in, Germany, Belize, Hong Kong, Falkland Islands, Cyprus, The Gulf, Northern Ireland, Canada, USA.

Since the inauguration of the Victoria Cross the Scots Guards have been awarded 11.

Exercise Sun Lion. Cyprus.

PEARSON plc

The fierce hand-to-hand fighting, reminiscent of the Great War clashes, encountered by G Company in bitter cold on the night of 13/14 June 1982; when they took Mount Tumbledown, overlooking Port Stanley, the key to the Falklands victory.

Top: Trooping the Colour, F Company 1997.

THE IRISH GUARDS

(THE MICKS)

On 1st April 1900, in recognition of the great bravery of the many Irish troops in the South African War, Queen Victoria created the fourth Regiment of Foot Guards, the Irish Guards. The First Colonel of the new regiment was Field Marshal Lord Roberts of Kandahar VC known and revered throughout the Empire as 'Bobs'.

The Irish Guards were the first new regiment to be created for many years. They had no uniform, no customs, no traditions. They were now part of Her Majesty's Foot Guards and had somehow to create something similar to the older regiments of the Brigade of Guards who bore so proudly their long history and distinguished reputation, yet something subtly distinctive and unique to the Irish Guards. And as we celebrate the millennium so the Irish Guards celebrate their own centenary.

The fledgling Regiment's first action was in the South African War when they formed a number of composite light mounted detachments from the Foot Guards volunteers. It was not until the First World War that the Regiment served as an entity. In the Great war the Irish Guards found two battalions and in the Second World War there were three battalions.

In 1914 the nation went to war. The Irish Guards were then stationed in Wellington Barracks, London, long the home of one or more Battalions of Foot Guards. War was declared on 4th August but even before then the Reservists had started to arrive. The ferries from Ireland were packed with men flocking to answer the call to the Colours who were determined not to be left out of the fight, for in those days over ninety percent of the Irish Guards came from Ireland, the majority from what was later to become Southern Ireland. Even today a significant proportion of the Regiment are Irish.

On 12th August, the fully formed 1st Battalion some 1,000 strong, marched to Nine Elms Station and there embarked for Southampton and for France. In July 1915 the 2nd Battalion of Irish Guards abandoned their training and reinforcement role at home and they too became a service Battalion in their own right. They joined the Guards Division who were fast earning their reputation of the elite of the elite. The 'Guards Way' was to become the watchword throughout the British Army of how soldiers should conduct themselves in war. The greatest legacy of 'the Guards Way' was the enormous number of Warrant and Non-commissioned officers whose early experience had been in the Brigade of Guards and who gained commissions in other regiments.

In common with other regiments of the British Army the sacrifice of the Irish Guards was immense. Over 8,000 Irish Guardsmen were killed or wounded in action, this from a new Regiment of only two Battalions. They were awarded four Victoria Crosses. Among the officers killed in 1915 was Lt John Kipling the only son of Rudyard Kipling who as an act of remembrance to his son and as an act of homage to Irish soldiers in general wrote the incomparable 'History of the Irish Guards In The Great War'. Recently reprinted, there is no finer testament to the unique character of the Irishman at war.

Reduced after the Armistice to a single Battalion the inter-war years found the Irish Guards serving in Turkey – where they were commanded by Lieutenant Colonel the Hon H R G Alexander, who was later to achieve fame as Field Marshal Earl Alexander of Tunis, and known universally as 'Alex'. They later saw service in Egypt and then Palestine, but towards the end of the 1930s war clouds were gathering again.

The Munich crisis of 1938 catapulted a complacent and sleepy nation into action. So certain was imminent conflict that in July 1939, the 2nd Battalion Irish Guards was reconstituted. First to see action though was the 1st Battalion in the ill-starred expedition to save Norway from the advancing Germans.

It was here in high Summer when there was no darkness that the Battalion embarked in an elderly Polish liner the 'Chobry'. Shortly after sailing she was attacked by German aircraft and by the greatest misfortune one bomb went straight down the funnel. It exploded near the officers' cabins killing the Commanding Officer, Second-in-Command, Adjutant and three of the five Company Commanders and severely wounding the other two. Separated by an inferno from their officers, with the exception of the Battalion priest, Father Cavanagh and with the ship sinking beneath them the Battalion formed up as though on parade in more peaceful circumstances and patiently waited for rescue. At great risk from exploding ammunition the accompanying warships came alongside. Then section by section, platoon by platoon, company by company and all in possession of their weapons the battalion boarded their rescuers.

Then it was the turn of the 2nd Battalion who with the British Expeditionary Force in full retreat from France covered the evacuation from Boulogne. There followed a period of intensive training. But a significant change was in the air, for an acute need for additional armoured units in the Army had arisen. So, in common with other battalions of the Foot Guards, the 2nd Battalion Irish Guards were converted to tanks.

However, it was the 1st Battalion who next saw action in North Africa, where the British 1st Army under command of 'their' General 'Alex' landed in Algeria and fought their way to east Tunis. From there they found themselves in Italy and then to the notorious Anzio bridgehead where they earned undying respect for their fighting skills under impossible conditions. This was to be the last time the 1st Battalion was engaged in the Second World War. So heavy were their casualties at Anzio that the remnants, all too few, were absorbed into the 2nd (Armoured) Battalion and the 3rd (Lorried Infantry) Battalion. This last having been formed in October 1940. These battalions both formed part of the Guards Armoured Division then poised for Operation Overlord, D Day and the invasion of Hitler's Europe.

On D 12 they sailed for France. With both tank and lorried battalions from the same Regiments in the Guards Armoured Division it was a natural progression to bring them together. So the Grenadier Group, the Coldstream Group and the Irish Guards Group were formed. United in background, in training and in family allegiance these regimental combinations were to provide the epitome of Infantry/Tank co-operation. This special unity was largely instrumental to the immense success of the Guards Armoured Division

A soldier of the 1st Battalion The Irish Guards provides the safety of NATO's umbrella to a young Albanian boy west of Pristina. The boy's eyes shine in delight at the prospect of peace under the watchful protection of the British Forces.

Right: HM The Queen Mother distributing her annual gift of shamrocks on St Patrick's Day.

as a fighting force. By coincidence within the Irish Guards group both battalions were commanded by cousins: Lieutenant Colonel J O E Vandeleur of the 2nd (Armoured) Battalion and Lieutenant Colonel G A M Vandeleur, the 3rd (Lorried Infantry) Battalion.

It was a signal honour that the Irish Guards Group was chosen to lead the advance of the British 2nd Army to relieve the airborne forces at Arnhem – an event immortalised in the film 'A Bridge too Far'.

In the Second World War nearly, 2,500 officers and men of the Irish Guards were killed or wounded. Two Victoria Crosses were awarded.

Since those far off days of 1945 the Irish Guards have served with distinction at Aden, Hong Kong, Belize, Berlin, West Germany and Northern Ireland.

Kipling wrote of the Irish Guards 'Their discipline is that of the Guards'. He could have added 'but there is a touch of magic about all they do – this is theirs alone'.

And they call it Mick 'magic'. It defies definition or the understanding of those outside the 'family' circle but it has sustained the Irish Guards throughout the one hundred years of their history, in sport, in war, in all they do. It has helped them take in their stride two bitter World Wars and countless lesser engagements since. It has helped them absorb changes in role and amazing changes in technology. It has created the ever-changing, never-changing Irish Guardsman we know today.

THE WELSH GUARDS

ORGANISATION OF THE REGIMENT

The Welsh Guards is the Fifth Regiment of Foot Guards and the junior regiment in the Household Division. The Regiment consists of Regimental Headquarters, the First Battalion, The Regimental Band, all those serving at training establishments and other posts around the world, and the Regimental Association.

THE FORMATION OF THE REGIMENT

The expansion of His Majesty's Army for the conduct of the Great War of 1914–18 provided an opportunity to fill the national complement of regiments of Foot Guards identified with the countries of the United Kingdom by the inclusion of Wales. His Majesty King George V signed the Royal Warrant of authority to raise the Welsh Guards on 26th February 1915. The motto of the Regiment is 'CYMRU AM BYTH' (Wales for Ever). The regimental cap badge is the leek. So ready was the response to the appeal from Wales and from Welshmen in other regiments of Foot Guards that the Battalion was able to mount its first Royal Guard on Saint David's Day, 1st March 1915. His Majesty sanctioned the title 'The Prince of Wales Company' for the right flank company of the Battalion on 19th March 1915.

THE GREAT WAR OF 1914–18

1st Battalion

After intensive training the Battalion sailed for the Continent on 18th August 1915 as part of the Guards Division, and fought its first action at Loos on 27th September. This action involved capturing the bare hill known as Hill 70 situated behind the mining town of Loos. Having taken the hill at great cost, the Battalion remained in the area for one month before being relieved. Only eight months and one battle old they had sustained almost 200 casualties.

The Battalion remained in Belgium and France taking part in the bloodiest conflicts of that war including Loos, and Ginchy in 1915, Flers Courcelette, Morva, Pilckem and Poelcappelle in 1916, the muddy Cambrai in 1917 and, in the final year, at Bapaume, Canal du Nord and Sambre. The names of all these places are Battle Honours of the Regiment and are emblazoned on the Regiment's Colours.

Sergeant Robert Bye was awarded the Victoria Cross for his bravery in eliminating a German machine gun blockhouse in July 1917.

The Battalion returned to England on 8th March 1919, with only 13 members of the original battalion which started out four and a half years earlier.

THE SECOND WORLD WAR

Between the wars the 1st Battalion saw service in Egypt, from 1929 to 1930 and were stationed in Gibraltar in 1939; when war was declared on 3rd September they were despatched directly to France.

In May 1940 the Allied Forces faced the might of the German war machine and the 1st Battalion fought a brilliant stubborn rearguard action at Arras, a town they were to liberate in 1944. The action was costly but the Battalion fought its way to the coast and evacuated with the remainder of the British Expeditionary Force at Dunkirk.

The New Second Battalion

Formed as an holding battalion in 1939, the new unit landed at Boulogne in May and after only two days bloody fighting in which they heroically delayed the advancing Germans, they were evacuated to England from Boulogne. They sustained heavy losses and many men were taken prisoner.

The Second Front

As part of the Guards Armoured Division both 1st and 2nd Battalions (the 2nd now armoured) landed at Arromanches on 18th June 1944. During the next three months the 1st Battalion paid dearly and sustained so many casualties that they were reinforced by X Company, Scots Guards. Following the final battles of Normandy and the recapture of Arras the two Battalions took part in the fastest advance in the history of armoured warfare.

On 3rd September 1944 the almost 100 miles dash from Douai to Brussels was covered by the Guards Armoured Division, with the 2nd Battalion Welsh Guards at its head at the final stage, at speeds of 50 – even 60 miles an hour.

On 8th September the 1st Battalion fought a particularly fierce but successful battle, against counter-attacking Germans, at the small Belgian town of Hechtel. While the 2nd Battalion fought right up to the final day of the war and into Germany, a much depleted 1st Battalion were relieved on 23rd March 1945 and returned to England.

The 1st and 2nd Battalion Battle Honours, borne on the Colours, are: 'Defence of Arras', 'Boulogne 1940', 'Mont Pincon', 'Brussels' and 'Hechtel'. The Victoria Cross was awarded posthumously to Lieutenant The Hon Christopher Furness, for his gallantry during the battle for Arras in May 1940.

The 3rd Battalion

This famous Battalion was formed in October 1941. On 1st March 1943 they joined the 1st Guards Brigade in North Africa and took part with distinction in the battles of Fondouk Gap and at Hamman Lif, the final major battle in that theatre of war.

In March 1944 the 3rd Battalion landed at Naples and were immediately engaged in some of the bloodiest fighting of the war, at Cerasola, Cassino, Piccolo and north of Florence at Monte Battaglia.

Over a period of thirteen months this rugged battalion fought its way up the spine of Italy and into Austria when on 2nd May 1945 the Germans signed an instrument of unconditional surrender.

3rd Battalion Battle Honours borne on the Colours are: 'Fondouk', 'Hamman Lif', 'Monte Piccolo', 'Monte Ornito' and 'Battaglia'.

THE POST WAR YEARS

1945–55

In October 1945 the 1st Battalion sailed for Palestine where they remained until 1948; it was a difficult and tense situation and not the holiday everyone had hoped for. From 1948–50 the Battalion was based at Chelsea Barracks and in Spring 1950 they moved to Wuppertal in Germany to be part of 4th Guards Brigade. This was followed by two years in Berlin and in October 1953 the Battalion was stationed in Egypt for 2½ years.

1956–65

After returning from Egypt the Battalion was based at Pirbright for 3 years and in November 1960 moved to Hubbelrath in Germany to be in 4th Guards Brigade once again. In 1964 the Battalion moved to Chelsea Barracks and celebrated the fiftieth anniversary of the Regiment. Aden followed in 1965 for one year and then Windsor and Pirbright before deploying to Munster in 1970. The first tour of Northern Ireland followed in 1971 before moving back to Chelsea in 1974. More tours in Ireland and Cyprus took place in the late 70's whilst the Battalion was based at Caterham and Pirbright.

The Falklands

On 3rd April 1982 1st Battalion Welsh Guards, were warned of possible participation in the South Atlantic; they were the first Household Division troops to be stood by.

Between 7–9 May all freight, rations, vehicles and drivers were loaded on to two ferries, MV Nordic and MV Baltic. The remainder of the Battalion embarked on The QE2 on 12 May.

On 27 May the QE2 dropped anchor in Gvytviken Bay South Georgia and the Battalion cross decked from the QE2 to the Canberra, and sailed to the Falklands.

The Canberra arrived in San Carlos Bay on 2nd June and on 7 June the Battalion embarked on two LSLs Sir Tristram and Sir Galahad. The latter sailed for Bluff Cove and The Prince of Wales's Company and Number 3 Company sustained heavy casualties as they were in the process of unloading equipment and disembarking from the ship on the following day.

Notwithstanding this setback 1st Battalion Welsh Guards regrouped for the final push on Port Stanley where they captured Sapper Hill overlooking the town.

Recent Years

In 1984 the Battalion moved to Hohne in Germany and then back to Pirbright in 1987. Two years in Ballykelly were followed by 18 months at Tern Hill in Shropshire. The Battalion are based at Wellington Barracks in London. Regimental Headquarters remains in Wellington Barracks with a small office in Cardiff.

HIS ROYAL HIGHNESS THE DUKE OF CORNWALL

Survivors from the bombed blazing landing ship Sir Galahad come ashore in Bluff Cove, Falklands 8 June 1982.

Top: The Prince of Wales's Company 1st Battalion Welsh Guards, mounting Queen's Guard, Forecourt of Buckingham Palace.

THE ROYAL SCOTS
(The Royal Regiment)

The Royal Scots, the oldest Infantry Regiment of the Line in the British Army, was formed in 1633 when Sir John Hepburn under Royal Warrant raised a body of men in Scotland for service in France. By 1635 he commanded a force of over 8,000, including many who had fought as mercenaries in the 'Green Brigade' for King Gustavus Adolphus of Sweden. It was by virtue of the Royal Warrant that the entire Regiment was considered as British; a regular force in a standing Army which could be recalled to Britain at will. And in 1661, the Regiment was summoned to Britain to bridge the gap between the disbanding of the New Model Army and the creation of a Regular Army, organised along the same lines as the British units in foreign service. The Regiment was thus the original model for all others.

In 1680 the Regiment was posted to Tangier and won its first battle honour. On the Regiment's return to England in 1684 the title 'The Royal Regiment of Foot' was conferred by Charles II. During Monmouth's rebellion in 1685, five companies formed part of the force concentrated against the rebels who they met at Sedgemoor. The following year, the Regiment was divided into two battalions and was not to have less until 1949.

The Regiment saw service under Marlborough during the war of the Spanish Succession and followed this with garrison duty in Ireland where it remained until 1742. From this date the two battalions were usually to be separated and posted far apart. The 1st Battalion moved in 1743 to Germany to take part in the Austrian War of Succession, and was involved in the Battle of Fontenoy. In the following year, the 2nd Battalion became involved in the fight against the Young Pretender which culminated in the Battle of Culloden. In 1751 the army was numbered and thereafter the Regiment was officially designated the First or Royal Regiment of Foot.

The war of Austrian Succession had not settled the chief issue between Britain and France, that of colonial supremacy. Both in India and America the fighting continued and most of the Regiment's active service in the 35 years which followed was to be in the New World. From Canada to the West Indies, during the Seven Years War, the 2nd Battalion found itself involved in many actions including the capture of Montreal in 1760 and Havana in 1762. Then, after a period in home service and in the Mediterranean, it was the turn of the 1st Battalion for service in the West Indies. Disease rather than the enemy accounted for most deaths; between 1793–96 the British lost 40,000 men in the West Indies of which The Royals lost 5 officers and 400 men, well over half the battalion strength.

During the Napoleonic Wars the Regiment was increased to a strength of four battalions. The 1st Battalion spent the entire period of the war in the Americas and the 2nd Battalion took part in the capture of Egypt (1801), then moved to the West Indies (1803–05), before travelling to India, the first time that any part of the Regiment had been there. They were to stay until 1831. In contrast the 3rd and 4th Battalions, remained in Europe with the 4th Battalion on home service until 1812 supplying drafts for the other three battalions. The 3rd Battalion first saw action at Corunna in 1808 and then

took part in the Peninsular War. There followed the battles of Quatre Bras and Waterloo which cost the battalion 363 casualties out of a strength of 624. Two years later it was disbanded; the 4th battalion having suffered a similar fate the previous year.

The next ninety years produced a considerable number of moves for both battalions with action in India in 1817–31 where the 2nd Battalion was stationed. The Crimean War was the next major campaign for the Regiment; the 1st Battalion arriving in time for the Battle of Alma. The Regiment's first VC was won by private Prosser during the Siege of Sevastopol for two acts of heroism. In 1900 the 1st Battalion joined British forces in South Africa for service in the Boer War. Most of the time was spent on mobile column work, patrolling and raiding expeditions.

World War I saw the number of battalions increased to 35 of which 15 served as active front line units. More than 100,000 men passed through these battalions, of which 11,000 were killed and over 40,000 wounded. Seventy-one battle honours and 6 VC's were awarded to the Regiment as well as innumerable individual medals. The active service battalions were involved in all areas from the Western Front to the Dardanelles, Macedonia, Egypt and North Russia.

In 1918 HRH Princess Mary became Colonel in Chief, a position she was to hold until her death in March 1965. Demobilisation soon reduced the Regiment's strength to peacetime numbers but in the years that followed there was little rest from active service as the two battalions moved between Ireland, Egypt, Burma, China and the North West Frontier with short periods in home service.

At the start of World War II, the 1st Battalion embarked for France as part of the B.E.F. Forced into the retreat which was to end at Dunkirk, they never made the road to freedom. After a desperate defence across the Bethune-Merville road and after suffering appalling losses, many were taken prisoner and few escaped home. The 2nd Battalion, based in Hong Kong, saw action when the Japanese attacked in December 1941. Here too, The Royal Scots fought like tigers but the result was inevitable. At the end they had just 4 officers and 98 other ranks left and taken prisoner. The 1st Battalion was reconstituted after Dunkirk and took part in the Arakan campaign in Burma in 1943 and the Battle of Kohima in 1944. A new 2nd Battalion (originally the 12th) was formed in May 1942 and served in Italy and Palestine whilst the 7th/9th and 8th fought in Europe after D-Day.

Since 1945 the Regiment has continued to serve in many parts of the world, including Germany, Korea, Cyprus, Suez, Aden and Ireland. In 1949 the two regular battalions amalgamated, the first time since 1686 that the Regiment had been without a second battalion. In 1983 the Regiment celebrated its 350th Anniversary and Her Majesty announced the appointment of her daughter, HRH The Princess Royal to be Colonel in Chief. In December 1990 the battalion deployed to Saudi Arabia as an Armoured Infantry battalion to take part in the Gulf War and it is now part of 24 Airmobile Brigade.

THE DRAMBUIE LIQUEUR COMPANY LTD

A Sergeant of B Company searches Iraqi prisoners, Gulf 1991.

Top: The 3rd Battalion at Waterloo, 1815.

Left: The Royal Scots marching to the Battle of Alma, 1854.

THE PRINCESS OF WALES'S ROYAL REGIMENT
(Queen's and Royal Hampshires)

FORMATION

The Princess of Wales's Royal Regiment (Queen's and Royal Hampshires) is the senior English Infantry Regiment of the Line. It was formed on 9 September 1992 by the amalgamation of The Queen's Regiment and The Royal Hampshire Regiment and is the County Infantry Regiment of Surrey, Kent, Sussex, Hampshire, Isle of Wight, the Channel Islands and Middlesex.

HISTORICAL BACKGROUND

The Queen's Regiment traced its history back to 1572 when Queen Elizabeth I reviewed the Trained Bands of London from which the 3rd Foot descended. Its precedence in the British Army dated from the raising of the 2nd Foot in 1661 for the defence of Tangier, acquired by King Charles II on his marriage to Princess Catherine of Braganza.

The Regiment was formed in 1966 from:

The Queen's Royal Surrey Regiment
an amalgamation in 1959 of:

The Queen's Royal Regiment (West Surrey)
2nd Foot, 'The Mutton Lancers'

and

The East Surrey Regiment
31st and 70th Foot, 'The Young Buffs'.

The Queen's Own Buffs, The Royal Kent Regiment
an amalgamation in 1961 of:

The Buffs (Royal East Kent Regiment)
3rd Foot, 'The Buffs'

and

The Queen's Own Royal West Kent Regiment
50th and 97th Foot, 'The Dirty Half Hundred'.

The Royal Sussex Regiment
35th and 107th Foot, 'The Orange Lillies'

The Middlesex Regiment (Duke of Cambridge's Own)
57th and 77th Foot, 'The Diehards'.

The Royal Hampshire Regiment, 'The Tigers', stems from an amalgamation in 1881 of the 37th (North Hampshire) Regiment and the 67th (South Hampshire) Regiment. The 37th descended from Meredith's Regiment, raised in Ireland in 1702. The 67th was formed in England in 1758 and its first Colonel was James Wolfe, later to be General Wolfe of Quebec fame. The distinction 'Royal' was granted to The Hampshire Regiment in 1946 in recognition of past services.

THE REGIMENT TODAY

The Princess of Wales's Royal Regiment is part of The Queen's Division of Infantry. The Regiment has two Regular battalions (1st and 2nd) available for service worldwide, one TA battalion (3rd) with its headquarters in Canterbury, and two Companies in other TA Regiments.

HRH The Princess of Wales was appointed Colonel-in-Chief on the Regiment's formation in 1992. She relinquished this post in 1996 and HM Queen Margrethe II of Denmark, formerly The Allied Colonel-in-Chief, was appointed sole Colonel-in-Chief in February 1997.

THE REGIMENT'S LINK WITH THE ROYAL HOUSE OF DENMARK

In 1689 the Lord High Admiral's Regiment, the 3rd Foot, was disbanded. The Holland Regiment took its place as the 3 Regiment of Foot, and Prince George of Denmark, who was the husband of Princess (later Queen) Anne and Lord High Admiral, was appointed Honorary Colonel. From 1689 until his death in 1708, The Holland Regiment was known as Prince George of Denmark's Regiment. The link with Denmark then lapsed until 1906 when King Frederik VIII of Denmark was appointed Colonel-in-Chief, The Buffs (East Kent Regiment), as the 3rd Foot had become. This appointment re-established the link with the past and was also intended as a compliment to Queen Alexandra who was a Danish Princess. Since then, successive Kings of Denmark have been Colonels-in-Chief of The Buffs during their lifetime. His late Majesty King Frederik IX became, in 1961, Colonel-in-Chief The Queen's Own Buffs, and in 1966, Allied Colonel-in-Chief The Queen's Regiment. Her Majesty Queen Margrethe II assumed the appointment of Allied Colonel-in-Chief of The Queen's Regiment in 1972; her appointment was

transferred to the Princess of Wales's Royal Regiment 9 September 1992. Her Majesty assumed the appointment of sole Colonel-in-Chief in 1997.

REGIMENTAL DAYS

Three important anniversaries are celebrated as Regimental Days:

Albuhera Day on 16 May honours the exceptional bravery of the 3rd, 31st and 57th Regiments of Foot at the Battle of Albuhera in 1811 during the Peninsular War.

Minden Day on 1 August recalls the Battle in 1759 when the 37th Foot was one of six battalions of British Infantry which defeated massed squadrons of French cavalry for the first time.

Salerno Day on 9 September celebrates the famous landing in Italy in 1943. Uniquely at this battle there were two brigades of Queen's battalions and one brigade of Hampshire battalions. For this reason the present Regiment was formed on this anniversary.

BADGES

Regimental Badge

The Regimental Badge is a composition of the badges of the forebear regiments. The Dragon was awarded to The Buffs, in recognition of their Tudor origin, by Queen Anne, probably in 1707. It was a rare distinction for a Regiment to be thus honoured in those days and it is one of the earliest known Regimental badges.

Below the Tudor Dragon is the Hampshire Rose as worn by the Trained Bands of Hampshire who fought so gallantly for King Henry V at Agincourt in 1415.

The surrounding device inscribed with the motto 'Honi Soit Qui Mal Y Pense' (Shame on him who thinks ill of it), is a garter, as awarded to the Knights of the Order of the Garter, England's oldest Order of Chivalry, founded by King Edward III in 1348. The garter is taken from the badges of the Royal Sussex Regiment and the officers' badge of The Royal Hampshire Regiment.

The feathers above the Tudor Dragon are the ostrich plumes worn by The Black Prince at the Battle of Crecy in 1346. The 15th Prince of Wales considered the East Middlesex Regiment to be deserving of his plumes for its exploits in India. The award was given the King's approval in 1810 and was subsequently included in the badge of the Middlesex Regiment.

Sleeve Badge

The Royal Tiger badge which is worn on the left sleeve was authorised for wear by the 67th Foot by King George IV in 1826 when the Regiment returned to England after 21 years in India under active service conditions. The Regiment's nickname is the 'The Tigers'.

FIGHTING RECORD

The forebear regiments of the Princess of Wales's Royal Regiment fought in nearly all the major campaigns and wars in which the British Army was engaged. They won no less than 56 Victoria Crosses, an outstanding record and were awarded over 550 Battle Honours including 'Tangier 1662–80', the oldest on any Colour.

TRADITIONS

The Regiment has many historic traditions. Among these are:

The Loyal Toast which is drunk seated because of the Regiment's Naval connections, each mess member and guest responding to the toast in rotation.

The Silent Toast to the 'Immortal Memory' of all who fell at the Battle of Albuhera and have subsequently been killed serving with the Regiment. This is drunk by officers and sergeants together every Albuhera Day.

The Minden Rose which is worn in the headdress of all ranks on Minden Day to commemorate the 37th Foot who picked roses as they returned from the battle.

The Sobraon Sergeant who is a specially selected member of the WO's and Sgts' Mess who takes charge of the Regimental Colour on each anniversary of the Battle of Sobraon (10 February 1846) in memory of the heroic action of Sergeant McCabe of the 31st Foot at this action.

A member of the Regiment with friends.

Top: The Regiment's 'Drum Display' and silver.

Left: Inspection by HRH Diana, Princess of Wales, as Colonel-in-Chief, 1992 to 1996.

THE KING'S OWN ROYAL BORDER REGIMENT

The King's Own Royal Border Regiment, the County Infantry Regiment of Cumbria and North Lancashire is the successor to three famous Regiments the 4th, 34th and 55th Regiments of Foot. The 4th Foot, later the King's Own Royal Regiment (Lancaster), was raised by King Charles II on 13 July 1680 for service in Tangier. The 34th Foot was raised on 12 February 1702 amd the 55th formed at Stirling in 1755. The latter two regiments received the county titles of Cumberland and Westmorland respectively in 1782 and in 1881 became the 1st and 2nd Battalions of The Border Regiment.

When William of Orange landed at Torbay in 1688, the 4th Foot were one of the first Regiments to go over to him, for which the Regiment was granted the distinction of wearing the Lion of England as its badge. The Regiment served as marines in the early 1700s and took part in the capture of Gibraltar and Barcelona and was awarded the Battle Honour Gibraltar.

The 34th Foot served in Flanders 1743–5 during the War of the Austrian Succession. At the Battle of Fontenoy on 30 April 1745, the 34th played a distinguished role covering the retreat of the allied army. Although no battle honour was awarded for the defeat, the Regiment received a laurel wreath for its gallant action. This Wreath and the Lion form the present cap badge.

The 4th and 34th took part in the campaign against the Jacobites, both being present at the battle of Culloden in April 1746, where the 4th bore the brunt of the Highland charge. The 4th, 34th and 55th all served during the Seven Years War 1756–63 and in North America during the War of Independence.

In the Peninsular War the 4th and 34th served with distinction. The 4th were in the rearguard of Sir John Moore's Army at Corunna in 1809, fought in the siege at Badajoz in 1812, was instrumental in forcing a breach in the walls at San Sebastian in 1813, served in the American War and returned to Europe in time to serve at Waterloo, having marched 48 miles in 30 hours with its Brigade. The 2nd Battalion of the 34th fought their French opposite number the 34th Regiment of the Line at Arroyo dos Molinos on 28 October 1811. In the total victory the 34th captured the French Regiment's drums and Drum-Major's Staff. The Battle honour Arroyo dos Molinos is unique and, operational commitments permitting, the French Drums are paraded on the anniversary of the battle to this day.

In the China War the 55th played a distinguished part and captured the Imperial Dragon Standard at Nanking. For this it received the Honour China and the device of a dragon, borne on the Colours and insignia. All three Regiments served in the Crimean War 1854–56 and suffered awful casualties from sickness and the conditions. Five of the newly instituted Victoria Cross were awarded to members of the Regiments. The 4th and 34th were in the Indian Mutiny, the 55th later went to India and the 4th saw service in Abyssinia in 1868 and the Zulu War of 1879.

As part of Cardwell's reforms in 1873 north Lancashire was assigned to the 4th Foot and the Depot built at Bowerham in Lancaster. The 34th and 55th were linked the same year and their Depot was established in Carisle Castle. In 1881 the numbers in the titles were dropped and the 4th King's Own became the King's Own (Royal Lancaster Regiment) and the 34th and 55th the Border Regiment. Into this new regimental system came the volunteer forces to form Militia and Volunteer Battalions, the predecessors of the Territorial Army. Regular, Militia and Volunteer soldiers of both Regiments fought in The Boer War of 1899–1902, including the battles at Colenso, Spion Kop and Tugela Heights and during the long period of guerrilla warfare for the last 18 months of the War.

At the outbreak of War in 1914 each Regiment had two regular and two Territorial battalions. By its end over 60,000 officers and men has served in thirty-two battalions, of which nineteen fought in France, Flanders, Italy, Macedonia (Greece), Gallipoli, Mesopotamia (Iraq) and on the NW Frontier. Among the hundreds of awards for gallantry were 13 VCs, but the war cost the Regiment nearly 14,000 lives. From 1919 to 1939 the two regiments saw service in Ireland, India, China, England, Egypt and Palestine.

During the Second World War, both Regiments expanded and eleven battalions served in the infantry role, as glider troops, gunners and in armour in North-West Europe, Italy, the western Desert, Malta and Sicily, Iraq and Syria, India and Burma. 1 King's Own were the first unit to be flown into battle when they were air-lifted in 1941 from Karachi for the defence of the RAF base at Habbaniya in Iraq. 1 Border served as a glider borne battalion in 1st Airborne Division and took part in the first allied glider landings on Sicily on 9/10 July 1943. For this the Battalion was awarded the glider badge, which is still worn on the uniform today. It later served with distinction at Arnhem in September 1944. 4 Border, having served in France in 1940, joined 2 King's Own and were well travelled, fighting the Vichy French in Syria, the Italians and Germans around Tobruk in the Western Desert and finally the Japanese in the Chindit operations of 1944. 2 and 9 Border served with distinction in Burma, as did 56 Anti-Tank regiment (King's Own).

After WW2 each Regiment was reduced to one Regular and one TA Battalion. It was a period of peace-keeping with service in India, Palestine, East Africa, Germany, Egypt, Korea, Hong Kong and Aden. In October 1959 the 1st Battalions of the King's Own and Border Regiments amalgamated at Barnard Castle to form The King's Own Royal Border Regiment.

Peace-keeping has been at the heart of Regimental operations over the last 40 years. The 1st Battalion went to the Cameroons in 1960, has served in Germany, British Guiana, Bahrein with Company tours in Aden in 1967, Cyprus and numerous tours in Ireland including three residential tours 1971–3, 1985–87 and 1992–95; the last of almost three years was the longest carried out by any infantry unit since the start of The Troubles in 1969. They have served in the Falklands, Cyprus again with the UN and Belize and in 1980 celebrated its Tercentenary with the presentation of New Colours by Princess Alexandra. In 1995 they converted to an armoured infantry role with the Warrior APC and, between training in the UK and Canada completed a tour in Bosnia 1997–8. Currently a large battle group from the Battalion are based in Macedonia with the NATO Extraction Force. The Territorials have gone through several major re-organisations since 1959 and the 4th Battalion has consistently been one of the best TA Battalions in the UK. Over 30 of its members recently served with the 1st Battalion in Bosnia. Sadly in 1999 it was reduced to two companies in one of the new NW TA Battalions, but this continues a 140 year tradition of volunteer service in Cumbria and North Lancashire.

Colours – The Crown with underneath, the Royal Cypher surrounded by the garter; the garter and cypher surrounded by the Fontenoy laurel wreath; the whole surrounded by the union wreath, under the tie of which is the Dragon superscribed CHINA; in each of the four corners of the Lion of England. Sixty of the Regiment's 150 Battle Honours are borne on the Colours.

Affiliations

The King's Own Calgary Regiment, Canada
The Royal Queensland Regiment, Australia
The 15th Battalion Pakistan Frontier Force
The Julia Brigade, Italy
HMS Cumberland and HMS Trafalgar

A.F. BLAKEMORE & SON LTD

1st (Airborne) Battalion in action at Osterbeek during the Battle of Arnhem, September 1944.

Top: Mortally wounded ensign points the way forward to the 4th King's Own, siege of San Sebastian, 1813.

Left: Muleteer serving as a Chindit, Burma 1944.

THE ROYAL REGIMENT OF FUSILIERS

'The Fusiliers' is the short title for the Regiment. Although one of the newest infantry regiments in the British Army, formed by order of Her Majesty The Queen on 23 April 1968, it draws upon the traditions and history of its four antecedent regiments (The Royal Northumberland Fusiliers, The Royal Warwickshire Fusiliers, The Royal Fusiliers and The Lancashire Fusiliers (V, VI, VII & XXth). The Regimental Headquarters is in Her Majesty's Tower of London, indeed RHQ is the only military unit remaining in the Tower. Here it was that the Royal Fusiliers, City of London Regiment, was formed in 1685.

Today the famous red and white hackle of the Royal Northumberland Fusiliers, formed 326 years ago in 1674, is worn by Fusiliers of all ranks.

Also in the Tower of London is the Regiment's mascot, Bobby. He is an Indian Black Buck antelope and is the only wild animal mascot authorised for a regiment in the British Army. Before 1968 Bobby had been the mascot of the Royal Warwickshire Fusiliers.

The Lancashire Fusiliers, famous for their 'six VCs before breakfast' at Gallipoli, are the forth of their antecedent regiments. In addition to Gallipoli the Fusiliers celebrate the battle of Minden on the 1st of August each year.

The Colonel-in-Chief of The Royal Regiment of Fusiliers is Field Marshal His Royal Highness The Duke of Kent KG, who was appointed in 1969 by Her Majesty The Queen. The connection of the House of Kent with the Regiment originated in 1789 when his Royal Highness Prince Edward, who was created Duke of Kent on 23rd April 1799, was appointed the 12th Colonel of the 7th Royal Fusiliers. Prince Edward was the father of Queen Victoria and the great great great grandfather of the present Colonel-in-Chief. The present Duke of Kent's father was appointed Colonel-in-Chief of the Royal Fusiliers in 1937, after the death of his father, King George V, who had been Colonel-in-Chief of that regiment since 1900.

Other unique attributes of the Fusiliers are their Northumbrian Pipers, and the Wilhelmstahl Colour.

The Northumberland Pipes are a regimental asset which testifies to the link between the Fusiliers and the Duke of Northumberland and the Percy family. A small number of proficient and dedicated volunteers maintain the Northumberland Pipes within the Regiment.

In addition to the Queen's Colour and the Regimental Colour, the Regiment also has the gosling green Wilhelmstahl or Drummer's Colour. This is a commemorative banner sanctioned by King George V which the Royal Regiment of Fusiliers inherited from the Royal Northumberland Fusiliers.

Archives and treasures are displayed in our four Regimental museums in Alnwick Castle, St John's House Warwick, the Tower of London and in Bury.

In the last decade Fusiliers fought with distinction in the Gulf, indeed the 3rd Battalion, since disbanded, earned outright the Battle Honour Wadi Al Batin on 26 February 1991. The 1st Battalion deployed to Bosnia as part of Operation Grapple in 1995. The 2nd Battalion has also served in Bosnia but as part of the NATO stabilisation force. In the year of the Millennium the 1st Battalion are serving their country on an unaccompanied tour in South Armagh – the 32nd tour in the province for the regiment. The 2nd Battalion serves as armoured infantry with their Warrior fighting vehicle as part of 7 Armoured Brigade, 'The Desert Rats'.

Over the past 300 years the Regiment has established alliances, affiliations and bands of friendship with other Regiments, Ships and Units. The Fusiliers are proud to carry forward these alliances into the new Millennium:

(The list below includes Allied HM Ships some of which are to be decommissioned following SDR).

Allied Regiments

Allied Regiments of the Canadian Army
The Royal Canadian Regiment, Petawawa, Ontario
The Lorne Scots (Peel, Dufferin and Halton Regiment) Brampton, Ontario
31 Combat Engineer Regiment (The Elgins), St Thomas, Ontario
The Royal Westminster Regiment, New Westminster, British Columbia
Fusiliers du St Laurent, Rimouski, Quebec

Allied Regiment of the Australian Military Forces
5th/6th Battalion The Royal Victoria Regiment, Melbourne

Allied Regiment of the New Zealand Army
6th Battalion (Hauraki) Royal New Zealand Infantry Regiment, Tauranga

Allied HM Ships
HMS Birmingham
HMS Coventry
HMS London
HMS Northumberland

Allied Squadron Royal Air Force
13 Squadron Royal Air Force

Bobby, on parade outside his London residence, The Tower.

Right, top: Badajoz, 6 April 1812 – the 5th, led by Lieutenant-Colonel Ridge, who lost his life, storm the breach.

Right, bottom: Regimental Standards are paraded at a Fusilier Gathering, Germany 1998.

THE KING'S REGIMENT

THE CITY REGIMENT OF LIVERPOOL AND MANCHESTER

Formed in 1685, the King's Regiment comprises the 1st or regular battalion, stationed with its families in Weeton, Lancashire, and the 5th/8th or Territorial Army battalion which has bases in Liverpool, Warrington and Manchester. The Colonel in Chief is HM Queen Elizabeth the Queen Mother and the Colonel of the Regiment is Brigadier Jeremy Gaskell OBE. The Regiment and its many friends are pleased to know that after the Strategic Defence Review, the Regiment will retain a TA presence in Liverpool and in Manchester.

The Regiment has Battle honours from service all over the world, from Marlborough's battles in the 18th Century to Korea in 1953. These battle honours trace the history of a Regiment always at the forefront of fighting since the modern army was created. They include honours gained in the American War of Independence during which a battalion both fought and garrisoned the Canada/US border. A battalion fought in Egypt in the Napoleonic wars and captured a French colour. Another battalion fought with Wellington in the Peninsula. A battalion was awarded the rare battle honour 'New Zealand'. In the Crimea, a battalion led the charge at the battle of Inkerman, routing the Russians, despite the loss of most of the officers.

The Regiment saw extensive service in the Boer War. This was the first major operation when volunteer battalions raised troops to fight alongside their regular army counterparts. At the siege of Ladysmith, battalions of both the King's (Liverpool) and the Manchester Regiment fought alongside each other in the successful defence. Two of the Regiment's VCs were won at the siege and 'Ladysmith' is the Regiment's premier battle honour.

In the 1st World War the Regiment raised the second largest number of battalions of any Regiment in the Army – 87. The 'Pals' battalions of the Regiment were the only battalions to gain their objectives on the first day of the Somme, fighting alongside each other. Battalions fought in France and Flanders, in Gallipoli, Salonika, Mesopotamia, Italy and after the Armistice, in Russia against the Bolsheviks. In the 2nd World War, the Regiment served worldwide. Regular and TA battalions fought in France in 1940, took part in the heroic defence of Malta and throughout the Italian campaign including the Cassino battles. Two first line Territorial battalions, the 5th (Rifle) and the 8th (Irish), landed in the first few minutes of the D-day operation. A war service battalion, destined originally for garrison duty fought with great distinction in the first Chindit expedition in Burma and a regular battalion fought with equal bravery, providing the glider borne spearhead of the second Chindit expedition. At Singapore, a regular battalion was taken prisoner by the Japanese and endured appalling hardship before the end of the war. Another regular battalion fought as a machine gun battalion in Kohima and Imphal as part of the 2nd Division. In the final operations in North West Europe, a regular battalion fought to the end of the war as a machine gun battalion and a Territorial battalion was used in an almost unique role as the main part of a 'T Force – a battlegroup assembled to capture installations, documents, equipment and individuals of value to the allies.

In the last 50 years, regular battalions, often reinforced from Territorial battalions, have served on operations in Malaya, Kenya, Kuwait, Northern Ireland, Hong Kong and Belize. Garrisons have been provided for Guyana, the Falklands and of course for extended periods all over Germany. Prior to the end of the Cold War, battalions had trained intensely to take their place in the NATO order of battle and face the Warsaw pact threat. Men from Liverpool and Manchester have been decorated for gallantry in all theatres and most recently in Northern Ireland. Individuals from both battalions of the Regiment continue to serve in former Yugoslavia. Both battalions have sent Kingsmen to exercise throughout the world, including recently Canada, the USA, Ascension Island, Egypt, Jordan, the Caribbean.

The Regiment's volunteer battalion tradition stems both from its 5th (Rifle) Battalion The King's Regiment (Liverpool), which was originally the third to be raised in the country and the first in the North West of England, and the 8th Battalion The Manchester Regiment. This tradition is maintained in the 5th/8th Battalion which includes the Liverpool Scottish Company, tracing its origins to the Liverpool Scottish battalion whose doctor in the 1st World War gained one of only three bars ever awarded to the Victoria Cross. In total, 23 Victoria Crosses and one George Cross have been awarded to men of the Regiment, including one of the very few VCs to have been awarded between the 1st and 2nd World Wars.

The 1st Battalion comprises 35 officers recruited from all over the Country and nearly 600 men recruited almost exclusively from Liverpool and Manchester. In addition there are many thousands of former serving officers and soldiers settled in the North West of England and throughout the United Kingdom who retain the closest links with the Regiment through the two Regimental offices in Liverpool and Manchester.

The Regiment has a fine sporting record, having won the unique Army double of Boxing and Football champions in its Tercentenary year of 1985. Many of the Regiment's Boxers have fought for their country and the battalion football team had the privilege of training with England's winning 1966 World Cup Squad. Many of the Regiment's serving and former personnel have represented the Army or their country at the highest levels of sport. One, Shea Neary, is currently a world boxing champion. He developed his boxing skills as an amateur in the Regiment.

Liverpool, Manchester and the Borough of Tameside have honoured the Regiment with the granting of the freedom of the Cities and the Borough. This very close link is exemplified by the warmth and goodwill extended to the Regiment by civic and commercial institutions in both cities and the Borough. The Regiment is immensely proud of its unique position as the Army's only City Regiment.

Two Corporals volunteer for the 'camel corps'.

Right, top: The Lord Mayors of Liverpool and Manchester present Colour Belts and admire the Queen's Colour (left) and the Regimental Colour.

Right, bottom: Training in Egypt with the Egyptian Army.

THE ROYAL ANGLIAN REGIMENT

The Royal Anglian Regiment is the Regiment of the ten Counties of East Anglia and the East Midlands. It was formed in 1964 from the Regiments of the East Anglian Brigade, which themselves had been formed through a series of amalgamations between 1958 and 1960. The Regiment is therefore the successor to the seven famous former County Regiments of Norfolk, Lincolnshire, Suffolk and Cambridgeshire, Bedfordshire and Hertfordshire, Leicestershire, Essex, Northamptonshire and Rutland.

The former Regiments as they are called, included the 9th Regiment of Foot, later The Royal Norfolk Regiment, which was raised in 1685, and whose Britannia badge had been awarded for its great bravery at the battle of Almanza in Spain in 1707 during the Wars of the Spanish Succession.

The 10th of Foot, later The Royal Lincolnshire Regiment, had also been raised in 1685 and had been awarded its Sphinx emblem and Honour Egypt for service under Wellington in 1801. Its most famous Battle Honour was gained at Sobraon in 1846 during the Sikh Wars in India.

The 12th of Foot, later The Suffolk Regiment, had been raised in 1685 and had won the battle Honour Minden in Germany in 1759 during the Seven Years War. It was awarded the emblem of the Castle and Key of Gibraltar for its part in the Great Siege of 1779–83.

The 16th of Foot, later The Bedfordshire Regiment, was raised in 1688 and was awarded the additional title of Hertfordshire in 1919. Its most famous Battle Honour was gained at the Battle of Blenheim in 1704 during the Duke of Marlborough's campaigns against the French.

The 17th of Foot, later the Royal Leicestershire Regiment, was raised in 1688. In 1777 it was awarded the unbroken Laurel Wreath Emblem for its bravery at the Battle of Princetown in the American War of Independence and in 1825 the insignia of the Royal Tiger superimposed with the word Hindoostan for exemplary service in India.

The Essex Regiment was raised in 1741 and incorporated the 44th and 56th Regiments of Foot. It took part in the Great Siege of Gibraltar from 1779–83 and was awarded the Castle and Key emblem. At the Battle of Salamanca in 1812 in the Peninsular War it captured a French Eagle, the highly treasured emblem of a French Regiment.

The 48th/58th Foot, later The Northamptonshire Regiment, was raised in 1741. It took took part in the Great Siege of Gibraltar and was awarded the Castle and Key emblem. Its most famous Battle Honour Talavera was gained in 1809 during the Duke of Wellington's campaigns in the Peninsula.

The Cambridgeshire Regiment which eventually became part of the Suffolk Regiment has an unusual history. A contingent of about 50 from Cambridgeshire went to South Africa with the Suffolk Regiment in 1900. In 1908 the Territorial Force was created and the Militia disbanded. The normal organisation of a Regiment was two regular battalions, one Special Reserve (ex Militia) and one Territorial Force (ex Volunteers). There were no regular Cambridgeshire battalions so the 1st Battalion, which formed in 1908 was a territorial battalion and the regiment of the county. Territorial battalions of The Cambridgeshire Regiment fought in both World Wars. In 1947 The Cambridgeshire Regiment was reformed as a Light Anti Aircraft Regiment RA TA, both becoming a Parachute Light Regiment RA TA. When the TA Airborne Division was disbanded they once more became infantry. In 1961 they became part of The Suffolk Regiment and were subsequently disbanded. In 1971 a TA company was raised in Cambridge as part of the 6th Battalion The Royal Anglian Regiment, so the traditions of the Cambridgeshires continue in this sub unit.

The seven Former Regiments amalgamated between 1958 and 1960 to form the 1st, 2nd and 3rd East Anglian Regiments. This was followed in 1964 by those Regiments and The Royal Leicestershire Regiment becoming the four Regular Battalions of The Royal Anglian Regiment, the first Large Regiment of Infantry to be formed in the British Army. At the same time the Former Regiments' seven TA Battalions were affiliated to the new Regiment and were later to become The Royal Anglian Regiment's 5th Battalion in 1967 and the 6th and 7th Battalions in 1971.

The 17th of Foot, later the Royal Leicestershire Regiment was raised in 1688 by Colonel Solomon Richards. The Regiment went to India in 1804 and remained there continuously for nineteen years engaged in numerous operations on the North West Frontier. In 1825 King George IV approved the wearing on its colours the figure of the Royal Tiger with the word Hindoostan superscribed. The Royal Leicstershire Regiment fought with distinction most recently in the Korean War and moved from the Forester Brigade to become the 4th battalion (Leicestershire) of The Royal Anglian Regiment when it was formed on 1 September 1964. The battalion lost its Leicestershire title in 1968 and was reduced to a Representative Company in 1970 and eventually disbanded in 1975. The 'Tigers' are remembered today by the wearing of the tiger emblem on Royal Anglian regimental buttons.

By 1996 the four Regular and three Territorial Army battalions of The Royal Anglian Regiment were reduced to two Regular Battalions the 1st and 2nd, and two Territorial Army Battalions, the 6th and 7th. This remains the Regiment's current organisation.

In spite of the contractions over recent years that result in four Battalions representing 10 counties, the history and traditions of the Former Regiments are not forgotten. They live on in the ceremonial, customs and dress of the present Regiment – the black lanyard to commemorate the death of General Wolfe, the black cap badge backing that commemorates the death of Sir John Moore at Corunna, the wearing of Minden roses, the Salamanca Eagle which is still paraded on important occasions, the Sphinx, Tiger, Britannia and Gibraltar Castle and Key emblems that illustrate and celebrate the rich 300 year long history of the Regiment.

In its operations, too, the Regiment maintains the high reputation of its predecessors with involvement in garrison, peace-keeping and counter-terrorist duties around the world. Since the early 1960s this has included involvement in operations in the Malayan Emergency, Indonesian Confrontation, British Guiana, Libya and with the Commonwealth Monitoring Force in Rhodesia. The 1st Battalion's capture of Jebel Huriyah in 1964 was to signal the end of the Radfan Campaign, while all Regular Battalions saw active service in Aden in the final years leading up to Independence.

In recent years the Regiment has seen its share of active service. The regular battalions have completed over thirty tours in Northern Ireland, a number of tours with the United Nations in Cyprus plus others in the Gulf and Former Yugoslavia. In 1996 whilst serving in the Banya Luka area of Bosnia Corporal M. Rainey was awarded the Military Cross for his actions when his platoon, mounted in Warrior Fighting vehicles was engaged by Serb forces. Many members of the Territorial battalions have served alongside their regular counterparts further strenghtening the links between the regulars and territorials and with the Counties from which the Regiment recruits.

The 'Vikings' and 'Poachers', the Regiment's Regular 1st and 2nd Battalions, the 6th (Volunteer) Battalion and the 'Tigers', the 7th (Volunteer) Battalion, continue to maintain the traditions and reputation of their illustrious Former Regiments in a uniquely modern form while maintaining close links with their County roots.

The 1st Battalion Colour Party parades with Minden Roses on Minden Day, 1 August.

LINCOLNSHIRE COUNTY COUNCIL

A 2nd Battalion soldier or 'Poacher' on patrol in Bosnia.

Top: Deputy Colonel-in-Chief HRH The Princess Margaret with Commanding Officers after presentation of new Colours, Duxford 1995. To the rear, the flags of the present and former Regiments.

THE DEVONSHIRE AND DORSET REGIMENT

The Devonshire Regiment (11th Foot (1685–1958))

To help to defeat the rebellion under the Duke of Monmouth in 1685, the loyal residents of Devonshire, Somerset and Dorset were formed into a regiment under the Duke of Beaufort; this regiment became the 11th or North Devonshire Regiment of Foot. The first battle-honour gained was Dettingen (1743) – the last battle in which a King of England (George II) commanded his army in the field. In the Peninsula War (1808–14), the Regiment saw much service, with many honours gained, under the Duke of Wellington; and in particular distinguished itself at the battle of Salamanca (1812) when its gallantry and heavy casualties earned it the nickname of 'The Bloody Eleventh', still used to this day. It gained honours on and beyond the Indian Frontier, including Afghanistan between 1879 and 1897, before both Regular battalions were heavily engaged during the Anglo Boer War of 1899–1902. During the Siege of Ladysmith the 1st Battalion distinguished itself at Wagon Hill for its courageous charge on 6th January 1900 and Lt Masterson won the VC in this successful action.

During the First World War, 25 battalions of the Devons served in France and Flanders, in Italy, at Salonica and in the Middle East, winning many more battle honours. It was during the Battle of the Somme in 1916, that both Pte Veale (8th Bn) and LCpl Onions (1st Bn) won the VC. If one action is singled out, it must be the gallant stand 'to the last man and the last round' of the 2nd Battalion at Bois des Buttes, on 27th May 1918, following which the French Government conferred the Croix de Guerre on the 2nd Devons in recognition of their great service to the Allied cause. The Croix de Guerre ribbon is worn on the sleeve of uniforms to this day.

In the Second World War whilst the 1st Devons were fighting in Burma, the 2nd Devons with the 1st Dorsets, took part in three assault landings – Sicily, Italy and Normandy in the famous 231 (Malta) Infantry Brigade, after being besieged in Malta. The 12th Devons fought as an airlanding battalion in the 6th Airborne Division. After the War, the Devons saw active service in Malaya (1948–50) and then in the Mau Mau terrorist operations in Kenya (1953–55).

The Dorset Regiment (39th and 54th Foot) (1702–1958)

The 39th Foot was raised in 1702 with several other regiments, owing to the outbreak of the War of the Spanish Succession. The 54th Foot was raised in 1755. A Battle Honour unique in the British Army, Plassey (1757) was won by the 39th under Lord Clive in India, and with it the proud motto 'Primus in Indis'. Later, the 39th was one of the four British Infantry regiments to serve throughout the great siege of Gibraltar (1779–83), and was the only one to serve also in the previous siege of 1727. The central feature of their cap badge was the 'Castle and Key'. In 1801, the 54th Foot also gained a unique battle honour, Marabout, in Egypt, against Napoleon's Army. Flushed with success, the 54th arrived at Gibraltar, in time to put down a mutiny in the garrison and so assist in saving the life of the Duke of Kent, Queen Victoria's father, who was Governor of the Fortress. Since then the House of Kent has been associated with the Regiment through the Colonels-in-Chief.

Like the 11th Foot, the 39th also saw service in the Peninsula, particularly distinguishing themselves at Albuhera and Vittoria. During the nineteenth century, battle honours were won in the Crimea War (1854–6), in India and Burma, and in the South Africa War; and in the Tirah Campaign of 1897, LCpl Vickery won the VC. The epic of the SS Sarah Sands occurred when the 54th were en route to India during the Mutiny of 1857; the officers and men of the regiment were primarily responsible for saving the blazing ship, filled with gunpowder, and bringing her eventually into Mauritius. A most complimentary Order was read at the head of every Regiment in the Army as a result, by order of the Commander-in-Chief.

During the First World War, 10 battalions of the Dorsets served in France and Flanders, (the 1st Battalion starting at Mons), in the Gallipoli Peninsula and in the Middle East. In Mesopotamia the 2nd Battalion greatly distinguished itself, as did the battalions on the western Front.

In the Second World War, the 1st Dorsets served alongside the 2nd Devons in 231 (Malta) Brigade and the 4th (TA) Battalion, which, with the 5th, formed part of the 43rd Wessex Division, sacrificed itself in going to the rescue of the Airborne troops at Arnhem. The 2nd Battalion, like the 1st Devons, served in Burma.

The Devonshire and Dorset Regiment (11th, 39th and 54th Foot) (1958 to date)

The amalgamation of the two famous old County Regiments took place in Minden, Germany in 1958, and the presentation of its first Stand of Colours by the then Colonel-in-Chief, HRH The Duchess of Kent, in Plymouth in 1962. The new cap badge embodied the Castle of Exeter and 'Semper Fidelis'

from the Devons, and 'Primus in Indus' and the Sphinx with 'Marabout' from the Dorsets.

During the 1st Battalion's existence, it has served in BAOR, Cyprus, the UK, British Guiana (Guyana), Libya, Malta, British Honduras (Belize), and Northern Ireland. Most of this service, including 10 tours to Northern Ireland, one of which as a Resident Battalion, have been active service of one kind or another, the latest of which was to Bosnia in 1995; operational in Northern Ireland, 'peace-keeping' in Cyprus, Belize and Bosnia and 'internal security' in British Guiana and Libya. The role in BAOR for much of this time has been that of a NATO Mechanised Battalion in 1 (BR) Corps, however from 1991 to 1998 this changed to an Armoured Infantry (WARRIOR) role in 1 (UK) Armoured Division, part of NATO's Allied Rapid Reaction Corps. During this time the 1st Battalion trained in Kenya, Canada, Sicily, Italy, France and Poland where they were the first British troops to exercise on Polish soil since before the Second World War. The Battalion is now stationed at Warminster as the Army's Infantry Training and Demonstration Battalion.

The Regiment's Territorial Army Battalion, the 4th Battalion, was re-formed in 1987, 20 years after disbandment of the old County TA battalions in 1967. The battalion inherited the title 'The 1st Rifle Volunteers' marking the formation of the Exeter and South Devon Rifle Volunteers in 1852, the first ever Volunteer Battalion. The present 4th Battalion, whose Headquarters is in Exeter, has Rifle Companies in Plymouth, Dorchester and Poole, and Headquarter Company and Support Group in Exeter and Paignton. Their role is that of a General Reserve Battalion for Home Defence or in 3 (UK) Division in support of NATO.

The Regiment has the Freedom of 13 cities and towns in its two Counties. The Devonshire Regiment Chapel and The Devonshire and Dorset Regiment Chapel are both in Exeter Cathedral and the Dorset Regiment Chapel in Sherborne Abbey. The present Colonel-in-Chief, HRH The Duke of Kent KG, was appointed in 1977. Regimental Headquarters is in Exeter, the Regimental Museum at The Keep Military Museum in Dorchester with displays in four Freedom Towns/Cities in Devon, namely Plymouth, Exeter, Torbay and Barnstaple.

Military Museum of the Regiment – The Keep, Dorchester.

Right, top: The last stand of the 2nd Devons at Bois des Buttes, 27 May 1918.

Right, bottom: 1st Battalion in Bosnia – exercising with LAW 80.

THE LIGHT INFANTRY

The Origins of Light Infantry

Although there had been 'light troops' in the British Army in the 1740s, it was the colonial war between France and England in North America which established the concept of 'Light Infantry' in the British Army.

In the North American Wars of the 1750s, the heavy equipment, conspicuous red and white uniforms and close formation fighting of the British Army proved to be wholly unsuitable when operating in close country against Indians and French colonists, who had highly developed fieldcraft and marksmanship skills. A small corps of 'Light' troops, recruited from the settlers, was formed in 1755. It consisted of specially trained men, carefully selected for their toughness and intelligence, able to scout and skirmish, concentrating and dispersing with great stealth and speed. Their dress, equipment and tactics were adjusted to meet this new role.

So effective were these 'Light' troops that steps were taken to increase the number available. Regiments formed 'Light Companies' of soldiers specially selected for their toughness, intelligence, military skills and ability to act on their own initiative. The bugle horn, which subsequently became the emblem of light troops, replaced the drum as the means of communication for the often widely dispersed Light Companies. The invasion of Spain by Napoleon in 1802 was to cause a further, rapid evolution of the Light Infantry concept under the leadership and training of the brilliant young general, Sir John Moore.

General Sir John Moore

John Moore joined the 51st Regiment of Foot, later to become The King's Own Yorkshire Light Infantry. In 1790 at the age of thirty he was appointed to command of the 51st serving in Ireland, Gibraltar and Corsica. It was in 1802 at Shorncliffe in Kent that he began to develop further his ideas for the training of infantrymen, grouping regiments to fight together as Light Infantry and eventually forming the Light Division which fought with such distinction in the Peninsula War.

Development of the Light Infantry

During the early nineteenth century it became the practice to grant, as a honour, the much coveted title of 'Light Infantry' to regiments which particularly distinguished themselves in action. The regiments which were to form the present Light Infantry were all granted this distinction and subsequently incorporated it into the Regiment's name. Those regiments, and the year in which they became Light Infantry, were:

1808

>68th Foot
>The Durham Light Infantry

1809

>51st Foot
>The King's Own Yorkshire Light Infantry

>53rd Foot
>The King's Shropshire Light Infantry

1822/4

>13th Foot
>The Somerset Light Infantry (Prince Albert's)

1858

>32nd Foot
>The Duke of Cornwall's Light Infantry

Formation of the New Regiment

The new regiment, The Light Infantry (LI), was formed on Vesting Day – 10th July 1968 – from the four regular battalions: 1 Somerset & Cornwall Light Infantry (SCLI), 1 King's Own Yorkshire Light Infantry (KOYLI), 1 King's Shropshire Light Infantry (KSLI), 1 Durham Light Infantry (DLI) and the Light Infantry Volunteers. The Light Infantry was so structured that the traditions and customs of its forbears were embodied equally in all battalions. The long-established and much cherished links with the counties from which the regiments sprang were retained.

These important links with the counties, and the Light Infantry interest therein, were maintained through the establishment of Light Infantry Offices in Durham, Pontefract, Shrewsbury, Taunton and Bodmin. Gradually also have been established the Territorial Battalions in the former Counties – 5th Battalion The (Shropshire and Herefordshire) Light Infantry, 6th Battalion

The (Somerset and Cornwall) Light Infantry and 7th Battalion The (Durham) Light Infantry. In 1996 the 8th Battalion The (Yorkshire) Light Infantry was reroled as a Reconnaissance Regiment under DRAC and re-named the King's Own Yorkshire Yeomanry (Light Infantry) (KOYYLI).

The silver bugle capbadge, drill from the 'at ease' position, rapid marching pace and green beret bear testimony to the ancestry of The Light Infantry. Distinctions of dress serve as an ever-present reminder of the former great regiments; red backing to the capbadge from the DCLI, sashes tied on the right from the SOM LI, the Inkerman chain from the DLI and the wearing of white roses on Minden Day from the KOYLI. The Regiment has the distinction of not being required to drink the Loyal Toast; a privilege which had been conferred upon both the KSLI and the DLI.

On 22nd July each year the Regiment celebrates its Regimental Day, the anniversary of the Battle of Salamanca (1812), a battle in which all the former regiments fought. The Light Infantry is intensely proud to have as its Colonel-in-Chief Her Majesty Queen Elizabeth The Queen Mother, an association which began in 1927 when, as Duchess of York, Her Majesty became Colonel-in-Chief of the KOYLI. It is also the Regiment's very good fortune to have as Deputy Colonel-in-Chief, Her Royal Highness Princess Alexandra, who had been colonel-in-chief of the DLI.

The Early Years

When the Light Infantry was formed on 10th July 1968 the 1st Battalion (1 LI) was in Gravesend and, within a month, moved to Ballykinler in Northern Ireland. The 2nd Battalion (2 LI) was in Berlin – at that time a divided city. The 3rd Battalion (3 LI) was based at Terendak Camp near Malacca in Malaysia as part of 28 Commonwealth Brigade, with companies detached on internal security duties in Mauritius; an operation for which the Battalion was subsequently awarded the Wilkinson Sword of Peace. The 4th Battalion (4 LI) was in Cyprus as part of the United Nations Force in Cyprus (UNFICYP).

The early years of the Regiment were to witness a constant conflict between the primary role of battalions and the short notice demands of a rapidly deteriorating situation in Northern Ireland.

The Years of Consolidation 1979–1989

Over the next ten years the Regiment was to consolidate both its structure and its reputation. Headquarters The Light Division was to play an increasingly important part in manpower and training matters, and the Light Division ethos was to develop rapidly as cross-posting between The Light Infantry and The Royal Green Jackets increased. Although Northern Ireland continued to place a heavy burden on the Infantry, the initial impact and the knock-on effect on postings, training and leave had been largely contained.

In February 1989 1 LI moved to Berlin and had nearly a full year of duties in the allied garrison before the Berlin wall was breached on 9th November 1989 which was to signal the subsequent collapse of communism and end of the Warsaw Pact as an effective military alliance.

On 31st May 1991 Her Majesty Queen Elizabeth The Queen Mother presented new Colours to the three regular battalions at Tidworth.

As a result of the Government decision to reduce the size of the Army it was decided that the reduction of The Light Infantry by one regular battalion should be achieved by the merger of the three existing battalions. In February 1993 the now 1 LI formed in the barracks originally occupied by 2 LI and 3 LI renumbered as 2 LI, remaining in Germany and subsequently serving in Bosnia on a very successful operational tour of duty with the UN and NATO forces.

Despite all these changes and evolutions The Light Infantry today remains as the largest Infantry Regiment with 2 regular and 3 territorial battalions. It embodies the characteristics of all the Counties from which it is formed and is immensely proud of the connection and heritage it derives from them.

Right, top: Peace in Our Time – 2nd Battalion in Bosnia, 1995/6.

HUGO GRENVILLE

Right, bottom: The 51st (2nd Yorkshire West Riding) Light Infantry at Waterloo, 18 June 1815.

BRIAN PALMER

THE PRINCE OF WALES'S OWN REGIMENT OF YORKSHIRE

The Prince of Wales's Own Regiment of Yorkshire (PWO) is the direct successor to The West Yorkshire Regiment (The Prince of Wales's Own) and The East Yorkshire Regiment (The Duke of York's Own). Both the original regiments were raised on the same day, 22 June 1685, and later took precedence as the XIV and XV Regiments of Foot respectively.

The West Yorkshire Regiment first recruited in Yorkshire in 1873 although the East Yorkshire Regiment had done so since 1782. These recruiting areas have remained substantially unchanged ever since and virtually all PWO soldiers are Yorkshiremen with the majority coming from Bradford, Leeds, York and Hull. The Regiment's permanent headquarters is situated in the centre of York, opposite the medieval Clifford's Tower, and there are Regimental Chapels in both York and Beverley Minsters. The title The Prince of Wales's Own was granted to the XIV Regiment in India in 1876 by the future King Edward VII and it was taken as the present Regiment's title on amalgamation in 1958. The cap badge, the White Horse of Hanover is considerably older. It was once worn by the whole Army and when this was discontinued in 1765 HM King George III granted the Regiment permission to retain the old badge as a distinction.

During the last three centuries the Regiment has served on every continent. In the early 1700s it fought in Europe under Marlborough at such major battles at Blenheim and Oudenarde. In 1759 on 13 September the XV Regiment, serving under General Wolfe, took part in the storming of Quebec, the action which decided the future of Canada. Since then the 13 September has always been known in the Regiment as 'Quebec Day' which is celebrated as an occasion whenever possible. Black distinctions of dress are also still worn in memory of Wolfe who was killed on that day. Later in the Century many actions were fought in the War of American Independence and against both the French and Spanish in the West Indies. In 1793 during an attack against the Flanders the CO of the XIV Regiment ordered the drummers to play 'Ca Ira', a Revolutionary French tune, with the words 'Come on lads, lets break the scoundrels to their own damned tune'. The enemy did break and by order of the Duke of York the Regiment adopted 'Ca Ira' as its Quick March which it has retained to this day. The Nineteenth Century saw many more battles. The Regiment was at Waterloo and fought the Russians in the Crimea, it also took part in campaigns in India and Afghanistan as well as fighting the Maoris in New Zealand. At the end of the Century the Regiment took part in the Boer War fighting in the Orange Free State, Natal and the Transvaal. It was shortly before the Relief of Ladysmith that Capt Mansel Jones won the first of the Regiment's thirteen Victoria Crosses.

During the Great War some 59 battalions were formed, 38 by the West Yorkshires and 21 by the East Yorkshires. Most of the fighting was in France although battalions fought at Gallipoli, Sulva, Salonika and in Italy. Fifteen West Yorkshire and nine East Yorkshire battalions fought in the gruelling three month Battle of the Somme in 1916 and at Ypres the following year there were ten West Yorkshire and five East Yorkshire battalions. During the War eight Victoria Crosses were won and the 8th (Leeds Rifles) West Yorkshires gained a collective Crois de Guerre. In the Second World War battalions of the two regiments campaigned extensively in North Africa, Burma and in Europe. Among many notable occurrences the East Yorkshires had the unique distinction of being the only regiment in the British Army with two battalions in the initial assault on D Day. In Burma both the 1st and 2nd West Yorkshires were heavily engaged in the defence of Imphal, the siege of which was lifted on 22 June 1944, the 259th Anniversary of the formation of the Regiment. The day has subsequently been kept as 'Imphal Day'.

The Prince of Wales's Own Regiment of Yorkshire formed in Dover on 25 April 1958 by the amalgamation of the two former Regiments and in September of that year the 1st Battalion moved to the Western Aden Protectorate and later to Aden. In April 1959 the battalion was sent to Gibraltar and remained there until 1961 when it moved to Germany, initially in Wuppertal, later in Berlin. In September 1965 another tour in Aden was carried out returning to Colchester in 1966. The battalion undertook an emergency tour in Aden yet again in 1967 returning once more to Colchester. This was followed in 1969 by a short tour in Northern Ireland. A tour in Cyprus from 1970–1972 was followed by two years in Northern Ireland and in June 1974 the battalion was stationed in Germany for four years. In August 1978 the battalion moved to Bulford and became part of the NATO Allied Command Europe Mobile Force. In 1983 it moved to Berlin where new Colours were presented in 1984 followed by a tour of two years in Northern Ireland beginning in April 1985. In May 1985 Her Royal Highness The Duchess of Kent was appointed Colonel-in-Chief and attended the Regiment's Tercentenary Celebrations on 22nd June 1985. The battalion moved to Catterick in North Yorkshire in May 1987. In 1990 they moved to Osnabruck in BAOR and whilst there provided detachments to serve in the Gulf War with 1st Armoured Division. Following a tour in Belfast from November 1991–May 1992 they served in Bosnia with the United Nations Protection Force for a six month tour until November 1993. Since then they have served in Warminster and in Chester with a further tour in Northern Ireland and training carried out in Canada and Kenya.

1st Battalion The East Yorkshire Regiment (Duke of York's Own) on a Route March, North West Frontier of India, 1936.

Top: Battle of Famars, 1793.

Left: Corporal Dobson, after receiving his Military Cross from The Queen for Bosnian service – the first non-commissioned rank to receive this award.

THE GREEN HOWARDS
(Alexandra, Princess of Wales's Own Yorkshire Regiment)

The Regiment was raised by Francis Luttrell of Dunster Castle, Somerset, on 19 November 1688, for service under William of Orange.

It was in 1744 that the Regiment became known as 'The Green Howards'. At that time the Regimental Colonel was General the Honourable Charles Howard, the second son of the 3rd Earl of Carlisle. It was usual, then, for a Regiment to be identified by the name of its Colonel and we were therefore known as 'Howards Regiment'. However, in this campaign we were brigaded with another Regiment whose Colonel was also called Howard so some distinction had to be made. As we wore green facings to our uniforms it was natural that we should become 'The Green Howards' whilst the other Regiment whose facings were buff in colour were known as 'The Buff Howards'. The nick-name 'The Green Howards' stuck and survived until 1920 when it became part of the official title of the Regiment.

The Regiment first became associated with, and affiliated to, the North Riding of Yorkshire in 1782 when it was granted the title of The 19th (or First Yorkshire North Riding Regiment) of Foot. Our close association with our home-town of Richmond began in 1873 when the Regimental Depot was built there. In 1875 the late Queen Alexandra, then Princess of Wales and formerly a Princess of the Royal House of Denmark, presented the Regiment with new Colours to replace those carried throughout the Crimean War and which are now displayed in the Regimental Museum. The Regiment then became The Princess of Wales's Own. On the introduction of the territorial system in 1881 it was again altered to The Princess of Wales's Own Yorkshire Regiment and after the South African War in 1902 the word Alexandra was added. Finally in 1920 it became The Green Howards (Alexandra, Princess of Wales's Own Yorkshire Regiment). Our cap badge was designed by Princess Alexandra herself to incorporate the Dannebrog (the Cross of Denmark) and her personal cypher, the whole being surmounted by her coronet. The date 1875 commemorates the Regiment becoming the Princess of Wales's Own and the Roman numerals XIX denote the 19th Regiment of Foot.

In 1914 Queen Alexandra was appointed our first Colonel in Chief, and was the first Lady to be granted that distinction in the British Army. She was much loved and had been associated with the Regiment for 50 years before her death in 1925. The link with the Danish Royal House was renewed in 1942 when Queen Alexandra's son-in-law, King Haakon VII of Norway (who had married her daughter Princess Maud) consented to become Colonel in Chief. King Haakon was born Prince Carl of Denmark and became King of Norway when Norway dissolved the century old union with Sweden in 1905.

King Haakon was Colonel in Chief for 15 years between 1942 and 1957. He was very popular and much respected as was his son King Olav V, who succeeded him in 1958 until his death in 1991. King Harald V, a great great grandson of Queen Victoria, was appointed Colonel in Chief on 7th Februury 1992.

The Regiment first saw active service in 1690 at the Battle of the Boyne in Ireland, but soon after found itself in Flanders at Steinkerke and Landen and it was present at the Siege of Namur in 1695. It returned to Flanders during the campaigns of the Duke of Marlborough in 1707–14 where it earned at great cost its first battle honour – Malplaquet in 1709.

In 1744, the Regiment moved for the third time to Flanders to take part in the second half of the War of the Austrian Succession, again fighting the French.

Between 1761 and 1854, the Regiment took part in many campaigns. Amongst these were the Expedition against Belle Isle 1761 – the American War of Independence in 1781 – the siege of Ostend 1794 – the campaign in Ceylon and the operations against Tippoo Sahib between 1796 and 1820, thereby missing out completely the War against Napoleon in Europe.

The Regiment next played a distinguished part in the war against Russia in the Crimean Peninsula. It was present at the Battles of Alma, Inkerman, and the Siege of Sevastopol. The Battle of the Alma is celebrated on the 20th September every year for it was during this action that the Regiment stormed and captured a Russian position consisting of strongly fortified earthworks and fourteen guns and known as The Great Redoubt. It was here that seven drums were taken from the Russian Borodino, Minsk and Vladimir Regiments. Five of these are held by the 1st Battalion and are customarily carried on parade each year on Alma Day. It was also during this war that Corporal John Lyons and Pte Samuel Evans of the 19th won Victoria Crosses at the Siege of Sevastapol.

In 1868 the Regiment was present in the Hazara Campaign against the tribes of the Black Mountains on the North West Frontier. They were in action in the Sudan in 1885 against the forces of the Mahdi and at the engagement at Ginnis on 30 December when they last wore the red coat of the British Infantry in battle. In 1892 they saw action in Burma which was followed in 1897 when they were again in action on the North West Frontier of India, in the Tirah Campaign.

Two years later the Regiment played a prominent part in the South African War, 1899–1902, and it was during this campaign that Sgt Alfred Atkinson won the Victoria Cross at the Battle of Paardeberg. It also took part in the operations for the Relief of Kimberley and many other smaller engagements.

During the 1st World War of 1914–18, twenty four battalions of the Regiment were raised and twelve officers and men won the Victoria Cross. Battalions of the Regiment took part in most of the principal battles and campaigns of this war, and over 65,000 men served in its ranks of these over 7,500 lost their lives and nearly 24,000 were wounded. The Regiment was awarded 56 battle honours.

Between 1918 and 1939, the Regiment took part in the war of North Russia 1918–19, the 3rd Afghan War of 1919, the operations in Palestine during 1938, the Waziristan operations of 1937–39, and many other internal duties overseas including those in Shanghai between 1927–1932.

In the 2nd World War of 1939–45, 12 Battalions of the Regiment were raised. The Regiment had units in all the principal theatres of War and two Battalions were first to land in the assault on D Day 1944. Members of the Regiment won three Victoria Crosses, nineteen Distinguished Service Orders, fifty Military Crosses, sixteen Distinguished Conduct Medals and ninety-two Military Medals. Twenty five battle honours were awarded.

Between 1949 and 1952 the Regiment served with great distinction in the campaign against the Chinese Communist Terrorists in Malaya.

In the years since 1952, the Regiment has served in Austria, West Germany, Suez, Cyprus, Hong Kong, Libya, Malaysia, Belize, Berlin and the UK. It has distinguished itself in operations in Northern Ireland and one Regimental Officer was killed in action whilst serving with very great bravery in the Falkland Islands, 1982. A small contingent from the Regiment was deployed as Medical Assistants to Saudi Arabia in the Gulf War of 1991. The Regiment has also spent training periods in Canada, Kenya, Norway, Denmark and Australia.

As a mark of appreciation of the Regiment's service to the County and the Country for over 300 years, six Yorkshire Boroughs have accorded the Regiment the honour of being Honorary Freemen. These are Beverley, Bridlington, Middlesbrough, Redcar, Richmond and Scarborough. Where applicable these have been renewed by the authority that replaced them. Illuminated scrolls of appreciation have also been received from Northallerton and Pickering.

HRH Princess Alexandra, Princess of Wales, who designed the Regiment's cap badge.

Right: CSM Stan Hollis with the only Victoria Cross won on D-Day, 6 June 1944.

JOHN SMITHS LTD

THE ROYAL HIGHLAND FUSILIERS
(Princess Margaret's Own Glasgow and Ayrshire Regiment)

1. The Raising of the Regiment

The Royal Highland Fusiliers was formed on the 20th January, 1959, by the amalgamation of the Royal Scots Fusiliers and the Highland Light Infantry. These two famous regiments were formerly three – the 21st Fusiliers, the 71st Highlanders (Light Infantry) and the 74th Highlanders. Their service covers that of the British Army itself. During fifteen reigns, from King Charles II to Queen Elizabeth II, there are few battlefields of importance on which they have not been present, either together or separately. The extremely formidable fighting tradition which the Regiment inherits and which has few, if any, equals, is briefly described in this section.

The three Regiments were raised at different times and under three different circumstances.

The Raising of the 21st

Scotland in the late seventeenth century was in a state bordering on chaos, rent asunder by warring clans in the north and fanatical Covenanters in the South. As a preliminary step to the re-establishment of law and order, on the 23rd September 1678, Charles Erskine, fifth Earl of Mar, received a commission to raise a Regiment of Foot. This Regiment, afterwards the 21st Foot or Royal Scots Fusiliers, was known as the Earl of Mar's Regiment and colloquially as 'Mar's Grey Breeks' on account of it's hodden grey breeks. It continued to be referred to by the name of it's successive Colonels until about 1685, when it became known as the Scots Fusiliers, and after 1707 as the North British Fusiliers shortly afterwards becoming the Royal North British Fusiliers. The numerical title, although dating from 1688 did not come into general use until the reign of George 11. A further colloquial name, of which the Regiment is justly proud, is 'Marlborough's Own' by which it was known for many years after it's distinguished and prolonged service under the first Duke of Marlborough, during the War of the Spanish Succession.

For ten years after it's formation, the Regiment served continuously in Scotland and it was not until it marched South to support King James 11 against William of Orange in 1688 that it first crossed the border. This has considerable significance regimentally. In fact, the 21st was the fourth Infantry Regiment of the Line to be raised and was the first to be raised in Scotland.

The Raising of the 71st

Highland Regiments, except for the Black Watch were not raised for a further 100 years and the rebellions in 1715 and 1745 were still to come, as was the American War of Independence.

The political consequences of the latter War were grave. At it's start, France, though not at war with the United Kingdom, had been actively helping the colonists, and when things went well for their cause appeared likely to declare war in their support. Under these circumstances it became urgently necessary to raise new regiments. Among these was the 73rd Highlanders, afterwards the 71st and later the 1st Battalion of the Highland Light Infantry.

The Regiment was raised in 1777 in the northern countries by John MacKenzie, Lord MacLeod, and mustered at Elgin early in 1778. A second battalion was raised shortly afterwards by MacLeod's brother, George MacKenzie.

John MacKenzie had been imprisoned in the Tower of London for his part in the Jacobite rebellion of 1745. He was released on account of his youth, but titles and estates gone, he made his way to Sweden, rising to the rank of General in the Swedish Army. On the outbreak of the War of Independence he offered his services to King George III and received a commission to raise a regiment, which he succeeded in doing without difficulty, recruiting largely from his old estates, but also partly from Glasgow. The 73rd was the first Clan Regiment to be raised under the British Crown and remained the second senior Highland Regiment until 1958.

The Raising of the 74th

Towards the end of the Eighteenth century it became necessary to protect British interests and allies in Southern India from French intrigue which threatened to bring British trade to an end. New Regiments were needed and in 1787 the 74th Highland Regiment was raised in Argyll and opened its headquarters in Glasgow early in 1788. It was a Campbell Regiment, eleven of the original officers being of that name, including the Colonel, Sir Archibald Campbell of Inverneil. It sailed for India by companies and in 1789 fought alongside the 71st in the second Mysore campaign. In 1881 it became the 2nd Battalion, the Highland Light Infantry.

Major campaigns and battles include:

> Blenheim
> Fontenoy
> The American Revolution
> Assaye (The Duke of Wellington's hardest fought battle)
> Napoleonic Wars including Waterloo
> 1814 21st Foot burn White House in Washington
> Crimea
> Indian Mutiny
> Zulu and Boer Wars

The Regiment raised 49 Battalions in World War I and 17 Battalions in World War II.

During its distinguished service officers and soldiers of the Regiment were awarded 20 VCs

2. The Title of the Regiment

On 11th June 1958, HM The Queen graciously designated the new Regiment.

THE ROYAL HIGHLAND FUSILIERS
Princess Margaret's Own Glasgow and Ayrshire Regiment

The title, The Royal Highland Fusiliers was one of the several submitted to the Colonels of the Royal Scots Fusiliers and the Highland Light Infantry by the amalgamation committee as possible titles for the new Regiment. It was selected by the Colonels with the unanimous support of both Regiments. On consenting to become Colonel-in-Chief, HRH The Princess Margaret graciously gave permission for The Royal Highland Fusiliers to be further designated 'Princess Margaret's Own Glasgow and Ayrshire Regiment', subject to the approval of HM The Queen.

Fusiliers was the title given in the late seventeenth century to those regiments armed with the 'fusil', a light flintlock musket. In battle such regiments were originally charged with the protection of the artillery, which in those days fired from the Infantry line and being very cumbersome, was a favourite target for enemy cavalry. The name 'Fusilier' became an honourable distinction which was awarded to the 21st early in its service, although the Regiment was seldom used to protect artillery. It is interesting to note, however, that the Regiment's first Victoria Cross was won while carrying out this role in the South African War.

The conversion of certain selected regiments into light infantry was started in 1803, the idea being that they should skirmish in advance of the main line of battle, and shake up the enemy columns by rapid movement and well aimed fire. They were also used for other special tasks. The 71st Highland Regiment was converted to light infantry in 1809, but retained its Highland designation. Thus originated the name of Highland Light Infantry. The light infantry regiments rendered such outstanding service during the Peninsular War that the title was later awarded to regiments as a particular distinction, although by that time all infantry operated in open order.

This title, which the 71st Highland Light Infantry bore for 150 years, cannot be incorporated in the name of the amalgamated Regiment, for Fusiliers is the more ancient honour, and a regiment could not be both 'FUSILIER' and 'LIGHT INFANTRY'.

The Regiment has now served for forty years under its new title and continues to live up to the good name of its predecessors and was awarded the Battle Honour 'GULF 1991' for its involvement in that conflict.

Right, top: An outpost, Tirah 1897.

Right, bottom: The sinking of HMS *Birkenhead* off the Cape of Good Hope, 25 February 1852 – where the 74th established the principle: 'Women and children first'.

AARDVARK CLEAR MINE LTD
The World's Leading Mine Clearance Flail – Manufactured in Scotland

An outpost (in sangar) Royal Scots Fusiliers. Tirah 1897.

THE 22ND (CHESHIRE) REGIMENT

The 22nd (Cheshire) Regiment was raised in 1689 on the Roodee, Chester for service under William III. Its 1st Battalion next served in its home County in 1988. During the intervening three hundred plus years, it has spent much time on garrison duty in the Empire.

It has a tradition of having had a detachment at Dettingen. There it won the distinction of wearing the oak leaf when on parade with Royalty and also on certain Regimental days. The story is that a detachment of The 22nd protected the King, who was commanding the field, from being taken prisoner by the French. The King picked a sprig of oak from a nearby tree and presented it to them. This has since featured as the Regimental badge. The remainder of the Regiment, at the time was in the Mediterranean.

The taking of Louisbourg in Nova Scotia was its most famous eighteenth century event; the Grenadier Company going with Wolfe to Quebec. A 22nd Grenadier appears to have been present at the death of Wolfe along with Ensign Browne, as shown in the famous Benjamin West painting. The Regiment stormed Havannah at the end of the Seven Years War, but suffered terribly from yellow fever in West Florida before taking part in the American War of Independence.

A spell in India led to The 22nd being the only English Regiment in Sir Charles Napier's force to conquer the Scinde. The great battle at Meeanee on 17 February 1843 is celebrated as the Regimental Day. A month later the Battle of Hyderabad took place to secure the Scinde for the Indian Empire. The links established at that time with Napier's Rifles (Indian Army) and The Eagle Troop RHA have been maintained to the present. The Regiment spent most of the nineteenth century in the Indian sub-continent or its dependencies.

A 2nd Battalion was raised in 1814 for a short while and re-raised in 1858. It fought in the Boer War in South Africa in 1900. This Battalion was amalgamated with the 1st at the end of World War II.

In the Great War thirty-eight Battalions were raised by The Cheshire Regiment. At the outset of the War in 1914 the 1st Battalion was exposed to the brunt of two German Army Corps at the village of Audregnies near Mons. Their heroic stand saved the British Expeditionary Force from a disaster and is celebrated as a second Regimental Day on 24th August. This Battalion was in every major action in France throughout the war and won 35 battle honours.

The Territorial and Kitchener's New Army Battalions fought in France and Flanders, Gallipoli, Sinai, Palestine, Salonika and Mesopotamia. The 12th Battalion won the French Croix de Guerre. Over 8,000 officers and men gave their lives.

Between the wars the two Regular Battalions served in India, Sudan, Palestine and Malta and became noted for their sports and athletics prowess.

Just prior to the Second World War all battalions were converted to the support machine gun role and the Regiment became a Support Regiment for the duration of the War.

At the outbreak of War in 1939 the 4th, 5th, 6th and 7th Battalion TA were re-established. A 30th Battalion (Home Defence) and thirty-nine Home Guard Battalions made up the Regimental roll. The 30th moved to Italy as the 8th Battalion and garrisoned Rome.

The 2nd and 4th Battalions were at Dunkirk and the 2nd went on to North Africa and Italy before returning to be part of the initial landing at Normandy. The 1st Battalion was in North Africa and Malta during the siege, where it distinguished itself for its selfless devotion under constant bombing. One Company was responsible for the dockyard area and was a major factor, despite the attacks, in unloading the docked ships of the famous Malta convoys. It finally moved to join the battle for NW Europe. The 6th and 7th Battalions fought in North Africa and Italy.

In the many conflicts since the Second War the 1st Battalion has taken its full part. It served in Malaya and was involved in the final clearance of the Terrorists from the southern jungles. It served in the Canal Zone, Cyprus and Northern Ireland including three, two year tours.

The most recent operation was as the first Infantry unit into Bosnia under the United Nations. Here they helped bring a stabilising influence into the lives of all parties to the conflict. They were lauded by all for their abilities which reflected those of the best traditions of the British Infantry over the past decades.

The Regimental Headquarters is still in the Castle at Chester within sight of the place of its raising by Henry Duke of Norfolk in 1689.

The Regiment now consists of a 1st Battalion and 3rd (Volunteer) Battalion. This latter unit is an Infantry Fire Support Battalion, as history repeats itself once more.

ALVIS VEHICLES LTD

The 1st Battalion in action at Andregnies, August 1914.

DAVID ROWLANDS

Top: Vickers machine-gunners of The 6th Battalion, Montegemmano, Italy, 1944

DAVID ROWLANDS

Left: Warrior in Bosnia, 1992.

THE ROYAL WELCH FUSILIERS

The Regiment was raised at Ludlow, the seat of the Council of Wales, by Lord Herbert of Chirbury in 1689. In 1702, when three regiments were selected to become 'Fusiliers', its title was changed to the *Welsh Regiment of Fusiliers*. In 1713 it became a Royal regiment, and a year later was titled the *Prince of Wales's Own Royal Regiment of Welsh Fusiliers*. From this it can be seen that the Regiment has had close links with Wales from its earliest days, and also with the monarchy. It is the only pan Wales line infantry regiment, and no other infantry regiment became connected with Wales until 1831.

The Regiment's first major battle was at the Boyne in Ireland in 1690. The first Battle Honour was earned at the siege of Namur in 1695. It fought with Marlborough at the battles of Blenheim, Ramillies, Oudenarde and Malplaquet, thus beginning a long period of involvement on the Continent. In 1714, as a result of its close connection with the Prince of Wales, it was authorised to bear three of his badges: The Red Dragon, The Rising Sun, and The Prince of Wales's Feathers on the Colours. For its part in the battle of Dettingen in 1743 the White Horse of Hanover is carried on the Regimental Colour. The Regiment featured prominently in the defeat of the French at the famous battle of Minden (1759) when the might of the French cavalry was broken by six British infantry battalions. It was present throughout the War of American Independence, fought at Bunker Hill (1775) and Yorktown (1781), where it earned the respect of its American enemy who built a memorial to the Regiment.

During the Napoleonic wars it saw action in the West Indies and captured a French eagle standard at Martinique, at Corunna where it was the last regiment to leave the town, in Egypt where in recognition of its conduct the Regiment bears a Sphinx on the Colour with the word 'Egypt', and in the Peninsular War where it fought, amongst other famous battles, in the bloody infantry battle of Albuhera. Wellington described the Royal Welch after Waterloo as 'the most complete and handsome military body I ever looked at.' In 1797 the 1st Battalion was sent to the Nore where a number of naval mutinies had occurred. On arrival an attempt was made to suborn the soldiers, but they resisted and sent a loyal address to the King. As a result the officers were given permission to dispense with the Loyal Toast except on St David's Day.

During the Nineteenth century the Regiment was engaged in the Crimea (1854–56) where, at the battle of the Alma, Sergeant Luke O'Connor won probably the first Victoria Cross awarded to a soldier. He was granted a commission, rose to the rank of Major General and, as Sir Luke O'Connor, became Colonel of the Regiment just before the First World War. The Regiment's Crimea Memorial is in Carmarthen. From the Crimea the Royal Welch went to India to assist in the suppression of the Mutiny. Later it was to be engaged in Ashanti (1873–74), Burma, the Second Boer War (1899–1902), and in China where it was the only British infantry regiment to be involved in the suppression of the Boxer Rebellion (1900). It was during this last campaign that a close link developed with the United States Marine Corps which exists to this day.

During the First World War the Regiment raised forty-two battalions, fought in France, Gallipoli, Mesopotamia, Salonika, Egypt, Palestine and Italy, won over 3,000 gallantry awards of which eight were Victoria Crosses, and gained eighty-eight Battle Honours. 10,000 men gave their lives. Amongst those who served was a galaxy of literary talent including, David Jones who wrote *In Parenthesis*, Siegfried Sassoon *Memoirs of an Infantry Officer*, Robert Graves *Goodbye to All That*, Frank Richards *Old Soldiers Never Die*, Llewelyn Wyn Griffith *Up to Mametz*, Doctor James Dunn *The War the Infantry Knew*, and Ellis Humphrey Evans who, as 'Hodd Wyn', won the Bardic Chair at the National Eisteddfod in 1917, but was killed in action at Pilckem Ridge only two weeks before he could claim his crown.

At the start of the Second World War the 1st Battalion suffered 759 casualties at Dunkirk in 1940. Later they went to Burma where they were joined by the 2nd Battalion following action in Madagascar against the Vichy French. Other battalions fought with distinction in North Africa, Italy, and Greece. The three Territorial battalions made a significant contribution to the liberation of North-West Europe and the final defeat of Nazi Germany.

Since 1945 the Royal Welch served in Berlin during the 'Airlift' of 1948, in Malaya in the war against the communist insurgents, in Cyprus against EOKA terrorists seeking union with Greece, in BAOR, in Northern Ireland, and in Bosnia in 1995 where their forebearance under pressure earned them international recognition and seventeen gallantry awards.

The Regiment has a unique distinction which identifies it from all others and that is the *Flash*, the five black ribbons on the collar of the tunic. A relic of the days when soldiers had powdered and greased pigtails which were enclosed in a 'queue bag'. When pigtails were abolished in 1808 the officers decided to retain the ribbons with which the queue was tied, and, using an old slang term for a wig, they were known as the 'Flash'. In 1834, William IV regularised its use 'as a peculiarity whereby to mark the dress of that distinguished regiment.'

No record exists of the origin of The Regimental Goat but it was apparently a custom of long-standing in 1777 when it was written that 'The Royal Regiment of Welch Fuzileers has a privilegeous honor of passing in review preceded by a Goat with gilded horns ... [and that] the corps values itself much on the ancientness of the custom'. Since 1844 the Goat has normally been presented by the Sovereign who, since George V, has been Colonel-in-Chief.

Finally, the Royal Welch Fusiliers are most fortunate in that they are one of only five regiments of line infantry never to have suffered an amalgamation.

Bosnia awards – investiture by Her Majesty The Queen, 1996.

Right, top: Crimea, Alma 1854 – Sergeant Luke O'Connor rescues The Colours, winning a VC. He also rose to Major-General and became colonel of the Regiment.

Right, bottom: The Goat proudly leads his Regiment, with the Pioneers just behind, through London.

THE ROYAL REGIMENT OF WALES
(24th/41st Foot)

On 11th June, 1969, **The Royal Regiment of Wales** was formed from The South Wales Borderers (24th Foot) and The Welch Regiment (41st/69th Foot) at an Amalgamation Parade in Cardiff Castle where new Colours were presented to the Regiment by its newly appointed Colonel in Chief, His Royal Highness The Prince of Wales.

The **24th Regiment of Foot** was formed in 1689 when a commission was issued to Sir Edward Dering, Baronet of Surrenden, Kent by King William III who needed new regiments to fight in Ireland. Thirteen years later the Duke of Marlborough became the Regiment's Colonel, and the regiment fought under his command with distinction in his famous quartet of victories at the Battles of Blenheim, Ramillies, Oudenarde and Malplaquet In 1782, the Regiment was instructed to style itself the 24th (2nd Warwickshire) Regiment. It was under this new name that it fought in the Peninsula under the Duke of Wellington and at the Battle of Chillianwallah during the Second Sikh War gaining one of its more famous victories despite taking a fearful number of casualties.

The Regiment fought in the Zulu War of 1879 and on 22nd January was heavily engaged at the Battle of Isandhlwana and at the Defence of Rorke's Drift. A total of 9 VCs were won by the Regiment in these battles, 2 by Lieutenant's Melville and Coghill who perished saving the Colours and 7, the most ever awarded to a regiment in a single action, by members of 'B' Company 2/24th at Rorke's Drift.

By 1873 the Regiment was recruiting heavily in Wales and had its Depot at Brecon, thus in 1881 when, under the Cardwell reforms the Army was given territorial titles, the 24th became The South Wales Borderers. It was under this name that the regiment fought in the Great War, winning the unique Battle Honour 'Tsingtao' and fighting alongside The Welch Regiment at Gheluvelt to halt the German onslaught that was driving towards the coast. The Regiment saw much action during the Second World War, with the 2/24th being the only Welsh Battalion to land on the Normandy Beaches on 'D' Day.

The **41st Regiment of Foot** was formed in 1719 when, fearing a possible invasion from the Continent and being short of money, the Government of the day decided to raise a 'Regiment of Invalids' from amongst the 'outpatients' of the Royal Hospital. This Regiment undertook guard duties and manned forts along the coast. Having been numbered the 41st in 1751, in 1787 the title 'Invalids' was dropped and it became a marching Regiment of the Line. In 1783 the 41st linked with the **69th** for recruiting purposes and later, under Cardwell reforms, the 69th became the 2nd Battalion, The Welch Regiment. In 1831 Royal Approval was given for the 41st to be styled The Welch Regiment bearing the Prince of Wales's Plumes and taking the motto 'Gwell Angau Na Chywilydd' (Death Rather than Dishonour), which has been inherited by The Royal Regiment of Wales.

In the latter half of the 18th century, the 69th won fame as Marines, for which the Regiment was allowed to bear on its Regimental Colour a Naval Crown inscribed 12th April 1782, another tradition carried on by the present Regiment. The 69th also had the honour of serving with the 'Iron Duke's' Allied Army during the Waterloo Campaign. It was involved at both Quatre Bras and at Waterloo itself, where it was positioned on the road a few hundred yards North of the centre of the battle between the Farmhouses of Hougoumont and La Haye Saint.

During the Crimean War, the 41st won 2 VCs, Captain Rowlands being the first Welshman to win the medal. During the Great War The Welch Regiment provided 34 battalions and in the Second World War produced a further eleven. In 1951 the Regiment saw active service in Korea.

Since 1969 the **1st Battalion**, The Royal Regiment of Wales has served in Osnabruck, Belfast, Berlin, Aldershot, Belize Lemgo, Warminster, Hong Kong, Tern Hill, Ballykelly and London and is at present stationed at Paderborn in Germany. It has carried out eight emergency tours of duty in Northern Ireland of about four months each and two full residential tours.

The **2nd (Volunteer) Battalion**, with its Headquarters in Cardiff, was formed in October 1993 by the amalgamation of the 3rd and 4th (Volunteer) Battalions of the Regiment. The Regiment is privileged to have been the first to be permitted to use the term '2nd' Battalion, a number usually retained for use in case a 2nd regular battalion should ever need to be raised.

The **3rd (Cadet) Battalion** was formed in 1997 from the Glamorgan Army Cadet Force and is now an integral and important part of the Regiment.

The Regimental Mascot

During the Crimean War of 1854–56, The 41st (Welch) Regiment of Foot adopted a goat as a mascot though the reasons for doing so are obscure. The tradition has been maintained ever since and the first officially recorded mascot, known as Billy, was presented by Queen Victoria in 1860 from the Royal Herd in Windsor Park. The goats still come from the Royal Herd, now

at Whipsnade Zoo, but when the Regiment was overseas and communications slow, they would come from local sources such as the one presented by the Sultan of Lahej in 1874 in Aden.

The 69th Regiment took up the custom on becoming the 2nd Battalion. The Welsh Regiment in 1881 and their exotic acquisitions included the mascot presented by the Amir of Tirah in 1889 on the North West Frontier and 'Taffy of Poouch' given by two aged tribesmen in India in 1933 in response to a 'bazaar' rumour that a replacement goat was required.

The mascots are officially mustered on the Regimental strength and Ration Roll under the name 'Gwilym Jenkins' though they have different known names in each Battalion. They earn promotion by time and some have seen active service, for instance at the Retreat from Mons, the First Battle of Ypres and Korea in 1951; their campaign medals are in the Museum to prove it.

On amalgamation, The Royal Regiment of Wales retained the distinction of the goat mascot and the serving goat of 1st Battlion, The Welch Regiment was renamed 'Taffy I', in the regular battalion. In the TA battalions, they became 'Dewi I' of the 3rd Battalion and 'Sospan I' in the 4th. In 1990, when Dewi IV died and could not be replaced from the Royal Herd because of serious inbreeding problems, now resolved from an injection of new stock from a herd from Llandudno, Mr and Mrs Brown, Cashmere Goat Breeders from Llancarfan, near Cowbridge came to the rescue with a splendid new mascot as Dewi V; when the 2nd Battalion was formed he returned to them on retirement and Sospan was posted from the 4th Battalion and renamed 'Shenkin'.

The Goat Major of 1RRW with TaffyIII.

Right, top: Battle of Isandhlwana, 22 January 1879.

Right, Bottom: Friendly power in Egypt: 1RRW Band in Muski, Cairo 1888.

ALCAN ROLLED PRODUCTS U.K.

THE KING'S OWN SCOTTISH BORDERERS

The King's Own Scottish Borderers (25th of Foot) is one of only five Infantry Regiments of the Line to have remained unchanged and unamalgamated since its foundation.

The Regiment was raised by the ruins of the Abbey Church of Holyrood in Edinburgh on the 18th of March 1689. The city was in turmoil. King William had landed in England from Holland to restore the monarchy vacated by King James, The Duke of Gordon held Edinburgh Castle for James, firing cannon-balls half-way down the Royal Mile, and John Graham of Claverhouse ('Bonnie Dundee') had defected to the Highlands. Enter David, Earl of Leven, who was urged by the Magistrates to raise a Regiment for the defence of the city. He immediately founded *Leven's Regiment*, the future KOSB, by beat of drum, 800 armed men being assembled in two hours.

The Castle was taken for King William. Soon after the Regiment was granted the Freedom of the City, a privilege which it frequently exercises 'with drums beating, bayonets fixed and Colours flying'. Further action soon fol-lowed at Killierankie which was fought uphill against Claverhouse's fearsome Highlanders. Although the battle was lost 'Bonnie Dundee' was slain and General Mackay said: 'I confess that Lord Leven, Colonel Hastings and their officers have distinguished themselves above all others'.

Soon – and oft to be repeated – *Leven's Regiment* embarked for Ireland and then to Holland where the Regiment won its first battle honour, Namur. Back in Scotland for 20 years *Leven's* (sometimes called *'The Edinburgh Regiment'*) did not take part in the campaigns of Marlborough but it fought in the other continental wars of the 18th century, the War of the Austrian Succession, the Seven Years War, and the French Revolutionary Wars. Of all these battles, the victory at *Minden* on the 1st of August 1759 is of special significance to the Borderers; it is still remembered every year on the 1st of August when red roses are worn in their headress by all ranks and families to recall the action of their forebears who plucked roses from the hedgerows on their advance to contact. It was a famous victory. Prince Ferdinand, the Allied Commander, remarked: 'It was here that the British Infantry gained immortal glory'.

Service followed in Minorca, Gibraltar, in both Jacobite rebellions of '15 and '45, the West Indies (twice), Egmont-op-Zee and Egypt. Since Leven's day the regiment had changed its name several times. For many years it was named after the Colonel of The Regiment, then for a short time it became, unbelievably, *The Sussex Regiment*, and at another time the troops were used as marines. A Second Battalion was formed in 1804. Thankfully, in 1805, sanity reigned and the Regiment took the title *The King's Own Borderers*. Some say that the Border referred to was not the English border but the border between the Lowlands and the Highlands.

It was not until 1873, under the Cardwell reforms which anchored regiments territorially, that the Regiment proudly attained its present title *The King's Own Scottish Borderers*, with its Headquarters in Berwick-on-Tweed, in the oldest occupied barracks in Britain, and its recruiting area the six counties of the Scottish Border – Berwick, Roxburgh, Selkirk, Dumfries, the Stewartry of Kirkcudbright and Wigtown.

Two years later the 1st Battalion was posted to Fyzabad in the Indian kingdom of Oudh. After a severe epidemic of cholera, they were heavily engaged in the Second Afghan War of 1878–79, followed by the Chin Lushai Expedition in Burma of 1889–90. Meantime, the 2nd Battalion was involved in the Sudan with the Sudan Defence Force, then back to India for the Relief of Chitral 1895 and the battle of Tirah 1897.

Back home again temporarily, the 1st Battalion recruited on the Borders and, after a short spell in Dublin, embarked for the Boer War in South Africa. There they were joined by a volunteer service company from the 1st Rox-burghshire, 2nd Berwickshire and 3rd Dumfriesshire Volunteer Battalions. Lieutenant G. H. B. Coulson was the first Borderer to be awarded the supreme decoration of the Victoria Cross for conspicuous gallantry in the Orange Free State. Sadly he died in the affray.

In the early part of the 20th century, both Battalions served either in India, or Ireland, North and South. Sterner challenges lay ahead with the outbreak of the First World War in 1914. The KOSB provided 14 Battalions of Infantry and they took part in over 80 battles on all the main battle fronts – the Western Front, Gallipoli and Palestine. Eight of the major battles are recorded as Battle Honours on the Colours. The casualties were appalling. From a population of 261,615 in the six counties of the Borders no less than 6859 were killed and 20,577 were wounded – 1 in 5 of the adult population killed or maimed.

Tales of gallantry abound. C/Sgt Skinner of the 1st Battalion had been wounded eight times before he fell at 'Passenchdale'. Awarded the V.C. he was regarded as one of the most remarkable men in the British Army. Six of the holders of the V.C. were pall-bearers at his funeral. Another V.C. was awarded to Company Quartermaster Sergeant W. Grimbaldestone for the storming of a blockhouse. A third V.C. was won by Sergeant McGuffie of the 5th (Dumfries and Galloway) Battalion from Wigtown for conspicuous lead-ership of his platoon at Piccadilly Farm near Ypres. But the V.C. which is best remembered in the Regiment is Piper Laidlaw of the 7th Battalion, a reservist in his 39th year, who came from Berwickshire. In the midst of heavy shell fire and a gas attack Piper Laidlaw coolly swaggered up and down the parapet playing the Regimental march *All the Blue Bonnets are over the Border*. He was then wounded and, in a sitting position, changed his tune to *The Standard on the Braes o' Mar*, the Regimental charge. Another piper distinguished himself at the battle of Loos – Piper Robert MacKenzie of the 6th Battalion, incredibly 60 years of age, played the Battalion 'over the top'.

Between the wars the two Battalions returned to peace-time soldiering in India, the Middle East and – as if drawn by a magnet – Ireland. As the support for 'the military' lessened they watched the inevitable approach to the Second World War in which the Regiment provided seven battalions. The 1st Battalion fought again in Flanders, were evacuated from Dunkirk and then returned triumphantly on D-Day with General Montgomery's 'Ironsides' 3rd Division. The 2nd Battalion, having served in India for many years, was launched into the fearsome battles against the Japanese in Burma and suffered severely in battle casualties and sickness. The 4th and 5th Battalions took part in the landings at Walcheren Island at the mouth of the Scheldt, and then advanced across the Rhine and the Elbe deep into the heart of East Germany. The 6th Battalion took part in a fierce battle at Hill 112 in Normandy and then advanced with notable successes in Holland right through to the Baltic. The 7th Battalion won immortal glory by dropping with the Airborne Division at Arnhem. The battalion went into action 740 strong – only 76 answered the roll-call when they returned. Although the overall casualties in the 2nd World War were mercifully less than 1914–18, nevertheless 1352 Borderers paid the supreme sacrifice and 4056 were wounded.

After the Second World War the 2nd Battalion 'went into suspended animation', a polite expression for disbandment, but the 1st Battalion was engaged in most of the post-war conflicts in the British Empire – Palestine, Korea, Northern Ireland (ten times), Malaya and Singapore, Aden, Borneo, besides standing firm in the Cold War in Berlin and Western Germany. In the Korean war, a further Victoria Cross was gained by Private William Speak-man, who happily is still alive to tell the tale. The 1st Battalion is presently serving in Cyprus.

On the 18th of March 1989, a significant event occurred when the KOSB's celebrated their tercentenary by marching down Princes Street in Edinburgh – Regulars, Territorials, Cadets and Old Comrades. It was a proud moment – a celebration of 300 years of service to King, Queen and country. The salute was taken by the Colonel-in-Chief, herself a Borderer, Princess Alice, Duchess of Gloucester who for 61 years has given dedicated service to her Regiment, *The King's Own Scottish Borderers*.

HRH Princess Alice, Duchess of Gloucester, has been Colonel-in-Chief since 1937.

COCA-COLA & SCHWEPPES

The OC presents Minden Roses to his men to commemorate one of the Regiment's proudest Battle Honours, Minden, 1 August 1759.

Top: The Raising of the Regiment – The King's Own Scottish Borderers begin 300 years of 'Blue Bonnets' over every border known to British history.

TERENCE CUNEO

THE ROYAL IRISH REGIMENT
(27th (Inniskilling) 83rd and 87th and The Ulster Defence Regiment)

The Royal Irish Regiment was formed on 1 July 1992 upon the amalgamation of The Ulster Defence Regiment and The Royal Irish Rangers. As a result the new Regiment immediately became the largest Infantry Regiment in the British Army.

Exactly twenty four years earlier, The Royal Irish Rangers were created from the amalgamation of three famous Irish Infantry Regiments comprising The North Irish Brigade, The Royal Inniskilling Fusiliers, The Royal Ulster Rifles and The Royal Irish Fusiliers.

Uniquely, on formation The Royal Irish Regiment consisted of two Regular Infantry Battalions (the 1st and 2nd), six Home Service Battalions and the 4th and 5th Territorial Army Battalions.

The Home Service Battalions, namely 3rd (Co Down & Armagh), 4th (Co Fermanagh & Tyrone), 5th (Co Londonderry), 7th (City of Belfast), 8th (Co Armagh & Tyrone) and 9th (Co Antrim) were formerly Ulster Defence Regiment Battalions which are, and remain, restricted to service in Northern Ireland.

The Regimental Headquarters and Depot at St Patrick's Barracks, Ballymena provide the administrative and training base.

On formation the 1st Battalion was stationed in Warminster and the 2nd in Lemgo, Germany. Later that year the 1st Battalion moved to Cyprus and, as part of the Army's restructuring, merged with the 2nd Battalion in 1993.

Simultaneously the two Territorial Army battalions amalgamated to form the 4th/5th Battalion, The Royal Irish Rangers (Volunteers).

In 1995 the 1st Battalion moved to Catterick from where it sent a Company detachment to Bosnia and conducted a six month tour in Northern Ireland, at which point all of the Regimental Battalions were serving together in the same theatre for the first time.

On a second Northern Ireland tour in 1998 the entire Regiment was under operational command of the Colonel of the Regiment, General Sir Roger Wheeler, who was then GOC Northern Ireland.

The Home Service battalions continue to play a key role in support of the Royal Ulster Constabulary. The courage and commitment of the men and women of these battalions, whether full or part time, are amply demonstrated by more than one thousand honours and awards received since the formation of the Ulster Defence Regiment. Sadly, 197 serving officers and soldiers including four Greenfinches have been killed by terrorists and some 450 wounded or injured. Forty seven former soldiers have been murdered, in some cases several years after leaving the Regiment.

The Ulster Defence Regiment

Following the outbreak of severe rioting and prolonged community and inter-sectarian violence in the Summer of 1969, Lord Hunt's Advisory Committee recommended the creation of what was to become the Ulster Defence Regiment. The Regiment was formed by Act of Parliament in January 1970 and became operational three months later on 1 April.

Initially it consisted of a Regimental Headquarters at Lisburn and seven battalions, one in each of the six counties and the seventh in the City of Belfast. Escalation of terrorist violence in 1971 led to the formation of four additional battalions.

Initially the Regiment was to be a part-time military force providing support to the Regular military forces in the Provinces, manning guards at key points, patrols and check points. However this role developed significantly.

In 1973, the first women were recruited into the Regiment. Known as Greenfinches, they quickly became wholly integrated and key elements of their battalions. Another significant change was the establishment of a full time Permanent Cadre. This development coincided with the assumption by the battalions of their own tactical areas of operational responsibility (TAORs) during the late 1970s in support of the Royal Ulster Constabulary.

The 1980s saw a general improvement in the security situation, enabling a series of amalgamations which reduced the eleven battalions to seven by 1991. This was achieved by the merger of the County Antrim Battalions (1984), the City of Belfast Battalions (also 1984), the 4th with the 6th and the 2nd with the 11th (both in 1991). Then in 1992, The Ulster Defence Regiment amalgamated with the Royal Irish Rangers to form The Royal Irish Regiment.

In its brief but distinguished history, the Regiment earned massive respect for its contribution to the fight against terrorist violence. Indeed it can claim the distinction of having seen more prolonged active service than any other regiment in the history of the British Army.

Irish recruiting scene, 1870's. A Recruiting Sergeant, a private and two drummer boys accompanying two strapping volunteers joining Britain's invincible Victorian army.

LADY BUTLER

Top: The Regimental Mascot, Brian Boru VI, leading the Band on parade in Donegall Place, with Belfast's City Hall behind.

Left: The Regiment patrols in the shadow of the Mountains of Mourne.

THE ROYAL GLOUCESTERSHIRE, BERKSHIRE & WILTSHIRE REGIMENT

On 27 April 1994, The Gloucestershire Regiment (28th/61st) and the Duke of Edinburgh's Royal Regiment (Berkshire and Wiltshire) united to form the Royal Gloucestershire, Berkshire and Wiltshire Regiment. The Regiment's illustrious history spans over 300 years.

The Gloucestershire Regiment

Although not officially connected with this county until 1782, The Gloucestershire Regiment's history extends back to 1694 when Col John Gibson raised a new regiment which later became the 28th of Foot. Fifty years later the 61st of Foot was formed, and within a few more years, both Regiments were linked with the county of Gloucestershire becoming the 28th (North Gloucestershire) and 61st (South Gloucestershire) respectively.

In 1881 these two proud Regiments, each with its own long history of battles and triumphs, became the 1st and 2nd Battalions of The Gloucestershire Regiment. To this new Regiment was added the Volunteer Battalions of the County which had been first raised in 1797.

The 28th and 61st, and their successors in the County Regiment, saw service on every continent. They fought under Marlborough, saw Wolfe shot before them at Quebec, and greatly distinguished themselves at the Battle of Alexandria in 1801. There, fighting at one point back to back, they enabled the British to achieve a famous victory for which they were awarded the right to wear the Back Badge worn to this day. They formed Sir John Moore's rearguard at Corunna, and fought throughout the Peninsular War. The 28th were the only English Regiment mentioned by the Duke of Wellington in his Waterloo dispatches.

The 28th fought in the Crimea, while the 61st took part in both the Sikh wars and the Indian Mutiny, winning high praise from the Duke of Wellington at Chillianwallah and their first VC at the Siege of Delhi. Both Battalions and the 4th Militia Battalion served in the Boer War.

24 battalions fought in the Great War 1914–18, winning 72 Battle Honours and five VCs. The cost, however, was high: 8,100 members of the Regiment giving their lives. In the Second World War, nine battalions took part, the 61st being annihilated defending the Dunkirk evacuation in 1940, and the 28th suffering a similar fate during the withdrawal in Burma in 1942.

Most recently the Glosters fought in Korea, winning the United States Presidential Citation at the battle of the Imjin River in 1951 for their valour. Until amalgamation the Glosters could boast that they carried more Battle Honours on their Colours than any other Regiment in the British Army.

The Royal Berkshire Regiment
(Princess Charlotte of Wales's)

The 49th of Foot was raised in 1743 to garrison Jamaica, but soon saw service in the American rebellion and in the early days of the Napoleonic Wars, when it had the honour of being present with Nelson at Copenhagen. It played a leading part in the defence of Canada in the war of 1812, fought in the Opium War in 1840 and earned its first three Victoria Crosses in the Crimea. The 66th Regiment of Foot was raised in 1756 and served in the West Indies, the Peninsular, Nepal and Canada, and was almost annihilated at the great disaster of Malwand during the Afghan War of 1879–80. The 49th and 66th were amalgamated in 1881 to become the 1st and 2nd Battalions of the Berkshire Regiment. Four years later, it had the unique honour of being made a Royal Regiment in recognition of the conduct of its 1st Battalion at Tofrek in the Sudan, and a few years later, the 2nd Battalion (raised in 1803) saw hard service in South Africa.

During the Great War 1914–18 the Royal Berkshires raised 13 battalions, were awarded 55 new Battle Honours, but lost nearly 7,000 men. They saw action at Mons, Ypres, Neuve Chapelle and Loos, and it was during the Battle of Loos and after that the 1st Battalion won two VCs. In 1916, seven Berkshire battalions fought in the Battle of the Somme, and the medical officer of the 6th Battalion was awarded the VC. The Regiment saw further action at the Battle of Doiran in April 1917, and this was followed by more fighting along the Lys, at Aisne, and repulsed a major Austrian attack at Piave in Northern Italy in 1918. In the months before the guns fell silent, action was seen at Arras, Cambrai and Selle.

In the Second World War, the Royal Berkshires raised 11 battalions of which six went overseas. They suffered heavy casualties in the retreat to Dunkirk and also saw action in Iraq, Egypt, Sicily and the Anzio landings. In 1944 the 1st Battalion were the first troops of the 2nd British Division to arrive in the Kohima perimeter, with the Japanese pounding the area for almost three weeks in their efforts to invade India. The water ration was a pint a day for all purposes – shaving and washing were forbidden. Nobody enjoyed more than two consecutive hours' sleep. Their training and fighting ability was put to the supreme test. The Royal Berkshires held firm, the Japanese acknowledged defeat and withdrew. Casualties amounted to 300, but they had played a key role in one of the decisive battles of the war. The Japanese never threatened India again.

The Wiltshire Regiment
(Duke of Edinburgh's)

The 1st Battalion (62nd of Foot) was raised in 1756 and quickly made a name for itself when four companies made a gallant stand among the ruins of Carrickfergus Castle against 1,000 French troops with artillery: they continued defending their position with bricks and stones after their ammunition was exhausted, and even used their buttons as bullets. The 62nd took part in the Sikh Wars and fought with great courage at the Battle of Ferozeshah on 21/22 December 1845 – a Battle Honour commemorated annually to this day when the Colours are handed over to the warrant officers and sergeants for the day in recognition of the fortitude of the sergeants in this Battle. In the words of the Duke of Wellington himself . . . 'The 62nd did all that brave men could at Ferozeshah'.

The 2nd Battalion (99th of Foot) was raised in 1824 in Glasgow, and saw arduous service in New Zealand in 1845/46. The 99th's sartorial perfection at this time is said to have given rise to the expression 'Dressed up to the Nines', an elegance other Regiments aspired to. They were to become successively the Lanarkshire Regiment the 99th (Duke of Edinburgh's) Regiment and the 2nd Battalion the Duke of Edinburgh's Wiltshire Regiment. The 62nd and 99th amalgamated in 1881 to form The Wiltshire Regiment.

The Wiltshires raised 12 battalions in the 1914–18 war, during which time they were awarded 60 new Battle Honours at a cost of 5,000 men killed. They served in almost every theatre of war – Egypt, Gallipoli, Mesopotamia, Palestine, Greece, Salonika and on the Western Front. It was at the Battle of the Somme that Capt RJF Hayward, who had already won the MC, was awarded a VC for 'displaying almost superhuman powers of endurance and consistent courage of the rarest nature' while commanding his company at Bapaume. Many Wiltshire battalions fought alongside battalions of the Glosters and Royal Berkshires throughout the Great War.

In the Second World War, The Wiltshire Regiment raised six battalions, of which four went overseas, with the 2nd Battalion serving in more theatres than any other battalion in our Regiments. The 1st Battalion served in India and Burma, while the 2nd Battalion saw action in Flanders, Sicily, Italy and Germany. It was while defending the bridgehead that Sgt MAW Rogers, having won the Military Medal in Sicily, won a posthumous VC in the breakout from Anzio. Soon after D-Day, both the 4th and 5th Battalions landed in Normandy and particularly distinguished themselves in the fighting round Mount Pincon and in the Seine crossings; once the bridgehead had been established, the whole of the British armour poured through and drove on to Brussels and Antwerp. Victory in Europe was soon to be achieved.

The Duke of Edinburgh's Royal Regiment
(Berkshire and Wiltshire)

The Regiment was formed on 9 June 1959 on the Isle of Wight through the amalgamation of the Royal Berkshire and the Wiltshire Regiments. After serving as part of the Strategic Reserve the Battalion moved to Malta from where, in 1964, it was ordered to Cyprus to conduct internal security operations when conflict broke out between the Greek and Turkish communities. In 1966, the Battalion moved to Germany to become one of the mechanised battalions of BAOR. Through the 1970s, the Battalion undertook a residential tour in Northern Ireland, an emergency tour in Cyprus from Shoeburyness, two years as the Infantry Demonstration Battalion in Warminster, and then returned to Osnabruck as part of BAOR.

During the 1980s, 1 DERR undertook operational tours from Canterbury to Northern Ireland and to Cyprus with the United Nations Forces, after which the Battalion returned once more to Northern Ireland for another residential tour.

The Royal Gloucestershire, Berkshire and Wiltshire Regiment

Within months of joining the British Army's order of battle on 27 April 1994 the 1st Battalion, stationed at Alma Barracks, Catterick, was sent to Bosnia as part of UNPROFOR for six months, mostly in the enclave of Gorazde. Following a brief return to Catterick, they then moved to Cyprus for two years, during which A Company Group spent six months in the Falkland Islands. In April 1997 they returned to Colchester as part of 24 Airmobile Brigade. The Battalion exercised in Canada in 1997 (Exercise Pond Jump 17), and was then deployed on operations in South Armagh, Northern Ireland.

The *Soldiers of Gloucestershire Museum* in Regimental Headquarters, at Custom House in Gloucester's Historic Docks.

Top: 2 RGBW (V) annual Camp, Sennybridge.

THE WORCESTERSHIRE AND SHERWOOD FORESTERS REGIMENT
(27th/45th Foot)

The Regiment is the county regiment of Derbyshire, Nottinghamshire, Worcestershire and the Dudley, Oldbury, Halesowen and Stourbridge area of the West Midlands. It consists of one regular battalion of some six hundred full-time soldiers and has part-time Territorial Army detachments in each of its main county areas.

Since its formation in 1970 the 1st Battalion has served extensively on operations in Northern Ireland, with UN Forces in Cyprus and with NATO Forces in Bosnia as well as on garrison duties in Germany, Cyprus, Belize and the United Kingdom. All units of the Regiment pride themselves on their high standards of marksmanship; between 1976 and 1997 the 1st Battalion won the Army's major marksmanship competition on a record fourteen occasions.

The Regiment values its close links with the Local Authorities throughout its county areas including the Freedom of nine cities and boroughs and is particularly grateful to the Cities of Derby, Nottingham and Worcester for housing its Regimental Museums. The present generation of those serving take pride in the proud history and traditions of their antecedent regiments which stretch back over 300 years and include 176 Battle Honours earned in all corners of the globe spanning the period from Marlborough's wars in the early 18th Century up to the Second World War. The four principal Battle Honours which the Regiment celebrates annually are the Glorious First of June 1794, the Battle of Badajoz on 6th April 1812, the Battle of the Alma 20th September 1854 and the Battle of Gheluvelt 31st October 1914.

The Worcestershire Regiment traces its history back to Farrington's Regiment formed in 1694 and Charlemont's Regiment raised in 1701, later the 29th and 36th Foot respectively. Throughout the eighteenth and nineteenth centuries the 29th and 36th Foot saw service in the Low Countries, North America, India, the Peninsular and France. In 1745 in America the 29th earned the nickname 'the ever sworded 29th' after the officers took to wearing swords in the Mess after being attacked by hitherto friendly Indians, and were later called 'the vein-openers' when they were responsible for the Boston 'Massacre'. Both the 29th and 36th served in the Peninsular where Wellington singled out the 36th after the Battle of Vimiera in 1808 as 'an example to the Army' and praised the 29th after Talavera as 'the best Regiment in this Army'. The 29th later served in the Sikh wars and the Indian Mutiny.

In 1881 the 29th and 36th became the 1st and 2nd Battalions The Worcestershire Regiment and shortly afterwards the local Militia and Rifle Volunteer Units were incorporated into the Regiment; elements of all these subsequently served together in South Africa during the Boer War.

During World War One the Regiment expanded to 22 battalions which fought in France, Flanders, Gallipoli, Mesopotamia, Macedonia, the Caucasus and Italy.

In World War Two the 7th and 8th Territorial battalions went to France and withdrew through Dunkirk in 1940; the 7th Battalion later served in India and Burma and fought with distinction at Kohima. The 2nd Battalion also fought in Burma. The 1st Battalion moved from Palestine on the outbreak of war to Sudan and later fought in Eritrea and the Western Desert before being taken prisoner at Tobruk. In 1943 it was re-constituted and took part in the Northern West Europe campaign.

After the war both regular and territorial elements were reduced to one battalion each. The 1st Battalion served in Germany, Malaya, the Caribbean, Gibraltar and Cyprus before amalgamation in 1970. The 7th Battalion was disbanded in 1967 since when the Territorial element has been expanded and contracted on several occasions.

The Sherwood Foresters traces its history back to Houghton's Regiment raised in 1741, later the 45th Foot. The Regiment won its first Battle Honour at Louisburg in Canada in 1758 while the Grenadier Company also took part in the capture of Quebec. In the following years the Regiment fought in the American War of Independence, the West Indies and Brazil. The 45th was one of the few regiments which fought with Wellington's Army in Portugal and Spain throughout the Peninsular War where it gained the nickname of 'Old Stubborns'.

The title 'Royal Sherwood Foresters' was first applied to the Nottinghamshire Militia in 1813, and it was not until 1866 that 'Sherwood Foresters' was authorised as a secondary title for the 45th (Nottinghamshire) Regiment.

The 95th (Derbyshire) Regiment was raised in 1823 and became the 2nd Battalion, Sherwood Foresters in 1881. After service in Malta, the Ionian Islands and Greece, the Regiment was sent to the Crimea where it gained fame at the Alma. During this campaign the Regiment captured some Russian drums at Inkerman, and to this day the Regiment's drums are embellished with black and white dicing, copied from these Russian drums. The 95th was the last British Army regiment to carry its Colours in a major battle and earned the nickname the 'Nail's because of its reputation for being 'as hard as nails'. Shortly after its return to England the 95th Regiment sailed for India and assisted in the quelling of the Indian Mutiny, where Private McQuirt won the first of sixteen VCs awarded to the Sherwood Foresters.

During World I the Regiment raised 33 Battalions. These fought with great distinction in Flanders, France, Gallipoli and Italy and nine VCs were awarded to members of the Regiment. At the outset of World War II (1939–1945) the 1st Battalion was on active service in Palestine and was later lost in the fall of Tobruk. The 2nd Battalion was soon in France with the British Expeditionary Force and was joined later by the 1/5th, 2/5th and 9th Battalions all fighting at Dunkirk. Meanwhile the 8th Battalion took part in the ill-fated Norwegian Campaign. The 1/5th Battalion were made prisoners of war when Singapore surrendered. In the Middle East, the 2nd and 5th Battalions fought with the 1st Army in Tunisia while the 14th Battalion took part in the Battle of El Alamein. Subsequently, all three Battalions took part in the severe fighting of the Italian Campaign.

Between 1945 and 1970 the 1st Battalion served in Germany, Egypt, Libya, Malaya, Singapore and Cyprus. Of the four original TA battalions the two were converted to anti-aircraft regiments in 1936, later becoming field squadrons, Royal Engineers (TA) in 1961. In the same year the other two were amalgamated, and later disbanded, only to be revived as the 3rd Bn The Worcestershire and Sherwood Foresters Regiment which represented the Regiment so well in Nottingham and Derbyshire for twenty eight years until it too was reduced to a company in 1999.

REGIMENTAL INFORMATION

The Colonel in Chief: HRH The Princess Royal

Motto: Firm

The Regimental Mascot. The Regimental Mascot, named Derby is a Swaledale ram from the Chatsworth Estate. The first one was acquired during the Indian Mutiny by the 95th.

The Regimental Memorial. The Crich Memorial Tower was built in 1922–23 near Matlock in Derbyshire originally to commemorate Sherwood Foresters who fell in the Great War. It is nearly 20m high and stands at 944m above sea level, from the top seven counties can be seen. On the first Sunday in July, the annual Pilgrimage is held at Crich.

A Warrior of The 1st Battalion patrols in Bosnia, 1996

Right, top: The Colours being trooped during the Presentation of New Colours by the Colonel-in-Chief, HRH The Princess Royal, 1995.

Right, bottom: Battle of Khohima, Burma 1944 – turning point of the war in Asia at a cost of 13000 casualties – 'When you go home tell them of us and say for your tomorrow we gave our today'.   TERENCE CUNEO

THE QUEEN'S LANCASHIRE REGIMENT

Lancashire's County Regiment

The Queen's Lancashire Regiment was formed on 25 March 1970 and proudly carries the honours and traditions of three of the Red Rose County's great Regiments:

> The East Lancashire Regiment
> The South Lancashire Regiment (Prince of Wales's Volunteers)
> The Loyal Regiment (North Lancashire)

These in turn were formed in 1881 by the pairing of six of the old numbered regiments of foot, respectively the 30th and 59th, 40th and 82nd, and 47th and 81st. Through its famous forbears we can trace an unbroken succession as Lancashire's County Regiment back to 1782.

The Regiment has had the honour and distinction of having Her Majesty The Queen, Duke of Lancaster, as Colonel-in-Chief since 1953.

Early History

The earliest of our predecessors, Viscount Castleton's Regiment of Foot, was raised in 1689 and first saw active service in Flanders. Later they spent many years as Marines, when they took part in the capture and defence of Gibraltar, 1704–5, and many other engagements on land and sea. The Regiment played a major part in the early history of North America, fighting first against the French and their Indian allies and then the American War of Independence and the War of 1812. The Battle Honour 'Quebec 1759' is celebrated annually to this day on 13th September, and the death of General Wolfe in this battle is commemorated by the incorporation of black in the Regiment's colours and officers' lace.

The Revolutionary and Napoleonic Wars

In the course of this epic struggle from 1793 to 1815 the Regiment widely deployed against France and her allies, winning particular renown in Spain, Egypt, Italy, South Africa, South America, the West Indies and Java, and earning 21 Battle Honours, including a Sphinx badge for their distinguished services in Egypt. They also saw service in the Mediterranean under Nelson's command, and to this day the Regiment is proud to maintain an affiliation with the Royal Navy. Among the Regimental trophies of this period is a Napoleonic Eagle captured at the Battle of Salamanca. At the Battle of Waterloo, 18th June 1815, the 30th and 40th were posted in the centre of Wellington's line where they withstood repeated attacks by cavalry and infantry and were pounded by cannon. Both battalions stood firm and towards the end of the day the 30th advanced in line to meet a column of Napoleon's Imperial Guard and routed them with one volley, while the 40th swept away the French infantry to their front and took part in the recapture of La Haye Sainte. Today the anniversary of Waterloo is observed with a traditional parade when the Colours are decorated and each officer and soldier wears a laurel leaf in his hat.

Soldiers of The Queen

In the century between the defeat of Napoleon and the outbreak of the Great War our predecessors were stationed world-wide, spending long periods in overseas garrisons guarding British trade routes and the frontiers of the rapidly expanding Empire, and fighting on every inhabited continent. Among their many campaigns some of the more notable were the Crimean War, when the Regiment's first two Victoria Crosses were won at the Battle of Inkerman, 1854, two Afghan wars and six other campaigns in and around India, and wars against Arabian pirates, New Zealand Maoris and South African Boers. Two Battle Honours are unique to the Regiment: 'Canton' in 1857 and 'Defence of Kimberley' in 1900. Further Victoria Crosses were won in New Zealand and Afghanistan.

The Great War 1914–18

In the course of the Great War 37 battalions of our predecessors saw active service overseas, fighting in France and Flanders, Gallipoli, Mesopotamia (modern Iraq), Palestine, Macedonia and East Africa. 112 Battle Honours were earned and twelve Victoria Crosses. The sacrifices made were immense, but two examples must suffice.

On 1st July 1916, in the opening hours of the Battle of the Somme, the 1st and 11th East Lancashires advanced steadily across open ground in the face of German machine guns and wire. Of 722 men of the 1st Battalion who went into action on that day only 237 came out, while the 11th Battalion (The Accrington Pals) lost 584 out of 720 in the attack. This memorable devotion to duty is commemorated in the Regiment annually to this day.

In Mesopotamia battalions of all three of our predecessor regiments battled their way up the River Tigris, earning three Victoria Crosses and particularly distinguishing themselves at the decisive assault crossing of the Diyala which led to the capture of Baghdad, March 1917.

The Second World War 1939–45

Three battalions of the Regiment held the perimeter during the Dunkirk evacuation and were among the last to leave, having earned the only Victoria Cross awarded for that operation. The Regiment then fought in Malaya and Singapore, played an active part in the capture of Madagascar and Tunisia, where a further Victoria Cross was won, and served in the arduous but ultimately successful Burma campaign. In Italy the Loyals won particular distinction by their stubborn defence of the Anzio bridgehead, in Normandy the South Lancashires were in the first assault wave on D Day, while in the bitter battles for the liberation of North West Europe the East Lancashires had a well-earned reputation for always taking their objectives, notably at s'Hertogenbosch in Holland, Grimbiemont in the Ardennes, and in the Reichswald.

In the course of the Second World War a further 52 Battle Honours were added to the Regiment's proud record.

The Post-War Years 1945–2000

Since 1945, the Regiment has seen active service in Palestine, the Canal Zone, Malaya, Aden, Bosnia and Northern Ireland, where 1st Battalion The Queen's Lancashire Regiment is currently stationed. In the final months of the anti-terrorist campaign in Aden, 1967, the Regiment amassed more gallantry awards than any other unit, while since 1970 there have been eight operational tours in Northern Ireland. There were also postings in Germany with the Rhine Army and, to set the seal on this period, in 1992–4 following the dissolution of the Warsaw Pact the Queen's Lancashires had the honour of being the last British battalion in Berlin.

The Regiment continues to cherish its close association with the historic County whose name it bears and enjoys the freedoms of Blackburn, Burnley, the Fylde, Haslingden, Preston and Warrington.

Capt H M Ervine-Andrews VC, 1st Battalion The East Lancashire Regiment, who was awarded the only Dunkirk VC for his gallant defence of the perimeter 31 May–1 June 1940.

LOVELL CONSTRUCTION LTD

Freedom March. The Queen's Lancashire Regiment exercising its Freedom by marching through Preston, 1997.

Top: Afghanistan 1880. Colours of the 59th Regiment under the walls of Ghuznee after the Battle of Ahmed Khel. This was the last occasion on which the Regimental Colours were carried in battle.

THE DUKE OF WELLINGTON'S REGIMENT (WEST RIDING)

The Regiment has been in existence for almost 300 years and today is one of the handful remaining in the British Army order of battle that have not been disbanded or amalgamated since the Infantry of the Line was reorganised in 1881. At that time the 33rd (or The Duke of Wellington's) Regiment and the 76th Regiment were amalgamated to form the 1st and 2nd Battalions The Duke of Wellington's Regiment (West Riding).

The 33rd can trace its descent from a letter addressed to the Earl of Huntingdon dated March 14th 1702 ordering him to raise a regiment of foot for the war about to break out with France over the succession to the Spanish throne. After initially taking part in the campaigns in Holland the regiment was sent to Spain where it was thoroughly 'blooded' in the major disaster at Almanza in 1707 when the tish were forced to surrender after their Portuguese allies fled the field. Then followed the Austrian War of Succession, where the Regiment earned its first battle honour at Dettingen, the Jacobite rising of 1745 and the American War of Independence as a member of the force Commanded by Lord Cornwallis, then also Colonel of the 33rd.

It was under Lord Cornwallis's colonelcy in 1782 that the Regiment was first formally linked with the West Riding of Yorkshire and became known as the 33rd (or 1st Yorkshire West Riding) Regiment. This was in recognition of its already long established practice of recruiting soldiers from this part of the country.

The appearance in 1793 of a young, 24 year old major, Arthur Wellesley later the Duke of Wellington, in the 33rd attracted little notice at the time. Six months later he purchased his Lieutenant Colonelcy. He remained in command of the Regiment until 1802. He took it first to Holland and then on to India which was in a state of turmoil following the collapse of the Moghul Empire, the intrigues of the French and the expanding influence of the East India Company. It was these years with the 33rd where he learned his trade as a soldier. In 1806 he succeeded Lord Cornwallis as Colonel holding the appointment until he relinquished it, with some reluctance, in 1813 to take up the Colonelcy of the Horse Guards. The 33rd subsequently also fought under him in 1815 at the Battle of Waterloo where it took part in the charge which routed Napoleon's Imperial Guard.

The 'Iron Duke' died in September 1852. Nine months after his death approval was given for the 33rd to become the only regiment of the British Army to be named after a subject not of Royal blood – The Duke of Wellington's Regiment.

In 1854 the 33rd were with the force that landed in the Crimea where, shortly afterwards, they were the leading regiment of the leading brigade which successfully stormed the Russian positions overlooking the river Alma, but at a terrible cost – 268 casualties, more than any other regiment that took part. They subsequently fought at Inkerman and Sebastopol and in the words of 'The Times' of 26th June 1856 'of the 33rd Regiment. . . . . no regiment has more largely shared in the losses, sufferings and the hard work of the expedition from the first to the last.'

The year 1857 saw the Regiment back in India and engaged in the actions to quell the Indian Mutiny. In 1867 they took part in the expeditionary force formed to rescue the Europeans who had been caste into chains by King Theodore, the half-insane ruler of Abyssinia. The task was achieved with great efficiency and on Easter Day 1868 his fortress at Magdala was stormed and King Theodore killed. The 33rd led the attack in the process earning two VCs.

The 76th was raised in 1787 for service in India. Most regiments have fought in India at one time or another, but no regiment won such distinction in so short a space of time. The 76th played an outstanding part in the campaigns which were to decide the mastery of India for the next 150 years. It fought first in the war against Tipu Sultan the ruler of Mysore in Southern India which resulted in the capture of Seringapatam. Then in the early 1800s it fought in a series of minor campaigns in Northern India before it's remarkable role as the only British infantry regiment in the force commanded by Lord Lake in the campaign against the Maharratta princes. The princes controlled the Deccan and much of Central and Northern India. Their aims were to substitute their rule for that of the Moghuls over India and they were holdng the Moghul emperor as a virtual prisoner in his palace in Delhi.

Lord Lake fought a brilliant campaign under exceptionally arduous conditions capturing the twin capitals of Hindoostan, Delhi and Agra, and releasing the Moghul emperor. For its services in India the East India company awarded the Regiment an honorary stand of colours making it today the only one to carry four colours on parade. Permission was also granted for the Regiment to use the badge of an 'Elephant' circumscribed by the word 'Hindoostan'.

The 76th returned from India in 1806. It was then ordered to the Peninsular and joined the army of Sir John Moore where it took part in the long, terrible, winter retreat to Corunna. From Spain they went to Holland, back again to the Peninsular in 1813 and then Canada for the War with the United States.

This was the last action the Regiment was to see before the Cardwell Reforms of the Army in 1881. It was these reforms that brought together the 33rd and 76th Regiments to become the 1st and 2nd battalions of The Duke

of Wellington's Regiment (West Riding). At the same time new barracks were built in Halifax to provide a recruit training depot for the Regiment. A role the barracks were to continue to fulfil until they closed in 1959.

The Regiment next saw action in South Africa where the 1st Battalion landed in January 1900, missing the blunders and disasters of the early days. They took part in the Relief of Kimberley and the Battle of Paardeberg that led to the surrender of Cronje, the senior Boer commander. A company of mounted infantry from the 2nd Battalion and the 3rd Militia Battalion also served in the war.

Great Britain declared war on Germany on 4th August 1914 and immediately mobilised the British Expeditionary Force which included within it the 2nd Battalion. The Battalion was early into action at Mons, Le Cateau, the retreat to Paris, the Marne and the first battle of Ypres. By the end of the war the 'Dukes' had put twenty one Regular, Territorial and Service battalions in the field. Of these, fourteen battalions fought on the Western Front during the long hard slog of trench warfare and in the process helped the Regiment to gain the Battle Honours of Somme, Arras, Cambrai and Lys. The only battalions to serve elsewhere were the 10th in Italy, the 8th who took part in the Gallipoli campaign and the 1st which, at the outbreak of war, was stationed in India and remained there for the duration as one of only 8 British battalions to garrison the country. The cost of the war to the Dukes, in killed alone, was over 8,000.

Between the wars the 1st Battalion was stationed almost entirely in the UK. Meanwhile the 2nd was overseas in Egypt, Singapore and then India where it took part in the Mohmand operations on the North West Frontier.

At the outbreak of the Second World War the 1st Battalion was sent to France to join the BEF and was subsequently part of the rearguard covering the retreat to Dunkirk. In 1942 and '43 it was in North Africa. In 1944 it participated in the landing at Anzio and saw some of the most desperate fighting of the war in the Italian campaign culminating in the battle of Monte Ceco on the Gothic Line. In February 1942 the 2nd Battalion was on the Indian North West Frontier when it was hastily mobilised as part of a force to reinforce Burma against the Japanese. Within two weeks of mobilisation they were in Burma defending the bridge across the river Sittang which was blown while they were still on the far side. The remnants of the battalion who managed to cross the river then endured the long 1000 mile retreat to India. After reorganising they were assigned to the Chindits and took part in the relief of Imphal in 1944.

Before the war, both the 4th and 5th TA Battalions were converted to Royal Artillery and Royal Engineers respectively. They served in these roles throughout the war though the 5th converted to RA also in 1944. The 6th and 7th Battalions each formed a 2nd Battalion. The 2/6th and 2/7th were sent to France in 1940, only partly trained and inadequately equipped, and soon found themselves facing a highly professional, well equipped enemy. After fighting their way to the coast with great distinction they were evacuated through St

Lieutenant Colonel The Hon Arthur Wellesley, commanded the 33rd Regiment 1793–1802; Colonel of the Regiment 1806–1813, later 1st Duke of Wellington.

Right, top: The 76th Regiment at The Storming of Deig, 1804.

Right, bottom: Winners of the first Army Rugby Cup 1906–7 – and 14 times since.

Malo and St Valery-en-Caux two weeks after the fall of Dunkirk. Neither Battalion was to serve overseas again. The 1/6th and 1/7th were in the 49th (Polar Bear) Division and took part in the Normandy landing in 1944. The 1/6th soon afterwards suffered heavy casualties and had to be broken up to provide reinforcements for the 1/7th. The 1/7th enjoyed a great reputation within the Division where it fought in the 'bocage', the capture of Le Havre and the liberation of Holland. The 8th and 9th Battalions were re-raised in 1940 and converted to RAC seeing action in North Africa, Italy, India, Burma and immediately after the war in Sumatra.

By 1947 both the 1st and 2nd Battalions were back in the UK and in 1948 they were amalgamated to form a single battalion – the 1st.

In September 1952 the 1st Battalion sailed for Korea to join the Commonwealth Division as part of the United Nations Forces. In one of the hardest fought battles of the Korean war the battalion held the key approaches to Seoul at the Battle of the Hook. This was the last major classic defensive battle fought by the British Army and the battalion suffered an intensity of artillery bombardment not seen since the trench warfare of the 1st World War.

Since their return from Korea the Regiment has experienced to the full the 'turbulence' that has been the lot of the British soldier since the Second World War ended. The Dukes have served in Gibraltar, Malta, Cyprus, Kenya, Northern Ireland, Germany and Bosnia where, in 1994, the 1st Battalion was the first unit into Gorazde. There it played a critical role in helping to prevent a similar 'ethnic cleansing' tragedy to that which befell Zepa and Screbrinica.

Within the Army the Regiment is particularly well renowned for its prowess on the Rugby field. The 'Dukes', besides having had many internationals in their ranks over the years, have won the Army Cup fourteen times – more than any other Regiment – and been runners up seven times.

Today the Regiment has a single regular battalion, the 1st Battalion, and two Territorial Army companies one in West Yorkshire and one in South Yorkshire. The Regiment continues to recruit its soldiers from the old West Riding. It is based on these long, historical ties to the people of the West Riding, and the honest, straight forward, hard working qualities they bring with them, that the Regiment's reputation for quiet professionalism is founded.

THE STAFFORDSHIRE REGIMENT
(The Prince of Wales's)

The Staffordshire Regiment (The Prince of Wales's) adopted its present title as a result of the amalgamation in 1959 of the South and North Staffords. These two Regiments which came into being in 1881 in the Cardwell Army Reforms, were in turn comprised of four numbered Regiments of Foot: 38th, 64th, 80th and 98th. Thus the present day Regiment traces its history back to 1705, a year after Marlborough's great victory at Blenheim, when Colonel Luke Lillington based himself at the Kings Head Hotel, Lichfield to raise a regiment for service in the West Indies. The Regiment, by then known as 38th Foot, was still based in Antigua when the Seven Years War began in 1756. In all it was to spend 57 years of continuous service in the West Indies, often short of pay, clothing, equipment and recruits. The Buff Holland Patch, worn today as part of the Regimental badge, was authorised as a dress distinction in 1935 for the South Staffords and represents the local cloth, a sort of sacking, which the Regiment used to make waistcoats and to line their tunics, possibly the first known use of tropical uniform.

During the Seven Years War the 38th fought alongside the newly formed 64th Regiment and they were together again 20 years later in the American War of Independence. To encourage recruiting regiments were first given territorial titles in 1782 and the 38th became First Staffordshire and the 64th Second Staffordshire. On return from the Americas both Regiments sent detachments to Staffordshire and began to incorporate the Stafford Knot into their badges. The Knot has been used by the Earls of Stafford since medieval times and, contrary to popular belief, was never designed to hang three men. Nor has it ever been the Staffordshire Knot despite the well known pun tune.

During the Napoleonic Wars the 38th and 64th fought in the Peninsular and the West Indies and were joined in holding a county title by the 80th Regiment (Staffordshire Volunteers) formed in 1793 almost entirely from the Staffordshire Militia. The 80th took part in the 1794 campaign in Flanders with the Duke of York and helped to eject Napoleon from Egypt in 1801, for which it received its first Battle Honour – The Sphinx superscribed Egypt, still carried on the Regimental Colour.

After the Napoleonic Wars the Army was returned to peace establishment and one of the regiments to be disbanded was the 98th Foot. It was reconstituted in 1824 and after distinguished service in China, under Colin Campbell later Lord Clyde, it was awarded the Battle Honour of a Dragon superscribed China, also carried on the Regimental Colour today. The four numbered regiments of foot spent much of the 19th century 'propping up Empire', between them serving on all five continents and taking part in many colonial wars. One such was the Sikh War of 1845 in which CSgt Matthew Kirkland was commissioned in the field at Ferozeshah for capturing a large black standard to which the Sikhs were rallying. The flag and two others from the war now hang over the Sikh War Memorial to the 80th Regiment in Lichfield Cathedral and each year, at the Ferozeshah Parade, the Officers hand over the Colours to the Sergeants as a sign of trust.

Staffordshire has always had a strong tradition of citizen soldiers fighting alongside the regulars. The Staffordshire Militia was granted the title of 'Kings Own' by George III, and Volunteer and Militia soldiers from both Regiments fought in the South African War of 1899. This tradition has continued and in the First World War the South and North Staffords raised a total of 35 Regular, Militia and Territorial battalions, losing nearly 10,000 men. As well as the Western Front, battalions fought in the Dardanelles, Mesopotamia, Southern Russia, Italy, India and Afghanistan. Seven members of the two Regiments were awarded the VC to add to the 3 won in the Indian Mutiny and the Zulu War. Perhaps the most noteworthy was LCpl Bill Coltman of the 1st/6th North Staffords who refused to bear arms for religious reasons and was awarded the VC, DCM and bar, MM and bar and an MID for his work as a stretcher bearer, probably the most decorated other rank of the war. Despite countless forays into No Mans Land to bring in casualties under fire, he was never wounded and died peacefully in 1974. His medals are in the Regimental Museum.

During the Second World War Staffordshire again raised many extra battalions. The 1st/6th South Staffords and 2nd North Staffords were at Dunkirk and both were to return to German occupied Europe, the first with the Territorial 59th (Staffordshire) Division in Normandy and the latter in Italy, where they marched on Rome after 5 months penned into the Anzio Beachhead. The 1st North Staffords fought the Japanese in Burma and in 1944 the 1st South Staffords fought behind Japanese lines in the 2nd Chindit Campaign where Lt George Cairns won a posthumous VC. The citation was lost with Wingate's plane and the VC was not awarded until 1948, following a radio broadcast about Cairns' bravery in hand to hand combat.

The other VCs won by the South Staffords in World War II were by the gliderborne 2nd Battalion at Arnhem, the only British battalion to gain two VCs in one battle in the course of the war. The battalion had also taken part in the Sicily air landings in 1943 for which it was awarded the dress distinction

of a gold glider badge, still worn today on the upper right sleeve by all ranks. Sadly it cost the lives of almost 300 men drowned when the gliders landed in the sea.

Since the Second World War the Staffords have helped to keep the peace in Hong Kong, Korea, Cyprus, Kenya, Uganda, Aden, The Gulf and Belize. It has spent more than 6 years on tours in Northern Ireland and played a full part in NATO's commitment to West Germany and Berlin. The greatest challenge of the last 50 years was that faced by 1 STAFFORDS during the Gulf War of 1990/91 when it formed the armoured infantry battalion of 7th Armoured Brigade. Warrior armoured vehicles were combined with the traditional weapons of rifle and bayonet across 300 kilometres of hostile desert, the dismounted infantrymen doing their job in the time-honoured way. After 100 hours of fighting the Battalion was described as 'one of the most successful formations in the British offensive and the one that was to see most action'.

On their return from the Gulf War the Staffords were to fight another battle, to avoid amalgamation under Options for Change. With massive support from the people of Staffordshire and the West Midlands the Regiment was saved. 'Worth Saving' by Bruce George MP and Nick Ryan tells the story of the campaign which made a star of Watchman III, the Staffordshire Bull Terrier mascot of the Volunteer Battalion. Sadly he died in 1998 and Watchman IV, still just a puppy, is being groomed to take over as the mascot of the whole Regiment.

The Regiment has borne the title Prince of Wales's since it was bestowed on the 98th Foot in 1876 but today is proud to have HRH The Duke of York CVO ADC as Colonel in Chief. The Staffords was his first colonelcy and, as a professional serviceman, he has taken a close interest in all its activities.

As well as a Regular (1st) Battalion, to be re-equipped with Warrior in 2000, the Regiment has Territorial Army bases at Burton upon Trent, Wolverhampton and Stoke on Trent as well as many badged detachments of ACF and CCF. RHQ is co-located with the Museum at Whittington Barracks, Lichfield and there are 15 branches of the Regimental Association (Old Comrades). The Regiment is proud to have the Freedom of ten County or Metropolitan Boroughs in Staffordshire and the West Midlands and many also run branches of Friends of the Staffordshire Regiment.

The Colonel-in-Chief consults Watchman III.

Right, top: Battle of Ferozeshah, 1845.   PETER ARCHER

Right, bottom: Warriors in action – debussing to take Iraqi positions at 'Objective Lead', Gulf 1991.   MICHAEL TURNER

THE BLACK WATCH
(Royal Highland Regiment)

The Black Watch owes its existence to the need of the government in the early eighteenth century to police the wild, remote and at that time lawless Highland regions of Scotland. Six Independent Companies of Highlanders were raised in 1725 to police or 'Watch' the Highlands. Fourteen years later these original companies were augmented by a further four to form the first Highland Regiment, its name derived from the contrast of the dark colour of its tartan with the red coats of other soldiers and from its policing role.

Three years after the first parade on the banks of the Tay at Aberfeldy the Regiment was ordered to London and thence to Flanders where it received its baptism of fire at the Battle of Fontenoy in 1745. Although this was a British defeat, The Black Watch gained great distinction by its conduct being described by a French officer as 'Highland Furies who rushed in on us with more violence than ever did the sea driven by tempest'.

The Regiment was next engaged in the French Indian Wars and especially at the Battle of Ticonderoga in 1758 where during the attack on the fort of that name more than half the men became casualties. By this time the Regiment had been allocated the numerical slot '42nd' in seniority, a number which it was to render illustrious all over the world. In recognition of its worth it was now granted the title 'Royal' and raised a Second Battalion. In 1786 this battalion became a separate regiment in its own right, the 73rd and was much in action in India and Ceylon, playing a prominent part in the capture of Seringapatam and Mysore.

Meanwhile after service during the American War of Independence and in Flanders the 42nd Royal Highlanders became involved in the Napoleonic Wars during the campaign in Egypt in 1801. There at the Battle of Alexandria the Regiment captured the standard of the French 'Invincible' Legion and won the honour of wearing the Sphinx on its colours and badge. No fewer than ten battle honours were awarded to the Regiment for its part in the continued fight against Napoleon's armies during six years of the Peninsular War. Both the 42nd and 73rd, which were to become respectively the 1st and 2nd Battalions of The Black Watch were present at the Battle of Waterloo and at the smaller but equally hard fought action at Quatre Bras two days previously.

Next in action during the Crimean War the Regiment played a particularly prominent part in the attack on the Russian positions at the Alma in 1854 before enduring all the dangers and tribulations of work in the trenches before Sebastopol. Scarcely was this war over before the Regiment was despatched to India to help quell the Mutiny. There they were first in action at Cawnpore and then early in 1858 at the relief of Lucknow. It was here that Lieutenant Farquharson won the first of the Regiment's fourteen Victoria Crosses.

For the remainder of the nineteenth century the Regiments activities were principally concerned with events in Africa. 'Ashanti', now part of Ghana, was the next battle honour to be added to the Colours. In a bad climate, through tough jungle terrain and against a resolute enemy the Regiment advanced to the capital Coomassie. In the words of the renowned American correspondent H M Stanley 'the regiment never halted nor wavered; on it went, until the Ashantis, perceiving it useless to fight against men who would advance, heedless of ambuscades, rose from their coverts and fled panic-stricken'.

In 1881 the 42nd was formally brought together with the 73rd, its former Second Battalion, to form the 1st and 2nd Battalions. The following year the 1st Battalion was deployed to Egypt and took part in the successful dawn attack on the rebel Egyptian position at Tel-el-Kebir. Two years later the Battalion was present at three fierce actions against the Mahdis' fanatical warriors in neighbouring Sudan. It was the turn of the 2nd Battalion to be first involved in action in South Africa in 1899, taking heavy casualties during the ill conceived attack on the Boer positions at Magersfontein.

By the outbreak of the First World War, in addition to the two Regular battalions, The Black Watch had four Territorial battalions, one each from the constituent parts of its Regimental area – 4th (Dundee), 5th (Angus), 6th (Perthshire) and 7th (Fife). During the course of the War almost 8000 Black Watch soldiers died in action and some 25000 had become casualties. Such harrowing statistics give but poor indication of the full horrors of the fighting on the Western Front by the eleven battalions of the Regiment in action there and by the 2nd Battalion in Mesopotamia – or of the terrible losses sustained at Loos, at Neuve Chapelle and many of the other 73 battle honours earned at such dreadful cost by the Regiment. Nor can the almost unique award of the French Croix de Guerre to the 6th Battalion or the awards of Victoria Crosses to individuals properly symbolise the sum of gallantry displayed by so many thousands of men who fought in The Black Watch during the Great War.

During the Second World War six battalions represented the Regiment in all the main theatres of war. The original 1st Battalion was captured at St Valery but was soon re-formed to fight in the 51st Highland Division with the 5th and 7th Battalions. After action in Somaliland, the 2nd Battalion were subjected to the first large scale airborne attack in the history of war during the German invasion of Crete. In the words of the German parachute battalion commander 'The battle continued with great ferocity, but The Black Watch never surrendered. Had it been any other regiment, *any other*, all would have been well'. Later this Battalion took terrible casualties in just one hour during the break-out from Tobruk and then went on to be converted into 'Chindits' operating in two separate columns in the most appalling conditions of heat, monsoon rain and disease behind the Japanese lines in Burma. Meanwhile the 6th Battalion was participating in the advance up Italy and the battles to capture Monte Cassino while those battalions with the 51st Highland Division after action in North Africa and Sicily were taking part in the fierce battles breaking out from the Normandy Bridgehead and then the hard fought actions on the Dutch–German border and beyond. The 7th Battalion had the distinction of being the first British troops to cross the Rhine in March 1945.

During much of the period since the Second World War the Regiment has been involved in the type of policing duties for which it was originally raised – in Kenya, in Cyprus and in Northern Ireland. It was more heavily committed in Korea where the most recent battle honour was won at the 'Hook' in 1952. It has also played a prominent part in the run down of the Empire for the 2nd Battalion were the last troops to leave British India and 50 years later in 1997 the 1st Battalion were in the spotlight of world media during the handover of Hong Kong.

Left: Sniper of the 5th Battalion in action, Germany February 1945.

Right, top: 'The Black Watch at Bay', Battle of Quatre Bras, 16 June 1815   W B WOLLENS

Right, bottom: The Pipe Major and Commanding Officer of the 1st Battalion in the limelight and rain during the handover of Hong Kong, June 1997.

HIGHLAND DISTILLERS – THE FAMOUS GROUSE

THE HIGHLANDERS
(Seaforth, Gordons and Camerons)

The Raising of the Regiment

The Highlanders (Seaforth, Gordons and Camerons) are the proud descendants of five famous Scottish regiments, raised in the late eighteenth century to counter trouble in the Colonies, and to meet the growing threat from France. In 1778 the Earl of Seaforth mustered at Elgin the 72nd Highlanders, recruited from Ross-shire and Lewis; and in 1787 Sir Robert Abercromby gathered the 75th Highlanders at Stirling. In 1793 Colonel Francis Humberston Mackenzie of Seaforth recruited a second Regiment from Ross-shire and Lewis; known as the 78th Highlanders or Ross-shire Buffs, they mustered at Fort George, Inverness. In the same year, Major Alan Cameron at Erracht mustered the 79th Cameron Highlanders at Stirling. In 1794 the Fourth Duke of Gordon with the help of his wife the Duchess Jean, recruited the 100th (later the 92nd) Gordon Highlanders at Aberdeen from his estates in Badenoch, Strathspey and Lochaber.

The Merging

The process of re-designation and merger between the Regiments began some fifty years later to meet the changing demands of national defence. In 1823 the oldest of the five Regiments, the 72nd, became The Duke of Albany's Own Highlanders. In 1881, under the Cardwell reforms, they joined the 78th Ross-shire Buffs to become Seaforth Highlanders. Simultaneously, the 75th (Stirlingshire) Regiment merged with the 92nd to become The Gordon Highlanders. The Cameron Highlanders, honoured by Queen Victoria in 1873 with the title 'Queen's Own' remained a single battalion regiment until 1897. These three distinct Regiments fought in every campaign of the late nineteenth and twentieth centuries, often as part of the same Highland Brigade.

In 1961 with peace in Europe established, and a decreasing role in the Colonies, the Seaforth Highlanders and The Queen's Own Cameron Highlanders merged to become Queen's Own Highlanders (Seaforth and Camerons). Thirty-three years later, with the Cold War ended and defence no longer such a national priority, the Queen's Own Highlanders and The Gordon Highlanders combined as The Highlanders (Seaforth, Gordons and Camerons), in Edinburgh on 17 September 1994.

Battle Honours

The new Regiment proudly carries, on colours and drums, 89 of the 366 ancestral battle honours won in worldwide campaigns over two hundred years. Officers wear the Sphinx of Egypt, where both Camerons and Gordons served in the early nineteenth century, as collar badges. The Indian Tiger badge is worn on the collar of the officers and drummers in ceremonial order, to commemorate the campaigns at Seringapatam and Mysore between 1799–1807 in which the 75th fought against Tipoo Sahib's Tiger battalions. In Central India in 1803, at the battle of Assaye, the 78th Highlanders were part of Wellesley's Army that defeated a much larger French-trained Maharrata force. The Seaforths earned that battle honour and now wear the Elephant superscribed 'Assaye' as a collar badge. Later in Belgium the 79th (Cameron) and 92nd (Gordon) Highlanders each played a central part in Wellington's victory at Waterloo in 1815. Piper Kenneth MacKay of the 79th courageously stepped outside the safety of the regimental square and inspired his Regiment to repel continuous charges by French cavalry. The 92nd charged against the French infantry clutching the stirrup leathers of the Royal Scots Greys: the Regiment's looped garter flashes symbolise this wild action.

Another honour was won at the relief and defence of Lucknow in India in 1857 in which the Seaforth Highlanders fought gallantly against the Indian Mutineers, winning six Victoria Crosses. Forty years later on the North West Frontier, the 1st Gordon Highlanders took the Heights of Dargai from Pathan tribesmen in a celebrated charge across open ground, encouraged by Piper Findlater who continued to play although shot through both ankles. His was one of two Victoria Crosses won that day. The following year, both 1st Seaforth and 1st Cameron Highlanders were together as part of Kitchener's force sent to suppress the Sudan after Gordon's death at the hands of the Mahdi at Khartoum. In 1898 the Dervishes were defeated at the battle of Atbara during which the Camerons closely supported the Seaforth Highlanders, and the battle honour 'Atbara' was won. All three Regiments fought in the Boer War, earning eight Victoria Crosses between them, and the battle honour South Africa 1899–1902.

With the twentieth century and the challenge of two World Wars, each Regiment expanded dramatically. By 1918 the Seaforths had raised nineteen battalions, the Gordons twenty-one, and the Camerons thirteen. Fourteen Victoria Crosses were won by the Regiments in the First War and close on 50,000 men lost their lives. Inevitably most Highlanders served in the fields of Belgium and France but some were further afield in Italy and Mesopotamia, Iraq and Macedonia.

The Second War started disastrously with five battalions captured by the Germans at St Valery and one by the Japanese in Singapore. But from 1942 all the Regiments fought with singular success from El Alamein through North Africa, Sicily, Italy and from the Normandy beaches to the Rhine. In the Far East too fortunes changed and battalions of Seaforth, Gordons and Camerons distinguished themselves in Burma. The Regiment's fortieth Victoria Cross was won in 1944.

In 1947 the three Regiments were reduced again to one regular battalion each, but they continued to serve with distinction in Korea, Java, Malaya, Borneo, Aden, Kenya, Cyprus, the Falkland Islands, Belize, Germany, and in Northern Ireland, from where the 1st Battalion The Highlanders has recently returned.

The Dress

The uniform of the new Regiment reflects its complex ancestry. As well as the peculiarities of the Assaye Elephant, the badges of the Indian Tiger and the Sphinx of Egypt, and the looped garter flashes, Highlanders' spat buttons are black, as is a thread in the shoulder cords, both in memory of the death at Corunna in 1807 of Sir John Moore under whom The Gordon Highlanders served. The many hundred medals and badges, records of honours, paintings, banners, uniforms, silver and personal momentos of all five antecedent Regiments are displayed in the Two Regimental Museums: The Queen's Own Highlanders Museum at Fort George, Inverness; and The Gordon Highlanders Museum at St Luke's, Aberdeen. The Regiment has two Headquarters: in Cameron Barracks, Inverness and at St Luke's, Aberdeen.

The regimental cap badge, with its symbolic stag's head and unique Gaelic motto Cuidich n' Righ (Save the King), is that worn previously by the Queen's Own Highlanders, with the royal blue hackle commemorating Queen Victoria's wish that the Camerons be designated her own Regiment. The tartan of each antecedent Regiment forms part of The Highlanders' dress: the kilt is Gordon, the trews Seaforth Mackenzie, and the pipers and drummers wear Cameron of Erracht tartan. Their uniform in various combinations is worn by the Territorial and Cadet Battalions, and the traditions of all three antecedent Regiments are followed.

The Family

The London Scottish, the Liverpool Scottish and the Lovat Scouts, territorial units, are part of the Regimental Family as are twelve Allied Regiments in Australia, Canada, New Zealand and South Africa. This Family also includes most importantly, the Old Comrades' Associations of Seaforths, Gordons, Camerons and Queen's Own Highlanders, known as the 'Old and Bold', who fought in two Great Wars and subsequent campaigns and whose example inspires the young men now serving in The Highlanders (Seaforth, Gordons and Camerons).

The Present

1st Battalion The Highlanders served, immediately after formation, for two years in Londonderry, Northern Ireland where they gained a superb reputation, and are now, at the turn of the century, part of 19 Mechanized Brigade at Somme Barracks, Catterick.

The Battle of Atbara, 8 April 1898. On the right The 1st Battalion Seaforth Highlanders charge the zareba (thorn fence); with the Queen's Own Camerons giving supporting fire.

Top: Charge of the Gordon Highlanders at Dargai, 20 October 1897.

Left: The Colours of The Queen's Own Highlanders and the Gordon Highlanders march on.

THE ARGYLL AND SUTHERLAND HIGHLANDERS
(Princess Louise's) (91st/93rd)

The Argyll and Sutherland Highlanders trace their origins to two separate and distinct regiments, the 98th (later 91st) Argyllshire Highlanders and the 93rd Sutherland Highlanders.

The Argyllshire Highlanders were raised against a background of the prospect of war against France in 1794. George III asked several Highland land owners to raise regiments at this time, including the Duke of Argyll. The Duke, however, was not well enough to carry out such an exacting task and he delegated it to his kinsman, Duncan Campbell of Lochnell. Lochnell had considerable problems with recruiting. Over 1,000 men were required in the space of three months and, although most of the officers were natives of Argyll, over two-thirds of the men had to be recruited from Lowland towns and from Ireland.

The 93rd Sutherland Highlanders, raised in 1799 by Major General William Wemyss, a nephew of the Earl of Sutherland, was recruited under unusual circumstances. General Wemyss had been particularly successful in recruiting two fencible regiments for home defence from Sutherland estates and lands. The last of these regiments had just been disbanded when Wemyss set to work to raise the Sutherland Highlanders. Over 250 men joined from the fencibles, while the other 390 or so were raised by levy and ballot on the Sutherland estates, where the men were actively discouraged from joining regiments other than the 93rd Sutherland Highlanders or the 78th Highlanders. In 1799 and early 1800, a census was taken of each parish on the Sutherland estates and the eligible men were summoned to appear on the open fields adjacent to the parish churches. The men were drawn up and the general with an aide passed through the ranks with a snuff mull and whisky. To those who were offered snuff, the signal was given that they were required for service and the 'contract' was sealed with whisky. Only in the isolated far north did this form of enlistment take place at this time.

For the next 80 years both Regiments fought with distinction all over the world. The 91st served in South Africa and in the Peninsula against Napoleon, during this time nine battle honours were gained.

The 93rd's most famous actions were in the Crimea at Alma, Sevastopol and Balaklava where they earned the nickname of the 'Thin Red Line'. During the Indian Mutiny they took part in the Relief of Lucknow and won seven Victoria Crosses, six in one day. They also played a heroic part in the Battle of New Orleans.

In 1872 Queen Victoria agreed to the designation 'Princess Louise's Argyllshire Highlanders' to mark the part played by the 91st at the marriage of Princess Louise to the Marquess of Lorne. In 1914 Princess Louise was formally appointed Colonel-in-Chief of the Regiment, a post she held until her death in 1939.

In 1881, as part of the Cardwell Reforms, the 91st and 93rd were amalgamated to form the 1st and 2nd Battalions of The Argyll and Sutherland Highlanders (Princess Louise's). Stirling Castle became the Training Depot for the new Regiment and all recruits were trained at the Castle until the end of National Service in 1964. Since that date the Castle has been home to the Regimental Headquarters and Museum.

Between 1881 and 1914 the two Battalions continued to see active service in India and the Boer War in South Africa, where the 1st Battalion earned a further three battle honours.

During the First World War the Regiment raised 27 Battalions, of which 2 Regular, 5 Territorial and 6 Service Battalions fought with great distinction in France and Flanders and the Middle East. A further 6 Victoria Crosses were won. The remaining Battalions carried out the tasks of home defence, reinforcement and training.

From 1919 to 1939 the two regular Battalions saw service in India, Egypt, Sudan, Jamaica, China and Hong Kong.

In the Second World War the 1st Battalion fought in Africa, Crete, Abyssinia, Sicily and Italy. The 2nd Battalion fought with great gallantry in Malaya and Singapore until the few survivors were made prisoners of the Japanese. The 5th and 6th Battalions were converted to Anti-Tank Regiments (91st and 93rd respectively) Royal Artillery, and saw service in France, Africa, Sicily, Italy and North West Europe. The 7th and 8th Battalions took part in the disastrous battles in France in 1940 and only a few survivors managed to get back to the UK. The 7th served in the 51st Highland Division for the remainder of the war in North Africa, Sicily and North West Europe. The 8th Battalion fought in North Africa, Sicily and Italy. The 9th Battalion was also converted to Royal Artillery and was in France in 1940 and North West Europe. The 15th Battalion was serving in Orkney in 1942 as a Home Defence Battalion and on the fall of Singapore became the Reformed 2nd Battalion and fought in North West Europe. A further two Victoria Crosses were won during the war.

In 1947 His Majesty The King appointed his elder daughter, Princess Elizabeth, as Colonel-in-Chief.

In 1948 the 2nd Battalion was amalgamated with the 1st Battalion which then saw service in Palestine, Korea (where Major Muir won the Victoria Cross), British Guiana, Berlin, Suez, Cyprus, BAOR, Singapore and Aden.

In 1968 news was received of the proposed disbandment of the Argylls. After a huge popular campaign which achieved world-wide support, the regiment survived but was reduced to company strength. In 1971, the 1st Battalion was reformed. It has subsequently seen service in Germany, Northern Ireland on numerous occasions, Cyprus, Hong Kong and the Falklands.

The Bicentenary of the Raising of the 91st was celebrated in 1994 when Her Majesty The Queen spent a day with the 1st Battalion at Folkestone.

In 1997 Her Majesty The Queen visited Stirling Castle to celebrate the fiftieth anniversary of her appointment as Colonel-in-Chief.

The Bicentenary of the raising of the 93rd was celebrated in 1999.

Mottos: Ne Obliviscaris (Do not forget) and Sans Peur (Without Fear).

Regimental Home: The Castle, Stirling.

Regimental Marches: Highland Laddie and The Campbells are Coming.

Principal Battle Honours: Cape of Good Hope 1806; Rolica; Vimiera; Corunna; Pyrenees; Nivelle; Nive; Orthes; Toulouse; Peninsula; South Africa 1846–7, 1851–2–3; Alma; Balaklava; Sevastopol; Lucknow; South Africa 1879; Modder River; Paardeberg; South Africa 1899–1902; Mons; Le Cateau; Marne 1914, 18; Ypres 1915, 17, 18; Loos; Somme 1916, 18; Arras 1917, 18; Cambrai 1917, 18; Doiran 1917, 18; Gaza; Odon; Rhine; Sidi Barrani; El Alamein; Akarit; Longstop Hill 1943; Italy 1943–45; Grik Road; Malaya 1941–42; Pakchon and Korea 1950–51.

Recruiting Area: Argyll and Bute; Dunbartonshire; Stirlingshire; Clackmannanshire; Renfrewshire.

Left: 'Over the Veldt' – 1st Battalion Pipes and Drums, South Africa 1901. KEOCH CUMMING

Right, top: 'The Thin Red Line' – The 93rd Sutherland Highlanders at Balaclava, 1854. ROBERT GIBB

Right, bottom: Re-entry into Crater – Aden 1967. PETER ARCHER

91

THE PARACHUTE REGIMENT

On 22nd June 1940 Winston Churchill called for the formation of 'a corps of at least five thousand parachute troops, suitably organised and equipped'. A Paracute Training School was formed at Ringway, and No 2 Commando chosen for training in parachute duties. As the scope of training increased, the title of No 2 Commando was first changed to '11th Special Air Service Battalion' and then to '1st Parachute Battalion' and then to '1st Parachute Battalion in the 1st Parachute Brigade', which had been formed under the command of Brigadier RN Gale, OBE MC in the previous month. In October 1941 Major General F A M Browning DSO was ordered to form an Airborne Division. Under his guidance The Parachute Regiment was formally established as a Regiment on 1st August 1942. By the end of the war it comprised 17 Battalions and a number of independent pathfinder units. Not all the Battalions were raised at home, three were formed in India and two in Egypt. The training and dropping of the Parachutists was entrusted to squadrons of 38 and 46 Groups RAF. Their history is closely linked to The Regiment.

In 1941, it was found possible to mount an experimental raid in Southern Italy against the Tragino aqueduct in Apulia. A year later on 17th February 1942, a successful attack was made by C Company of the 2nd Battalion on the German radar station at Bruneval on the coast of France. It was here that the Regiment increased its scope as the technique of Airborne Warfare developed and more resources became available. In North Africa the battalions of the 1st Parachute Brigade were dropped on widely separated objectives, and in the subsequent fighting earned for The Regiment, which now wore the maroon beret, the name of 'Red Devils' bestowed upon it by the enemy. In the attack on Sicily, the same brigade was dropped by night with the task of seizing Primosole Bridge. When 1st and 4th Brigades returned to England before the invasion of Northern France, 2nd Independent Parachute Brigade remained and later took part in airborne operations in Italy, Southern France and Greece.

The night of 5th/6th June 1944 marked the first divisional airborne operations of the war. It was then that the 6th Airborne Division, which included the 3rd and 5th Parachute Brigades, landed in Normandy, France. This Division was commanded by Major General R N Gale OBE MC, who had raised it. There followed the famous operation at Arnhem on 17th September 1944 by the 1st Airborne Division, which included the 1st and 4th Parachute Brigades and which, with the 82nd and 101st US Airborne Divisions formed the 1st British Airborne Corps, which took part in the crossing of the Rhine and the subsequent operations which led to final victory in May 1945.

Direct enlistment into The Regiment by other ranks was introduced in 1953. Direct Commissioning of officers was introduced in 1958 although a small proportion continue to be seconded from other regiments.

From 1945 to the 1960s The Regiment has served in most theatres, including the Far East, Palestine, Germany and the Middle East, playing a prominent part in Airborne operations at Port Said in 1956. During the 1960s The Regiment was involved in operations in Cyprus in 1964 (1 Para), Radfan in 1964 (3 Para), Borneo in 1965 (2 Para) and Aden in 1967 (1 Para). Since 1969 all three battalions have served in all parts of Northern Ireland on numerous short and long tours of duty. From April to June 1982 the 2nd and 3rd Battalions were involved in Operation Corporate in the South Atlantic. During this conflict on the Falkland Islands, both Battalions played a very important part in the Task Force, in particular at Goose Green, Darwin Hill and Wireless Ridge (2 Para), and Mount Longdon (3 Para). On conclusion of this operation two VCs were posthumously awarded, as were numerous other awards for gallantry. Since the Falklands War the Regiment has carried out numerous operational tours in Northern Ireland.

The Regimental capbadge is a set of wings either side of a parachute above which is the crown of the monarch. The Regimental mascot is a Shetland pony called Falklands. The Regimental motto UTRINQUE PARATUS means 'Ready for anything'.

The Future of the Regiment

These are exciting times. Speculation surrounding the Strategic Defence Review suggests that two battalions of The Parachute Regiment will join 3 regiments of the new attack helicopter – the Westland AH 64-D Apache – in a new Air Manoeuvre Brigade. The Brigade will be able to operate with the RAF's Support Helicopter fleet of CH 47's (Chinooks) and will be able to exploit the air flank across the spectrum of conflict. Operational roles may range from the rescue of British Nationals oversees to high intensity war fighting.

The Air Manouvre Brigade will retain the capability to deploy the Lead Parachute Battalion Group, but will also develop air assault concepts of operation which will fully utilize the potent firepower of the Apache attack helicopter. The Air Manoeuvre Brigade will be an extremely agile and versatile combat formation within which the Parachute Regiment will move forward with renewed purpose into the 21st Century.

Chutes fitted for Operation Muskateer drop, Suez November 1956.

Top: Normandy, 6 June 1944.

Right, top: On one of many visits to N. Ireland.

Right, bottom: A foot patrol of the 1st Battalion the Parachute Regiment is supported by heavily armed Para's on a six wheeled Supacat All Terrain Vehicle through the streets of Pristina, Kosovo 1999.

MEDIA OPS HQ LAND COMMAND

THE BRIGADE OF GURKHAS

Gurkhas have served the British Crown since 1815, and have fought and died alongside their British comrades in nearly every theatre of war around the world.

The connection began in war between the British, represented by the Honorable East India Company, and the fledgeling and expansionist warrior Gurkha state of Nepal. Gurkha raids into Northern India led to the Anglo-Nepal War of 1812–1814. The war ended in stalemate but was an unusual conflict for the time. Both British and Gurkha armies had become accustomed to previous enemies which broke and ran when faced with organised military opposition. Here, both faced an enemy which stood and fought bravely. Both sides treated prisoners honourably and refrained from the then accepted excesses of the victor. By the end of the war a mutual respect had grown between British and Gurkha, and the Gurkha suggestion that they would prefer to fight with the British than against them was swiftly accepted.

At first the three Gurkha regiments raised were 'Irregular': that is while they were armed, trained and commanded by British officers they lacked the status of being part of the regular army proper. It was the mutiny of the Bengal Army in 1857, when the survival of British power in India hung by a thread, that led to the full integration of Gurkha regiments. All Gurkha units remained loyal to the British Crown, and their actions, particularly during the siege of Delhi, led to them being placed on the regular order of battle. They were also given the rank 'Rifleman' rather than 'Sepoy', and were awarded the perhaps odd but unique privilege of access to British canteens, out of bounds to all other non-British troops.

Throughout the rest of the 19th century the Gurkha Brigade, now comprising ten regiments each of two battalions, a total of some 25,000 men, saw service throughout the sub-continent of India. They took part in operations in China, Tibet, Afghanistan, 'Asia Minor' and Cyprus.

In the First World War, over 120,000 Gurkhas joined the Army. Six battalions of the Gurkha Brigade fought in Flanders in 1914–15 and, at Neuve Chapelle in March 1915 were the first British units to break the German line; a Gurkha was awarded a VC following the battle, the first ever awarded to a Gurkha and one of only two awarded to Gurkhas during the war. They also fought in the Middle East and Mesopotamia, most notably during the Gallipoli campaign of 1915 when they alone secured the commanding heights of Sari Bair. As close allies the Nepalese Army helped to garrison India.

In the 1920s and 1930s, the Gurkha Brigade were a significant part of the garrison in India, and played an active and special role securing its borders and holding its remote regions. Gurkhas were involved in all the major operations on the North West Frontier of British India.

During the Second World War, a similar number of Gurkhas fought in Malaya, North Africa, Italy, Greece and Burma. As part of the 8th Army they were present at all the major desert battles, gaining particular fame at the break-in battle on the Mareth Line, where a 2nd Gurkha officer won the first of ten Gurkha VCs awarded. In the battles to retake Italy, Gurkhas were involved in all the key battles, gaining particular fame at Monte Cassino, Medecina and at the breaking of the Gothic Line. However, it was in Burma where their contribution was greatest, taking part in all the battles of the 14th Army. They participated in both the Chindit operations and their contribution at Imphal, Sangshak and the final break through into the Irrawaddy Delta and Rangoon were of major importance in this bitter campaign. In effect, the entire youth of Nepal was placed at the disposal of the British. With a population of only seven million, this meant that virtually every Nepali of the martial castes and of military age was serving the British Crown. Casualties were heavy, especially in Italy and Burma, and almost ten per cent were killed.

With Indian Independence in 1947, the ten regiments of Gurkhas were split between the armies of India and Britain. The 2nd, 6th, 7th and 10th Gurkha Rifles transferred to the British Army and were immediately involved in the 12 year (1948–60) campaign to defeat communist insurgency in Malaya. In December 1962 Gurkhas were deployed to Brunei to quell the rebellion there; this lead to the more protracted Confrontation with Indonesia during the period 1963–66. Gurkhas also saw action in the 1982 Falklands War and the 1991 Gulf conflict.

In June 1994 the four Gurkha infantry regiments amalgamated to form the Royal Gurkha Rifles and today, there are two battalions, one stationed in the United Kingdom and one in Brunei. As a *temporary* measure there are three independent companies of Gurkha infantry which support understrength British battalions; one of these companies is parachute trained. The Queen's Gurkha Engineers, Queen's Gurkha Signals and Queen's Own Gurkha Transport Regiment, each formerly of regimental strength, are now of squadron strength though there are plans to increase them. The Brigade of Gurkhas also provides the Demonstration Companies at the Royal Military Academy Sandhurst and the Infantry Training Centre, Wales. About a third of Gurkhas serve accompanied by their families. A small organisation is set up in Nepal to arrange for recruiting of Gurkhas, to pay pensions to retired servicemen and to handle welfare requirements.

Competition to get into the British Army is fierce in Nepal, where soldiering has always been regarded as an honourable profession. There are usually some thirty applicants for every recruit vacancy offered. Soldiers are recruited annually, with only the very best being selected to undergo the rigorous recruit training in the United Kingdom.

Recruitment for the British and Indian armies is authorised by virtue of the Tripartite Agreement with the Kingdom of Nepal; this agreement governs rates of pay, terms of service and international status. Gurkha soldiers of the British Army are available for service in any role and any location that Her Majesty's Government may wish them to be deployed.

The Gurkha Welfare Trust is the Brigade-sponsored charity and does much to alleviate hardship amongst ex-servicemen in Nepal. The history, traditions and ethos of the Brigade of Gurkhas are graphically portrayed in The Gurkha Museum at Peninsula Barracks, Winchester.

Kosovo: Soldiers of 1 Royal Gurkha Rifles guard the route north up the Kacanik Pass, towards Pristina. On 21 June 1999 two Gurkhas became the first NATO ground casualties when they died during operations to clear ordnance from a civilian area.

MEDIA OPS HQ LAND COMMAND

Top: Sarawak, 21 November 1965: Lance Corporal Rambahadur Limbu stormed alone up a steep hill to take a strong enemy position, before returning to rescue his wounded men; his devotion to duty and them winning a VC. He retired as a Captain in 1985.

TERENCE CUNEO

Left: A Gurkha Guard perform the Ceremony of the Keys, the traditional nightly locking up of the Tower of London.

TERENCE CUNEO

SHELL INTERNATIONAL LTD

THE ROYAL GREEN JACKETS

The Formation and Origins of the Regiment

On 1st January 1966 The Royal Green Jackets was formed as a single Large Regiment. Its creation followed logically from the composition of The Green Jackets Brigade in 1958, which grouped together three former single-battalion infantry regiments: The Oxfordshire and Buckinghamshire Light Infantry (43rd & 52nd), The King's Royal Rifle Corps (60th) and The Rifle Brigade.

It was no accident that these particular regiments, each having had such a distinguished record in the past, should have progressively, voluntarily and successfully come together, avoiding the stresses which often accompany amalgamations, because they shared a large measure of their history and their traditions. They, and The Royal Green Jackets as their heir, lay claim to being the innovators who developed much of the new thinking in the British infantry in the fields of tactics, training, equipment and man-management from the mid-eighteenth century onwards.

Early Days

The 18th century saw Great Britain and France intermittently at war, both on the continent of Europe and throughout their colonial territories, and the British Army was continually expanded and reduced to suit the needs of the moment. Thus it was that the 43rd was formed, with its HQ in Winchester, in 1741, while the 52nd was raised in Coventry in 1755. In that same year the 60th was established in North America, for service there, recruiting 4 battalions of 1,000 settlers each to enable the British Army to take on the French and their Red Indian allies in terrain unsuited to the Red Coats and their ponderous European tactics. The 43rd & 60th took part together in the vital battle of Quebec, at which General Wolfe gave the 60th their motto 'Swift and Bold', which is the motto of the Royal Green jackets today. Both the 43rd & 52nd, and later the 60th took part in the American War of Independence, while shortly afterwards a significant step was taken in the development of the Green Jackets with the formation in 1797 of the 5th Battalion the 60th, which was dressed in green uniforms and armed with the rifle rather than the smooth bore musket, the first attempt by the British to establish specialised Light Infantry for the European battlefield. Shortly afterwards the experimental Corps of Riflemen was formed in 1800, later to become the 95th and in 1816 the Rifle Brigade. Also dressed in green and armed with the rifle, the Rifle Corps served aboard Nelson's ships as sharpshooters at the battle of Copenhagen in 1801, earning its first battle honour and, later, a naval crown in its cap badge, retained to-day in that of the Royal Green Jackets.

In 1803 the 43rd & 52nd and 95th moved to Shorncliffe to constitute the Light Brigade under the command of Sir John Moore. His insistence on absolute professionalism and mutual respect between officers and men created a formation whose contribution was crucial to Wellington's victories in the Peninsular and whose traditions survive in The Royal Green Jackets to-day. Two battalions from each of these three regiments served in the Peninsular War in the Light Brigade and then the Light Division, usually in the van or flank of the Army, while the 5th Battalion of the 60th provided a rifle company to each Brigade as that Brigade's look-outs, skirmishers and sharpshooters. The four Regiments emerged from the Peninsular War with their reputation enhanced, and with 46 Battle Honours between them. The 52nd & 95th later fought with distinction at Waterloo, the 52nd under Sir John Colbourne charging in to the flank of the Imperial Guard when it had been halted by the fire of Maitland's Brigade of Guards, turning its advance into a disorderly retreat.

Imperial Campaigns

Space does not permit a detailed account of the former regiments' activities in the expansion and policing of the Empire, but all took part in the many campaigns in Africa and India, the 60th particularly distinguishing itself on the famous Ridge at Delhi during the Mutiny, gaining 7 VC's there, not quite equalling the feat of the Rifle Brigade in gaining 8 VC's in the Crimea. In all, 15 VC's were awarded to the former Regiments in the Mutiny. Further afield the 43rd found themselves in New Zealand for the Maori Wars of 1863, where a VC was won, while the 60th had a battalion in the Anglo-French Expedition to China to capture the Taku Forts in 1860.

The Boer War

All former regiments took part in the 2nd Boer War, with the 60th and Rifle Brigade very much involved in the defence and relief of Ladysmith, while other elements of these two regiments played a major part in the development of Mounted Infantry.

The First World War

The 43rd & 52nd had 12, the KRRC had 26 and the Rifle Brigade 21 battalions in World War I. The majority of these served on the Western Front, but battalions also served in Mesopotamia, Italy, Salonica, and Macedonia. Casualties were appalling in France and Flanders, and the gallantry of members of the regiments was rewarded with a great number of decorations, the most notable being the VC, DSO and MC of Major W Congreve and the VC, DCM, and MM of Sergeant W Gregg, both of the Rifle Brigade.

World War II

All the former regiments were caught up in the disasters of France in 1940; three battalions of the 43rd & 52nd took part in the withdrawals to Dunkirk, while the 2nd and 7th 60th and the 1st Rifle Brigade were all killed or captured in the defence of Calais between 23 & 26 May. The 60th & Rifle Brigade's motor battalion role involved them in the North African, Italian and N.W. European campaigns, while the 43rd also featured there, and in Burma. Mention must be made of the celebrated 'Snipe' action at El Alamein, when the 2nd Rifle Brigade destroyed some 51 enemy tanks in 16 hours, for which its CO, Vic Turner, was awarded the V.C. Meanwhile the 52nd had pioneered the new role of airlanding by glider, which gave them the honour and fame of airlanding and capturing the bridges over the Caen Canal (Pegasus Bridge) and the River Orne at midnight before D-Day, and involved them later in the airborne crossing of the Rhine.

The Post-War Years

Immediately after World War II the regiments continued their separate existence, with the 43rd & 52nd amalgamating in 1948. The 52nd & 60th had been in Palestine before then, while in 1949 the 43rd & 52nd were in Greece during the Civil War, in Egypt, and in Cyprus confronting the Enosis insurgents in 1956. The Rifle Brigade, no longer a motor battalion, took part in the Emergencies in Kenya and Malaya from 1954 to 1957.

The Green Jackets Brigade

On 6th November 1958 the Green Jackets Brigade was formed to comprise 1st Green Jackets (43rd & 52nd), 2nd Green Jackets (The King's Royal Rifle Corps) and 3rd Green Jackets (The Rifle Brigade). With its RHQ at the Green Jacket Depot at Winchester, where the Depot of the KRRC and Rifle Brigade had been since 1858, the three battalions were all engaged in the confrontation with Indonesia in Borneo in the 1960's, while at other times they had served in Cyprus, British Guiana, Belize and BAOR.

The Royal Green Jackets

On 1st January 1966 the three regiments of the Green Jackets Brigade became three battalions of a single 'Large Regiment', the Royal Green Jackets. Since then the regiment has had battalions in Hong Kong, Gibraltar, Belize and the Falklands, as well as in Great Britain, Germany and, of course, Northern Ireland, where 29 tours have been completed; while in the Gulf War the 1st Battalion sent a strong contingent to reinforce the Staffords. Under 'Options' in 1992 the Regiment was reduced to two regular and two Volunteer Battalions. Also under Options, the previous Rifle and then Light Division Depot at Winchester has been reduced to a company in the Army Training Regiment just outside Winchester, leaving only RHQ and the RGJ Museum in Peninsula Barracks.

The present Regiment is ever mindful of the achievements of its predecessors, reflected in its 252 Battle Honours and 55 Victoria Crosses. While no longer retaining the specialist roles of the past, it still seeks to retain the attributes encouraged so long ago by Sir John Moore so that it can confidently face the challenges of the present and the uncertainties of the future.

N M ROTHSCHILD & SONS LTD

The Defence of Calais, that held up the German Army while Dunkirk was evacuated, 23 to 26 May 1940: 'three days that saved the Army' – Winston Churchill

Top: The Rear Guard of The Light Brigade, led by Brigadier General Crauford, covers the retreat to Corunna, Peninsular War, 1808.

THE SAS

The SAS began life in July 1941 from an idea by Scots Guards Lieutenant David Stirling for small teams of parachute trained soldiers to operate behind enemy lines. This idea was put forward to the Army High Command and endorsed by them, since a deception organisation already in the Middle East theatre of operations wished to create a phantom Airborne Brigade. This was to act as a threat to the enemy planning of operations. This deception unit was known as 'K Detachment, Special Air Service Brigade', and Stirling's unit was to be known as **'L Detachment, SAS Brigade'**.

The term Special Air Service existed in Great Britain, due to the formation of a parachute battalion known as '11 SAS Battalion' – although the previous ten battalions did not exist, and this battalion was shortly to be renamed 1st Parachute Battalion.

Following extensive training at a camp near Kabrit, about a hundred miles east of Cairo, 'L Detachment' undertook its first operation on enemy airfields at Gazala and Tmimi on 16/17 November 1941. The 'Birthday' of the Regiment was subsequently 17 November. The operation was not particularly successful with two-thirds of the attacking parachutists killed or captured, but Stirling stood by his ideals and the unit was reformed and reorganised.

The Detachment now also had its own insignia – a cap-badge that was a winged representation of King Arthur's sword Excalibur, woven on a shield, with the Motto 'WHO DARES WINS'. The badge was worn on side-caps, and officer's field service caps, then white berets, changed to the sand-coloured or beige beret still worn today. Also Operational parachute wings were devised that even today are peculiar to the SAS in design.

The detachment continued to expand and using the transport of the Long Range Desert Group – an intelligence gathering penetration unit, and then its own American jeeps, attacked enemy airfields and convoys. Due to its successes in September 1942 it was officially designated **1 SAS Regiment.**

David Stirling was captured in January 1943, and his depleted regiment was formed into the 'Special Raiding Squadron' under his second-in-command Major R B 'Paddy' Mayne, DSO. This with the **'Special Boat Squadron', a Free French Squadron**, and the **Greek Sacred Squadron** formed the new **1 SAS Regiment.**

In May 1943 **2 SAS Regiment** was raised by the founder's brother Lt Colonel William Stirling at Philippeville, Algeria. Both Regiments went on to serve in Sicily and Italy through the summer of 1943.

The Special Boat Squadron remained in the Middle East theatre and operated in the Aegean and the Balkans. After the two SAS Regiments returned to the United Kingdom in 1944, it became known as the **'Special Boat Service'.** After the war its role was taken over by the Special Boat Service of the Royal Marines, which had also taken over the duties of the disbanded Army Commandos and their Special Boat Section.

In early 1944 1 SAS Regiment and 2 SAS Regiment both understrength returned to the UK, and joined in Darvel, Scotland a Headquarters unit of the new SAS Brigade, of the Army Air Corps. The other units in the Brigade comprised two French SAS Regiments (3 and 4), and one Belgian Independent Company. As part of the Army Air Corps the units in the Brigade were instructed to wear the AAC's maroon beret, however photographic evidence shows many of the desert veterans continued to wear their own beige berets.

The brigade was at the forefront of the action with the Normandy landings in June 1944, serving behind enemy lines in jeeps assisting the French Resistance, as well as in support of the Allied forces. It continued to serve through Belgium, Holland and into Germany until the end of the European War in May 1945. An SAS War Crimes Investigation Team served in Europe with the Judge Advocate General's Branch well into 1949, funded by the War Office, tracking down war criminals involved with the murder of SAS soldiers and agents working with the Resistance.

Following the conclusion of Far East hostilities in September 1945, 1 and 2 SAS Regiments that had returned from Norway in August were disbanded during October and November of that year – 1 SAS Regiment at Hylands Hall, Chelmsford, 2 SAS Regiment at Wivenhoe Park, Colchester, and finally the HQ SAS was wound up at Sloe House, Halstead in Essex.

The French and Belgian regiments were absorbed into their own armies in September 1945, and their successor units still exist to this day.

In June 1946 an Army Instruction was issued officially disbanding 'The Special Air Service Regiment, Army Air Corps'.

In 1947, the familiar Winged Sword badge, (also later known as the Winged Dagger) reappeared in the British Army order of battle, this time as part of the Territorial Army. This was on the formation in London of **21 SAS Regiment (Artists).** Then with the disbandment of the Army Air Corps in 1950, 21 SAS was given a Corps Warrant as an independent unit on which to form a new SAS Corps, alongside the Glider Pilot and Parachute Corps.

Meanwhile the Communist guerilla 'Emergency' in Malaya which began in 1948 had seen the creation in 1950 of the **'Malayan Scouts (SAS)'** which had volunteers from army units in that theatre. They were also joined by a volunteer squadron from 21 SAS Regiment, which had been on its way to fight in Korea. The Malayan Scouts were to act in small teams fighting the Communists in their own jungle areas, where large army units could not penetrate.

In 1952, the Malayan Scouts were absorbed into the Regular Army Order of Battle as **'22 Special Air Service Regiment'** The Regiment remains the only Post-War Regular unit of the SAS.

A second Territorial Regiment – **'23 SAS Regiment TA'** was formed in London in 1959, from a unit involved in special forces' reconnaissance duties. It was later based in Birmingham, with squadrons in the North of England and Scotland.

In 1960 22 SAS Regiment returned to the United Kingdom, and was based firstly at Malvern, and then Hereford, where it remains today.

22 SAS Regiment has been deployed in Borneo and Aden, during the 1960s. Then Dhofar and in Northern irteland through the 1970s to 1990s. By which time it has transformed into a multi-purpose multi-skilled unit, with anti-terrorism and peace-keeping duties, such as with the Iranian Embassy Siege in 1980. Apart from going to war in the Falklands in 1982 and Western Iraq in 1991, the Regiment has trained many other countries' special forces, as well as conducting joint exercises with them.

Although the Special Air Service does not possess a Regimental Colour, it has been awarded 15 Battle Honours from 'North Africa 1940–43' to 'Gulf 1991'.

Descent to jungle warfare.

Right, top: Long Range Desert Group, 1942 – adapted jeep with maximum fire-power, attacking enemy convoys and airfields and gathering intelligence.

Right, bottom: Abseiling into action – training other countries' Special Forces.

INDUSTRIA ENGINEERING PRODUCTS LTD

THE ARMY AIR CORPS

The Royal Flying Corps

In 1911, due to the foresight and energy of a dedicated band of officers, the War office established a military flying school at Larkhill on Salisbury Plain. The Royal Flying Corps (RFC) was established by 1912. At the beginning of World War One, the RFC had 63 aircraft formed into four squadrons to be employed on reconnaissance tasks for the British Expeditionary Force in France. With the formation of the Royal Air Force in 1918, Service flying passed from Army hands.

The Eyes of the Army

By the time war was once again looming in 1939, officers of an imaginative turn of mind had formulated the notion that light aircraft, by then more reliable and rugged, should be employed for reconnaissance and, particularly, for directing artillery fire. This was accepted and Royal Artillery officers flew light aircraft in RAF Air Observation Post (Air OP) Squadrons throughout World War II.

The Wings of the Army

In 1940, Winston Churchill ordered the Chiefs of Staff to recommend how best to form a new combat arm which was to be delivered to the battlefield by air. The result of this initiative was the formation in 1942 of parachute battalions and the Glider Pilot Regiment (GPR), whose soldiers wore the maroon beret and capbadge of the AAC. The GPR was created to fly troops and heavy equipment in large towed gliders into areas behind the enemy's front line.

The now famous glider operations of the Second World War speak for themselves. The many casualties suffered by the GPR reflected the hazards of glider operations, but their deeds and achievements were outstanding. As gliders became obsolete, pilots retrained onto powered light aircraft and served alongside Air OP Squadrons as part of the Army's eyes and ears. By the 1950s Army flying was about to enter a new phase.

The Renaissance of the Army Air Corps

On 1 September 1957, an Army Order authorised the re-establishment of the AAC. It was to be responsible for managing its own fleet of aircraft, for aircrew training and tactical development. Technical support was placed in the hands of the Royal Electrical and Mechanical Engineers and the Royal Army Ordnance Corps.

The new Corps was to be formed from the existing Air OP Squadrons and the Light Liaison Flights operated by the remaining GPR units. Thus the early tradition of Army flying would be reborn from the amalgamation of these two bodies who were, in any case, well known to each other. They were to bring their expertise, traditions and history together so the new Corps had, quite literally, a flying start.

The AAC has been involved in every campaign in which the Army has taken part and takes its place in the fighting Order of Battle as a Combat Arm within the British Army.

Divisional Operations

For divisional operations the AAC provides two regiments in the anti-tank role. 1 Regiment AAC is based at Gütersloh in Germany supporting the 1st (United Kingdom) Armoured Division. 9 Regiment AAC is based at Dishforth, Yorkshire and supports the 3rd (United Kingdom) Division.

The regiments are both equipped with three identical anti-tank squadrons, a HQ squadron and an aviation workshop.

Each anti-tank squadron has six Lynx Mark 7 anti-tank helicopters and six Gazelle Mark 1 helicopters. These squadrons provide fast, flexible and mobile combat power for the division. Lynx Mark 7 has a 13 times magnification thermal image sight and it is armed with the Tube launched optically tracked Wire guided (TOW) missile system which has a range of 3750 metres. When not fitted with TOW missiles the Lynx is used in the general support role and can carry up to nine soldiers.

The Gazelle, with a times 10 magnification sight, is used for reconnaissance. Both Gazelle and Lynx aircrew are trained to fly their aircraft by night vision goggles (NVG). The combination of flying with NVGs and the thermal image sight gives the AAC a round-the-clock fighting capability.

AAC units are ready to be committed wherever the Army is deployed. In 1991 an anti-tank regiment deployed with the British Army to fight in the Gulf War and successfully engaged Iraqi armour. More recently the AAC has deployed anti-tank squadrons in support of UN operations in the former Republic of Yugoslavia. A number of squadrons are permanently on stand-by for the Joint Rapid Deployment Force (JDRF).

Airmobile Operations

The AAC has two regiments within 24 Airmobile Brigade. Both regiments are based at Wattisham Airfield in Suffolk. Each regiment has two anti-tank squadrons, one Light Battlefield Helicopter (LBH) squadron, a HQ squadron and an aviation workshop. The anti-tank squadrons provide the combat power with their TOW missile systems. These squadrons are organised and operate in a similar manner to the anti-tank squadrons of a divisional aviation regiment.

The LBH squadrons are equipped with the wheeled Lynx Mark 9. This aircraft's main role is to move small teams of soldiers within the Brigade's area at low level, in formation by day and night. The LBH squadrons often work with infantry companies, air defence teams and engineers.

Much effort and time is devoted to honing the specialist skills of aircrew and groundcrew. Military helicopters can frequently only survive if they are flown stealthily and at a very low level. 'Nap of the earth' flying must therefore become second nature to army pilots. As with the anti-tank regiments a number are on permanent stand-by for the JRDF.

The Apache Longbow

The introduction of the Apache Longbow from 2000 onwards heralds a major change in the aviation support to the Army. The Apache wil be grouped into 3 regiments each of 2 squadrons of Apache and one squadron of Light Utility Helicopters (LUH) based on the Lynx Mk9. These regiments will be assigned to the Airmobile role under 24 Airmobile Brigade 3 and 4 Regiments will be based in Wattisham, and 9 Regiment in Dishforth. Divisional support to the 1st and 3rd (United Kingdom) Divisions will be provided by 1 Regiment AAC based in Gütersloh with a detached squadron in Netheravon.

The Apache Longbow with its deadly combination of lethal weaponry and sophisticated sensors, will provide one of the most capable weapons systems that the Army has ever fielded. This unique combination will give the Army significant operational advantages and will enhance operational effectiveness across the conflict spectrum. The integration of the target acquisition system, weapons and defensive aids suites ensures that it is capable of defeating most threat weapon systems before they have even had a chance to identify or engage the aircraft.

WAH 64 Apache Longbow.

Troops disembark from a Lynx on exercise.

Top: Lynx MK7 firing TOW on exercise.

THE ROYAL ARMY CHAPLAINS' DEPARTMENT

Emperor Constantine was converted to Christianity after seeing a cross in the heavens and a sign saying 'In hoc signo vinces' – 'In this sign conquer'.

The RAChD took this sign as their motto and incorporated it in their badge. They translated it into English as the ordinary soldier would not have understood Latin. Their badge also consists of a Maltese Cross (8 points) in silver upon a wreath of laurel (for victory) and oak (for strength), in gilt. In the centre of the cross a circle in gilt on a blue enamel ground with the motto. Within the circle a quatrefoil voided. The whole ensigned by the crown in gilt.

The Royal Army Chaplains' Department have two cap badges. As well as the Christian badge there is also a Jewish one which has the same wreath of laurel and oak, but instead of a Maltese cross, a cross of David, and no motto.

The RAChD is unable to give a precise date on which they came into existence, due largely to the fact that armies have had men of the church within their ranks for a very long time, ie: since around 430 AD and 'The Hallelujah Battle.' When William, Duke of Normandy, invaded Britain in 1066 he had some priests on his staff. His brother, Bishop Odo of Bayeux, lead his own 120 knights into battle, and because the church objected to priests shedding blood with the sword, he used a mace as a weapon! And in 1175 a decree by Westminster stated that clergymen should no longer carry arms or wear armour at all.

By the 14th century clergymen were fulfilling a priestly roll. At Crecy in 1346 three grades of chaplain were mentioned, but in the reign of Edward III, while he was in France, the Scots invaded England, and among the formation commanders of the army, which defeated these invaders, were the archbishops of Canterbury and York and the bishops of Durham and Carlisle. So the evolution of the role of the chaplain in the army did not always go in the same direction.

By the time of Henry VIII chaplains had become more established and in 1621 regimental Chaplains were mentioned in standing orders. Oliver Cromwell took things a stage further so that in the new model army of 1645 the status of chaplains was regularised and most regiments had their own chaplain. 1660 saw the establishment of the regular army in Britain and the articles of war of 1662 specified the duties of chaplains. These were:

'Zeal in his profession and good sense, gentle manners; a distinctive and impressive manner of reading divine service; a firm constitution of body as well as of mind'.

Regimental chaplains, chosen by, and paid for, by the commanding officer of the regiment, were the order of the day at that time, and for centuries after, but this was not very satisfactory. Matters came to a head in 1795 when Sir Ralph Abercromby was preparing to take an expeditionary force to the West Indies, and no chaplains were available to go; so the system of regimental chaplains was abolished and, by Royal Warrant dated the 23rd September, 1796, the Army Chaplains' Department was formed, under a chaplain general, the Rev John Gamble.

However there was a shortage of chaplains prepared to face the hardships and dangers of army chaplaincy, for the small financial return and in 1811 the Duke of Wellington complained that 'he had only one excellent young chaplain in this army, Mr Samuel Briscall, who has never been one moment absent from his duty'.

Chaplains have been involved in all campaigns ever since, including the Crimea, the Indian Mutiny, the Boer War, WW1, WW2, Korea, Suez, the Falklands, the Gulf, Bosnia and, of course, Northern Ireland.

In the Great War of 1914–18 chaplains had the opportunity to bring comfort to those in mental as well as physical pain. Many padres distinguished themselves on the fields of battle as well as in the R.A.P's and hospitals to which they were originally bound. Two well known names are 'Woodbine Willie' – The Rev Geoffrey A Studdert-Kennedy and 'Tubby' Clayton, the founder of TOC H.

Chaplains also served in the Indian Ecclesiastical Establishment and won one of their 4 VC's at Killa Kazi, on 11th December, 1879.

Less widely known but distinguished in a different way was the Rev Theodore Bayley Hardy who won the VC, DSO and MC, before dying of his wounds on 18th October, 1918, two days before his 55th birthday. His repeated acts of bravery, helping wounded men under fire, were an inspiration to everyone in his vicinity; as were those of the Reverend Noel Mellish, VC, MC and the Reverend W R F Addison, VC.

The second world war differed in several respects from the first. One of the differences was the large number of men who became prisoners of war in Europe and the Far East. The loss of freedom, boredom and shortage of food imposed a severe strain on most men. Those in the Far East in particular were often subjected to brutal treatment by their captors who had been brought up to despise prisoners of war. It is not surprising therefore that the role of the chaplains differed from that undertaken in World War 1.

A Roman Catholic priest who was highly respected was the Rev 'Dolly' Brookes. A platoon commander in the Irish Guards in WW1. He studied for the priesthood at Downside Abbey. He had served under General Alexander in the first world war and did so again in North Africa and Italy.

Several specialist formations were created during World War 2. Airborne forces were an example, and it was not long before chaplains were required to train as parachutists. One of these, the Rev J J A Hodgins initiated the padre's hour in which the chaplain had a regular period within the soldiers' training programme. Chaplains went by air into battle with the various airborne formations. One such being the Rev Fraser Mclusky, MC who parachuted into central France with the Special Air Service. They worked with the Maquis disrupting German communications miles behind German lines.

On the 22nd February, 1919 HM The King approved the Army Chaplains' Dept becoming the Royal Army Chaplains' Dept, 'in view of the splendid work performed by the army chaplains during WW1'.

During all this time Army Chaplains did not have their own HQ and Depot, and after WW2 King George VI offered them Bagshot Park, which had stood virtually empty since the death of the Duke of Connaught, and they stayed there for 50 years, from December, 1946 until 23rd September, 1996, when the lease finally ran out. During that time they had offered christian-based courses to officers, soldiers and civilians, and continuing ministerial and military training for their chaplains.

Sadly, they then had to find another location for their Headquarters and Depot. Several locations were suggested and dismissed, until finally it was decided to form a Tri-Service headquarters called the Armed Forces' Chaplaincy Centre. However the Royal Army Chaplains' Dept has maintained it's independence as an Army Department.

In the interim the Royal Army Chaplains' Dept went into 'rattle' accommodation at Upavon for three months. Then to Netheravon House for over two years, until the final move into Amport House, in 1999. During all this upheaval it continued it's work, both in the Headquarters and with regiments and corps at home and abroad.

Military Ministry – A Field Communion Service, painted to commemorate the Bicentenary of the formation of The Royal Army Chaplains, 1786–1996.

Top: The Reverend Theodore Bayley Hardy VC, DSO, MC being invested with the Victoria Cross in the field by King George V. Hardy was only at the front for 11 months: dying on 18 October 1918, two days before his 55th birthday and twenty-four before the Armistice. The nurse is his daughter.   TERENCE CUNEO

Left: The Reverend Tom Place, CF with his transport in Bosnia.

THE ROYAL LOGISTIC CORPS

The Royal Logistic Corps was formed on 5 April 1993 from the Postal and Courier branch of the Corps of Royal Engineers, the Royal Corps of Transport, the Royal Army Ordnance Corps, the Royal Pioneer Corps and the Army Catering Corps. The RLC embraces and draws strength from the history, traditions and multitude of logistic skills of the forming Corps and the Corps now comprises over 15,000 Regular officers and soldiers, which is some 16% of the trained strength of the Regular Army. It is supported in the Base by some 13,000 civilians and backed up by over 11,000 RLC members of the Territorial Army. The Royal Logistic Corps currently has units in over a dozen countries world-wide and is participating in every theatre of operations in which the British Army is engaged.

Logistics is one of the four main elements of combat power. The RLC provides specialist logistic services and material such as ammunition, food, fuel, water, vehicles, equipment and spares, at the right time, in the right place, in the right quantity and condition. The importance of logistics to the success-ful outcome of military operations is widely recognised and commanders must only plan to fight the battle that they can sustain. The Corps motto, 'We Sustain', reflects the logistic role of the RLC and our task to deliver the required level of logistics support to sustain military capability.

The RLC is responsible for the supply and distribution functions of the British Army, together with a host of other logistic services in peace, crisis and war. The skills and disciplines within The RLC necessary to effectively and efficiently provide this key component of combat capability are equally valuable to operations in peace and operations short of war.

The ability to deploy a force into a Theatre of Operations, and therafter to sustain and recover it, are fundamental pre-requisites for operational success and the major components of what is known as Combat Service Support (CSS). CSS embraces medical, provost, personnel, logistic engineering and equipment support in addition to civilian resources and logistic support. Logistic support includes supply, distribution, transport, catering, pioneer support and postal services and is that element of CSS provided by The Royal Logistic Corps. LS is complementary to Equipment Support, providing for the soldier, unit and formation. It is defined in the British Army as '*The sustainment of forces through the acquisition, control and distribution of material, and the provision of logistic services*'

In situations of conflict, other than war, when the UK's interests are at risk, the British Army may be required to conduct operations with the purpose of supporting overall policy to resolve or terminate the conflict. Such operations include peacekeeping and peace enforcement (collectively known as peace support operations), counter insurgency and limited intervention. Since for-mation, the RLC has played a major part in operations other than war, not only in the Former Republic of Yugoslavia, where RLC soldiers and formed units have been heavily committed, but also in Rwanda and Angola, where the efforts of the UN have been spearheaded by RLC units.

In peace, the purpose of military forces is to take part in activities in support of the civil authorities, either at home or abroad, to contribute to deterrence and to train for operations. These activities are generally characterised by the non-violent use of military capabilities and skills. The RLC is well placed to contribute to these operations and, for example, regularly provides individual tradesmen and specialist formed units to assist with disaster relief; and in Northern Ireland the Corps undertakes a wide range of duties in aid of the Civil Power, including counter-terrorist bomb disposal activity. In GB and throughout the world the RLC also make a major contribution to the wider Defence Explosive Ordnance Disposal capability in support of operational commanders and other government departments.

The Corps is an organisation that encompasses a food empire, a catering chain, a transport operation, a port operation, a vehicle spares company, a removal firm, a mail and parcel service, a fuel company, a private railway; and it operates internationally but it is the men and women in the Corps who are the most important resource. The trade skills required to produce a seamless web of Logistic Support are:

Air Despatcher	Postal and Courier
Driver (including Driver Tank	Railway Operator
Transporter and Staff Car Driver)	Vehicle Specialist
Driver Radio Operator	Ammunition Technician
Movement Controller	Chef
Pioneer	Petroleum Operator
Port Operator	Supply Controller and Supply Specialist

Adventure training and sport is strongly encouraged throughout the Corps. Both activities develop qualities of mental and physical toughness, initiative and leadership and play a vital part in helping to maintain physical fitness, morale as well as personal and unit pride. Since 1993 large numbers of RLC officers and soldiers have taken part in a wide range of adventure training

expeditions around the world; a few have represented their country at sport and many have represented the Army and Combined Services in sports as diverse as rugby, cross-country, athletics, skiing, bobsleigh, squash, motor cycling, angling and marathon running.

THE RLC TERRITORIAL ARMY

The RLC TA total over 11,000 Servicemen and women. They fall into two categories of Volunteer: the Independent, who is geographically based with a drill hall, and the Specialist, who has specific skills, is recruited UK wide and based in the home of the RLC TA at Prince William of Gloucester Barracks in Grantham. In addition to formed RLC TA units there are approximately 3,000 individual RLC TA tradesmen serving in independent units of other Arms and Services as Chefs, Drivers and Supply Specialists. All are highly trained, thoroughly professional and provide the specialist skills and endurance necessary to enhance Regular military capability – they have done so fre-quently in support of UN operations.

The Head of The Royal Logistic Corps is a 1 Star Director who has responsibility for regimental matters. Two staff branches are established to manage Policy, Doctrine, Training and Logistic Development. This leaves the Regimental Headquarters, under the Regimental Colonel, to lead on Regi-mental Affairs which includes liaison with the Royal Colonels and the Colonels Commandant, the provision of benevolence as well as sport, adventure training and Museum matters.

Right, top: Men of 5 Airborne Logistic Battalion on Operation Gabriel, Rwanda 1994.

Right, bottom: **'SUSTAINING FORWARD' – ARMY CATERING CORPS**
Prior to the Second World War feeding soldiers could, perhaps, kindly have been described as 'adequate'. Each Regiment had its complement of cooks, few of whom had volunteered for cooking duties. In late 1936, with tension growing in Europe, it was decided to increase the size of the Armed Forces. In 1937 Leslie Hore Belisha, Secretary of State for War, invited Sir Isadore Salmon, Chairman of J Lyons and Co, to become Honorary Catering Adviser to the Army. As a result of Sir Isadore's recommendations in the 'Salmon Report', a programme of improvements to army messing was initiated. Two years and nine months later the Army Catering Corps was formed by Special Army Order 35 of 1941. During the War the Corps became a highly success-ful organisation and on 5 October 1945 the Army Council took the decision to retain the ACC as an integral part of the post war army. At this time it numbered around 50,000.

Since the Corps' formation the Training Centre at Aldershot has become one of the biggest Cookery instruction schools in the world. Not only does it train Chefs in catering skills but each individual is trained as a soldier enabling him or her to serve in theatres as diverse as The Falklands and Belize. You will find a member of the Corps anywhere the British Army is serving.

During the Gulf War the 847 ACC personnel provided a 24 hour service using the No 4 and 5 field catering cooksets, catering for much greater numbers than originally intended. Whilst coping with the day to day cooking a great deal of time was spent completing Nuclear, Biological and Chemical Warfare practice drills.

For example, cooking for soldiers in transit through Blackadder Camp was a massive and exhausting operation: after 1st Division arrived a 15 man unit cooked for 2–3000 people, right round the clock. Elsewhere, a containerised bakery was producing 16,000 rolls a day. One television report claimed that the British Army had consumed some three million eggs and 1200 tons of potatoes by early February (plus 12 goats for the Gurkhas).

The painting depicts an actual kitchen located in Concentration Area KEYES on the Saudi-Iraq Border, between the towns of Hafa Al Batin and Qaysamah, serving a cooked meal on 17 January 1991 thus feeding elements of 7 Armoured Brigade before moving to their pre-attack positions. The No 4 cookset is shown (trailer) along with the No 5 cookset (free standing). In this location over 10,000 allied troops were fed during a period of 5 days.

TERENCE CUNEO

ROYAL ARMY MEDICAL CORPS

The Royal Army Medical Corps celebrated its centenary on 23 June 1998. It was formed by Royal Warrant bringing together the professional officers of the Army Medical Department and the soldiers of the Medical Staff Corps. As we shall see, in that one hundred years the Corps has given sterling service to the army, all over the world but it trod a long and turbulent path to achieve the respect it now enjoys.

Prior to the Restoration of the Monarchy in 1660, armies were raised for war and, subsequently, disbanded after hostilities. Thus there was no continuity or development of military medical skills. Few doctors put their experiences into print, and the little knowledge that accrued was by word of mouth. Medical posts were established only during campaigns, and did nothing to produce either an experienced medical service, or to aid the invalided soldier in peacetime.

Following the restoration, Charles II created a permanent standing army and with it a medical service. When the army took to the field an Army Medical Staff was established with the high offices of Physician-General, Surgeon-General and Apothecary-General to direct the affairs. Hospitals were established with functions similar to a modern field hospital. The Duke of Marlborough had 'Flying Hospitals', not dissimilar to the Field Ambulances of today, which marched with the regiments. They were staffed by medical personnel, which included soldiers wives as nurses and were provided with waggons for the transport of sick and wounded. These units ceased to exist after the Marlborough campaigns.

The Peninsula Wars, 1812–1814, saw the emergence for the first time of a medical staff officer of stature in James McGrigor, the Principal Medical Officer to the Duke of Wellington. His advice and organisation of medical services during the campaign were seen to contribute to both the ultimate victory and reduction of mortality of the wounded. He was able to persuade his commander of the greater need for medical support in the field. McGrigor introduced many innovative ideas with the ultimate result that medical care of the soldier on campaign was greatly improved. As a result Wellington gave McGrigor uncontolled management of medical matters during that war. McGrigor became Surgeon-General in 1815 and retained the appointment for 36 years.

Following Waterloo, with very little campaigning the medical services went into another decline until the Crimea. As a result of forgetting all the lessons learnt in the Napoleonic wars, medical support during this war with Russia resulted in the horror of suffering and loss that shocked even the Victorian public, causing a scandal that lead to the setting up of a Royal Commission to report on the medical services. An Army Medical School was established at Fort Pitt, near Chatham in 1860 and in 1865 moved to Netley on Southampton Water when the Royal Victoria Hospital was constructed. Military hospitals were also constructed in the main garrison areas such as at Woolwich, and Aldershot.

The Medical Staff Corps, formed in 1855 as a result of the shortcomings in the Crimean campaign, was succeeded by the Army Hospital Corps in 1858. (It would revert back to Medical Staff Corps in 1884). This new Corps was recruited from the line regiments and soldiers had to be both sober and literate. By 1860, Regimental Medical Officers were gazetted to, and wore the uniform of their regiment and there were no distinct personnel for duty in the regimental hospitals other than those provided by the regiment. There was also an entirely separate establishment for medical officers and soldiers in the general hospitals.

In 1891, a royal warrant granted substantive rank to medical staff officers up to the rank of Surgeon-Major General, and this was the first step in the integration of medical officers into regular army service. This continued until 1898 when, by Royal Warrant of Queen Victoria, The Royal Army Medical Corps was formed.

On its inception, the Corps comprised 953 officers (618 British Army – 335 Indian Army) and 2,642 rank and file. In support were 55 officers and 1,230 men of the Volunteer Medical Staff Corps. Within three months it was fully deployed in the Sudan, and supporting the British contingent at the Boxer Rebellion. A sterner trial soon followed in South Africa (the Boer war) where 6 Victoria Crosses were won, and where the Corps had some 22,000 wounded, and over 74,000 sick to deal with.

The lessons of the South African War were not forgotten, for the tradition and direction of the new corps was to be shaped by another great figure in the history of the Corps – Sir Alfred Keogh, Director General Army Medical Services from 1904–1910. Amongst his activities, Keogh organised the new Territorial Force Medical Services.

On the outbreak of the Great War in 1914 he was recalled as DGAMS, by which time the organisation, training and framework had become established, which enabled 160,000 all ranks of the RAMC to deal with over 2.5 million casualties in France, Belgium, Macedonia, Italy, Palestine, Russia and Mesopotamia [Iraq]. Nine VC's (including two bars) were added to the 6 of the South African War.

The Territorial Force raised by Sir Alfred Keogh provided 246 complete units for the war and made an important contribution in trained personnel. At the outbreak of the Great War, the Corps had a total Regular and Territorial strength of under 20,000. By 1916, this had expanded to 13,000 officers and 154,000 soldiers.

The RAMC entered the Second World War much better prepared than ever before. A service had to be provided world wide, in which weapons of destruction increased in lethality, variety and scale and were producing casualties in great numbers. New challenges faced the Corps, increased armoured warfare, parachute and commando forces, all of which would need medical support. Hostilities lasted 71 months during which over 5 million cases were treated, and 1,000 medical units mobilised world-wide.

Although no major conflict of great length has taken place since 1945, the Army has, amongst others, been committed in Korea, Malaya, Cyprus, Borneo, Aden, Suez, Northern Ireland, Falkland Isles, the Gulf and Bosnia. The Royal Army Medical Corps continues to provide medical support to the armed forces of the crown and has also become a leading authority on disaster medicine and humanitarian relief providing aid to countries throughout the world. As they enter the next century of service the RAMC continues to live up to its motto 'In Arduis Fidelis' – Faithful in Adversity'.

Army Hospital Ward with staff – late nineteenth century.

Right, top: AFV Ambulance of 1 Armoured Field Ambulance, 1998.

Right, bottom: Treating a civilian emergency, Kosovo 1999.

PFIZER GROUP LTD

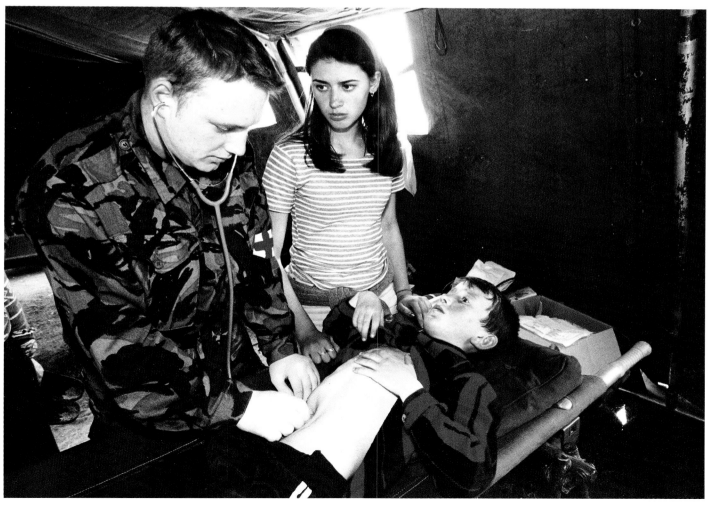

CORPS OF ROYAL ELECTRICAL AND MECHANICAL ENGINEERS (REME)

The task of REME is to ensure the operational fitness of Army equipment. This includes all the Army's weapons and vehicles, its aircraft and ships and virtually every piece of electrical, mechanical, electronic or optical equipment used by the Army. REME personnel form a major element of the Army's Equipment Support function.

There has always been a requirement for qualified tradesmen and engineers to support an Army but it was not until the dramatic increase in the numbers and complexity of mechanised equipment in World War II that it became necessary to form a corps specifically to deal with this and to make effective use of the skilled manpower scattered throughout the Army. REME was formed in 1942 and the battle of El Alamein tested the new Corps for the first time under battle conditions. Repair and recovery carried out close to the battle, often under fire, ensured that tanks in particular were rapidly returned to action. Field Marshal Montgomery paid tribute to the achievement of the Corps in the words *'REME exists to keep the punch in the Army's fist'*.

Since its formation, REME personnel have been attached to every regiment and corps and have been involved in every conflict and operation in which the British Army has been engaged. Their technical skills have also made them an essential component in the many peacekeeping and humanitarian operations carried out by the British Army in recent years.

A typical armoured regiment equipped with Challenger tanks includes a REME unit of a captain and 86 soldiers. REME units like these, varying in size and composition to suit the role, are found in artillery, engineer, signals, infantry, aviation, transport and other regiments. One factor which they all have in common is that they operate as an integral part of the unit which they are supporting and REME soldiers have to be as competent with their rifles as they are with the tools of their trade.

Mobile REME Battalions provide a more complex range of repair in support of combat units. The Close Support Companies can deploy Forward Repair Teams to carry out repairs in-situ on battle-winning equipment while the major repair capabilities are concentrated in General Support Companies which also include most of the electronic and optronic repair vehicles. One Battalion specialises in aircraft repair and the support of airmobile operations. Each REME Battalion is able to produce two or more workshop companies tailor-made to support a brigade on operations.

REME operates several specialist vehicles peculiar to itself. The biggest of these is the Challenger Armoured Repair and Recovery Vehicle, based on the Main Battle Tank. Its crane and winch enables it to recover tanks under the most difficult circumstances and to carry out power pack repairs in the field. Similarly, repair and recovery variants of the Warrior Mechanised Combat Vehicle support infantry and other units equipped with those vehicles. A range of wheeled recovery vehicles specifically designed for military use is also operated. Other vehicles have been developed to provide mobile repair facilities for power packs and for electronic and optical equipments which require specialised test equipment and clinically clean working conditions.

On operations, REME TA units and individual tradesmen have proved invaluable in providing additional support to the regular army.

The task of REME is not limited to providing engineering support in the field. It also plays an important part in the design of military equipment and in bringing it into service. Teams of REME experts work alongside designers and engineers in research establishments in order to ensure that new equipments are reliable and easy to maintain and repair. REME is also responsible for planning the way that a new equipment will be supported throughout its service and for monitoring equipment performance in order to improve future designs.

To provide the wide range of skills needed to carry out its complex task REME has a large training organisation which, by virtue of long experience and continuous refinement, has devised highly effective methods of training potential mechanics and technicians in the shortest possible time. Thereafter a full range of trade courses provides progressive training up to HNC level. At more senior levels, management training is provided by the School of Equipment Support (SES(A)) to servicemen of all Regiments and Corps and also to MOD civilians.

The home of REME is Arborfield, near Reading, where the Corps Headquarters, the REME Museum of Technology, the Corps Memorial Chapel and the Headquarters Officers' and Sergeants' Messes can be found. Here also are based the headquarters REME training Group, SES(A) and the School of Electronic and Aeronautical Engineering. The School of Electrical and Mechanical Engineering is based at Bordon, Hampshire, as is HQ REME TA.

Challenger Armoured Repair and Recovery Vehicle (CRARRV) creates an access route to swamp-bound casualty.

Right, top: The *cameraderie* not only of the Army, but shared technical problems and skills.

Right, bottom: Victim of the Bosnian weather enjoys a speedy rescue.

MARCONI ELECTRONIC SYSTEMS

ADJUTANT GENERAL'S CORPS

The Adjutant General's Corps formed on 6 April 1992 (the first new corps in the Army for fourteen years), following an Army Board decision to rationalise the Army's A services by creating one organisation to look after all personnel related functions. The result was that the Corps of Royal Military Police, the Royal Army Pay Corps, the Military Provost Staff Corps, the Royal Army Educational Corps and the Army Legal Corps amalgamated into one corps, the Adjutant General's Corps (AGC). At the same time, it was decided to disband the Women's Royal Army Corps and transfer all members to other corps of the Army, including the Adjutant General's Corps. The new Corps consisted of four branches, Staff and Personnel Support (SPS) Branch, Provost (Pro) Branch which included the Royal Military Police and the Military Provost Staff, Educational and Training Services (ETS) Branch and Army Legal Services (ALS) Branch. Later, all Royal Army Ordnance Corps staff clerks were transferred to SPS Branch and, by July 1993, the clerks from all the arms and services were subsumed into the Branch; as a result, all clerical and financial functions within the Army became the preserve of SPS Branch.

Initially, the Corps was headed by a Director General Adjutant General's Corps (DGAGC). The first Director General, Major General R D Grist OBE set up his directorate at Worthy Down where he operated as any other arms and service director. Subsequently, DGAGC became double hatted as Chief of Staff to the Adjutant General (COS AG) and, later still, the DGAGC post was removed, at which point COS AG became Assistant Colonel Commandant of the Adjutant General's Corps and a member of the Regimental Council.

The Corps now runs as a federation of four branches with the regimental focus provided by Commander Adjutant General's Corps Centre and the Regimental Colonel and Regimental Secretary at Worthy Down.

SPS Branch is the largest branch of the Corps, with some 475 officers and 4,000 soldiers. The role of the branch is to provide professional financial and administrative support to the Army. The Branch provides a regimental administrative officer (RAO), a detachment commander and an administrative office for all major units and many minor units throughout the Army and is represented in almost every Army station.

Provost Branch embraces Adjutant General's Corps (Royal Military Police) (RMP), AGC (Military Provost Staff) (MPS) and AGC (Military Provost Guard Service) (MPGS), which formed on 1 April 1997. Unlike the majority of the Corps, AGC(Pro) operates as formed units up to regimental size. RMP is responsible for policing within the military community, in barracks and in the field. MPS mans the Military Corrective Training Centre at Colchester, a tri-service establishment, and provides a guardroom inspection facility. MPGS provides guarding for selected MOD sites. Provost Branch is some 2,350 strong.

Educational and Training Services (ETS) Branch, with 335 officers, is involved with the educational development of officers and soldiers throughout their careers. It retains its traditional resettlement role, provides linguists and training development officers and has an operational role. New initiatives in the national educational and training sphere such as whole life learning and national vocational qualifications are now incorporated within ETS Branch's responsibilities to the Army.

ALS, the smallest branch with some 78 officers, is responsible for advising on all matters of military law and for providing prosecutors through the Army Prosecution Authority. ALS provides advice and instruction on the law relating to the conduct of military operations including the law of armed conflict and the Geneva Conventions and protocols. ALS also advises on Army aspects of developments in domestic and international law and is responsible for training the Army as a whole. ALS provides a legal aid service overseas.

Commander Adjutant General's Corps Centre (Brigadier) is located at Worthy Down. In addition to his regimental duties, he has garrison responsibilities for Winchester and Marchwood and some functional responsibilities, although these are mainly delegated to branches. The Regimental Colonel, Regimental Secretary and Assistant Regimental Secretary, all retired officers, are also located at Worthy Down. The antecedent corps, including WRAC, retain their regimental offices and associations. Those for RAPC, RAEC and WRAC are at Worthy Down, alongside Regimental Headquarters AGC while RHQs RMP and MPSC are at Chichester and Colchester respectively.

The Corps is greatly honoured to have Her Majesty The Queen as Colonel in Chief and Her Royal Highness The Duchess of Gloucester and Her Royal Highness The Duchess of Kent as her deputies. In 1993, all three visited Worthy Down for Corps Day, thought to be a unique gathering of three royal colonels in chief.

The Colonel Commandant on the formation of the Corps was Major General J J G Mackenzie who retired from the post on 23 October 1998, as General Sir Jeremy Mackenzie GCB OBE ADC Gen, after over six years in the post. He has recently been replaced by Lieutenant General Sir Mike Jackson. In addition, the Corps has an Assistant Colonel Commandant (currently double hatted with Chief of Staff to the Adjutant General) and four deputies, three retired and one serving, each with special responsibilities for one of the branches.

The Adjutant General's Corps is very fortunate to have its own Band which lives at the home of the Corps, Worthy Down. This derives from the Band of the Women's Royal Army Corps which was badged AGC in 1992. Originally an all-female organisation, the Band is now mixed and, indeed, was the first mixed band in the Army. The Corps Quick March is *Pride of Lions*, specially composed at the time of formation. Each of the branches has a branch march that is played on appropriate social and ceremonial occasions.

Dressing the Corps has provided a challenge not unknown in our still tribal Army and has involved a combination of standardisation and compromise. For example, the majority of the Corps, wears the AGC cap badge (which, uniquely, contains three lions in its design) although AGC(RMP), AGC(MPS) and AGC(ALS) wear the cap badges of their antecedents. Similarly, the Corps wears several differently coloured berets. A common feature is the stable belt, in the Corps colours of red and blue.

The Corps has acquired a good deal of stability and maturity in the six years of its existence and although there will undoubtedly be further changes, it has made its mark on the Army and shown a degree of professional expertise that safeguards its future. The Territorial Army is represented in all four branches of the Corps. The recent cuts to the TA have reduced the number of AGC(RMP) soldiers but have enhanced the roles of SPS and ETS branches. A pool of TA lawyers has recently been created to support ALS Branch. In each of the six years of its existence, up to 20% of the Corps has been serving on operations, including in Northern Ireland and Bosnia, at any time.

The Corps' motto is *Animo et Fide*, which means with resolution and fidelity and it enters the new Millennium in this spirit and with a firm determination to provide the best possible level of personnel support to the Army.

Female Combat Administrator: all AGC soldiers undergo comprehensive military training before assuming their primary roles.

Right, top: AGC permanent staff at ATR, Winchester

Right, Bottom: AGC Military Police in Bosnia.

THE ROYAL ARMY VETERINARY CORPS

The RAVC is a small technical support Corps. Involved in all aspects of military animal activity and related matters, the RAVC is technically responsible to the Director Veterinary and Remount Services.

The Army Veterinary Service was founded in 1796. The public, outraged that more Army horses were lost by poor farriery and husbandry than at the hands of the enemy, demanded action and the Committee of General Officers was obliged to address the issue. Professor Edward Coleman, was appointed Principle Veterinary Surgeon and graduates of the London Veterinary School, of which Coleman was the Head, were recruited to the regiments of cavalry. The first was John Shipp who joined the 11th Light Dragoons on 25 June 1796.

The AVS has been represented in most campaigns since. For 150 years the concern was equines. In 1946 came responsibility for managing the Army's dogs around the world. In Malaya, RAVC dog specialists played a significant support role to US Army dogs deployed in Vietnam and throughout the 1970's, veterinary officers helped establish the Oman State Veterinary Service, while in Northern Ireland the Corps became very active in the strategic use of dogs. In the Falklands, it fell to the RAVC to help the government restore its animal health regime and, in the Gulf War, it was an RAVC Veterinary Officer who commanded all water purification plants. Today, in Bosnia, RAVC personnel are helping the civil authorities with animal welfare and handlers and dogs are supporting the security force.

The Army Veterinary Service was founded in the infancy of the veterinary profession. Diseases encountered by Army veterinary officers were varied and often previously unknown. Much pioneering work was done. In the field, necessity demanded bold action in 'nothing to lose and everything to gain' situations. Many equine treatments and procedures are attributed to officers of the AVS.

A milestone was the foundation of the Army Veterinary School at Aldershot in 1880. It became a major influence in improving the skills of veterinary officers and training regimental personnel in good horse management. The School had an immeasurable impact on the care of military horses, changing military perceptions and developing strategies that ensured the veterinary response was effective and progressive.

The Army Veterinary Corps was formed in 1903 to unite most Veterinary Officers under one badge and to provide a soldier resource trained to assist and support them in their duties. The AVC was surely tested in WWI. It rapidly expanded from under 400 personnel to almost 30,000. Of 2.5 million equine admissions, mainly on the Western Front, 80% were treated and returned to duty, an achievement far exceeding any previous attainment. It earned the Corps its Royal prefix on 27th November 1918.

Mechanisation led to a decline in the post-war size of the RAVC. In 1921 it was only 772 all ranks but there was still a job to be done particularly in the Turco-Greek war in 1922 and the Shanghai Defence Force in 1927.

Many veterinary officers served in India which had an extensive animal establishment. Some animals were kept as part of the military food chain but there was extensive use, particularly of mules, in support of units operating along the North-west Frontier. Contagious diseases prevailed – Anthrax, Foot-and-Mouth, Glanders and Rinderpest were but a few that demanded constant veterinary vigilance, good husbandry practice and the development of vaccines to combat them. Rinderpest was one disease brought under complete control by the Army Veterinary Service in India. Mallein, the testing agent for Glanders, was developed by the RAVC and produced at the RAVC Laboratory Aldershot until the early 1970's.

A report on the RAVC in 1937, when the establishment was down to 190, concluded that 'the RAVC should be preserved in order to conserve the experience of the past against possible future needs and to modify and enlarge this knowledge by study and practice under changing conditions'. Well founded then these words remain just as sound today.

In 1939 on the outbreak of WW2, the 1st Cavalry Division went to Palestine with 20,000 animals – the RAVC was in business! In the UK large numbers of equines were assembled in anticipation of major operations in Norway. In Italy, India and Burma mules played a major role in support of the ground forces. The RAVC again expanded rapidly to nearly 4,500 personnel.

Dunng WW2 the Corps developed an interest in dogs that was to ensure its post-war viability. In 1942 the RAVC became responsible for the procurement of Army dogs running the Army Dog Training School set up at the Greyhound Racing Association kennels at Potters Bar. In 1945 the school moved to Belgium and then to Sennelager in Germany. The Defence Animal Support Unit RAVC continues to provide technical support for all animals on the continent, from that same Sennelager base.

In 1942 the Army Veterinary and Army Remount departments amalgamated and, in 1945, was charged with the overall management of Army animal resources. The RAVC Depot, re-located from Woolwich to Doncaster Racecourse for the war, needed a new home quickly – the Jockey Club wanted to resume racing! It moved to the Army Remount Depot, Melton Mowbray.

Comprising over 300 acres, used extensively throughout the war as an equine assembly area, it was readily adaptable to the needs of the RAVC Depot embracing the Army Dog Training School, School of Equitation, School of Fakery, Remount Depot and Veterinary Hospital. Melton Mowbray proved ideally suitable to such military activities, a fact validated by a number of studies in recent years.

War-time skills gained in the training and deployment of dogs was to significantly benefit the RAVC as the military use of equines decline rapidly. By the 1960's horses were primarily being used for ceremonial duties only.

The post-war years have been active for the RAVC. Dogs have been an invaluable aid to ground troops being used to good effect in Malaysia, Borneo, Egypt, North Africa, Kenya, Cyprus, Hong Kong and Northern Ireland. Their superior ability to indicate the presence of an intruder coupled with their agility and speed in chase and apprehension, make dogs a formidable deterrent rarely challenged by ill intent. Capable of covering an area that might otherwise require five separate foot patrols the dog and handler are an effective force multiplier. There is still no machine that can match a dogs ability to detect explosives or drugs.

The RAVC retains a duty to maintain the capability to respond quickly to the changing military need in animal deployment and military veterinary officers are taking a leading role in military biomedical research. Dogs make an important contribution and there are possible scenarios where pack transport might be a vital solution in future operations and these latter skills remain inherent in the training of RAVC personnel. In the liberated Falkland Islands a small pack horse section was provided by the RAVC and, in the current situation in Bosnia, commanders on the ground are mindful of the potential of such means. The RAVC is ready to respond.

Cost effectiveness and efficiency is something with which the RAVC is well acquainted and it strives to continue to make an effective contribution to the revitalised, post Strategic Defence Review, Army.

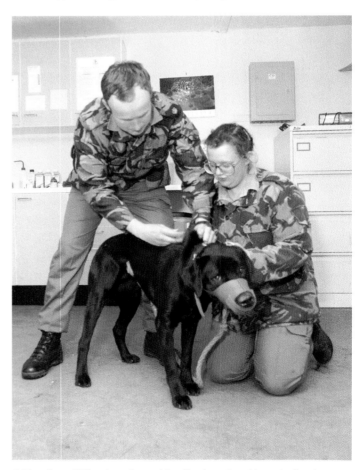

A Veterinary Officer inserting an identification microchip at the Services Veterinary Hospital.

Right, top: Her Majesty The Queen at the Army School of Equitation.

Right, bottom: RAVC Dog Trainer with his Service Dog, Luka, keeping the peace in Bosnia.

SMALL ARMS SCHOOL CORPS

The original School of Musketry owed its existence to the introduction of the rifle into the services in the 18th Century. The first rifle used by the British Army was the Ferguson Rifle in 1776. This was followed by the Baker Rifle which had been selected by the Board of Ordnance at Woolwich in 1800. The Baker Rifle was used to arm the newly formed Corps of Riflemen in that year and was later issued to the 60th (Royal American) Regiment of Foot. Both were forerunners of the present Royal Green Jackets. The advantages and disadvantages of a rifle compared to the smooth-bore musket, with which the majority of the services were issued, were very apparent. The rifle was lighter and more accurate, however, the rate of fire was slower and the firer had to master a considerable number of new skills such as judging distance, aiming and aiming off for wind if the best use of the rifle was to be achieved. The Baker rifle was replaced with the Brunswick Rifle in 1838. By this time it was considered that the advantages of the rifle far outweighted the disadvantages and the search was on to procure a rifle for issue to the whole army.

In 1851, the Master General of Ordnance, the Marquess of Anglesey, with the agreement of the Duke of Wellington, decided that the Infantry, Marines and other troops using Infantry weapons should be issued with the 'Minie Rifled Musquet' (later to be designated the Rifle, Musket, Pattern 1851). In the following year, when Viscount Hardinge took over as Master General of Ordnance, the search was on to obtain a lighter and more efficient arm for the services. He invited some of the principle gunmakers to submit pattern 'musquets' for trial. Amongst the contenders were the Baker and the Minie as well as the eventual winner, the Enfield Rifle (Rifle, Musket, Pattern 1853). When the Duke of Wellington died in 1852 and Viscount Hardinge took over as General Commanding in Chief his interest in 'rifled muskets' did not diminish. He was well aware of the shortcomings in training and decided to formalise the rather ad hoc procedures which were then in place. The main requirement was to obtain a suitable range, consequently, in February 1853, a 1400 yds range was purchased at Hythe in Kent. The first step in establishing the School of Musketry, and with it the forerunners of the present day Small Arms School Corps, was in place.

Although instruction and trials took place at Hythe in 1853 it was not until 1854 that the 'School of Musketry' was first mentioned in the Army List. The tasks of the 'Musketry' instructors on the staff of the 'School' were to teach the drills and tactics of the newly introduced rifled musket (the 'Minie' Rifle) and to conduct trials on weapons and their ancillaries. These tasks have continued with the introduction of each successive rifle as well as with pistols, sub-machine guns, machine guns, mortars, anti-tank weapons and associated training matters to the present day. The School of Musketry was renamed the Small Arms School in 1919. In 1926 the Infantry Support Weapons, which had been partially taught at Hythe, began to be taught at Netheravon in Wiltshire and was named the Netheravon Wing, Small Arms School. In the same year the Small Arms School was renamed the Hythe Wing, Small Arms School. This occasion was marked with the introduction of the title 'Small Arms School Corps' and the present badge was introduced in 1929. Prior to this the badge was a pair of crossed rifles surmounted by a crown. The Depot SASC moved from Hythe to Warminster in 1969, was renamed HQ SASC and placed under direct command of the Director of Infantry in 1996. The Corps is one of smallest units in the British Army and is manned by volunteers recruited from the army, particularly the Infantry. At present it consists of approximately 130 members, 25 of which are commissioned officers. They are very much to the forefront of training the trainers in all matters small arms, mortars, anti-armour weapons, armoured infantry weapons and range safety and are still involved with trials on similar equipment. SASC personnel serve at virtually every Army Training Centre in the UK and overseas, including some NATO and Commonwealth countries. They also provide advice and assistance to the Field Army world wide and serve with some regular Infantry Battalions.

MRTRIGAT firings.

Top: SMI Gallagher firing the AW .50 inch (Long Range Large Calibre Rifle) in Alaska.

Left: Top shot SMI Tony Reece – with some silver.

THE ROYAL ARMY DENTAL CORPS

The Royal Army Dental Corps (RADC) today is a small and highly professional Corps of officers and soldiers, both male and female. The Corps fulfils the essential role of achieving and maintaining the dental health of military personnel in peace and war, both at home and overseas. The Corps is organised around the concept of a dental team in which each member plays a vital role. Working together, these professional teams deliver high standards of dental care and treatment all over the world – in hospitals, dental centres and in the field. Soldiers and officers of the Corps are trained in the most up-to-date techniques and use the latest equipment.

The Corps badge and crest is based upon a story in the legend of Cadmus, son of Agenor King of Phoenicia. Cadmus, who had sent his men in search of a spring, discovered that they had been devoured by a dragon. Cadmus slew the dragon with one blow of his sword whereupon a voice bade him extract the dragon's teeth and sow them in the broken ground. Cadmus knew the order came from the immortal Gods and immediately obeyed. The teeth were no sooner planted than a crop of men sprang from the soil, fully grown and armed to the teeth.

'Ex Dentibus Ensis – From the Teeth, a Sword'

In the Regular Army of 1660 dental awareness was almost non-existent and treatment was restricted to extraction for the relief of pain. However, it was essential that musketeers had sound incisor and canine teeth in order to be able to open the gun-powder charge and pour it's contents into the muzzle of his weapon. For two centuries the possession of sufficient teeth for this purpose was the infantry dental standard. So the deliberate extraction of front teeth in a man of military age became a criminal offence.

The introduction of breech-loading rifles with metal cartridges in the 1860s ended this first military dental requirement. The British Dental Association was concerned: 'It could be argued that since the old cartridge has been abolished and the infantry have no biting to do, the Government has no concern with the teeth of soldiers or sailors. This, however, is a selfish and superficial view. It is well known that a toothless soldier is not apt for half the duty that a well-stocked jaw can do for the country. A soldier with defective teeth too costs the Government in doctors' bills, because it has been demonstrated that it requires the full force of an undiseased jaw to masticate the 'hard tack' thoughtfully provided for the military staff of life'. 'The equipment of each regiment with a Dentist will save Gunpowder, for it is well known that to alleviate his misery the soldier is prone to fire off his tooth by means of a powder. This picturesque, but perilous form of Dentistry sometimes blows out the offending tooth, and not unfrequently the unoffending jaw-bone. Now, there are few that will seriously contend that a jawless soldier is either a useful or decorative object in garrison or field'.

Despite constant pressure from the British Dental Association: 'It has long been a notorious fact that practically the only dental treatment the soldier has received has been that of the extraction of every aching tooth or administration of a pill to relieve pain. It is also an undoubted fact that too frequently the army medical surgeon leaves even this limited and ancient kind of dental treatment to the hospital sergeant though where, when and how this latter functionary acquires his knowledge must be left to your imagination.' It was not until the Boer War that Whitehall was persuaded to act upon the sick wastage due to dental disease. Four dentists were sent to South Africa but they were given no Army status and were required to supply their own instruments. Their subsequent report focussed attention on the poor dental state of many recruits.

At the beginning of the Great War of 1914–18, dental treatment in the British Army, was very limited. No arrangements had been made, either at home or in the field, for the dental treatment of the vast army which was shortly to be formed. Not one dental surgeon accompanied the Expeditionary Force to France. In 1914, instructions were issued by the War Office to the effect that no serving soldier was to be discharged on account of decay or loss of many teeth if, by dental treatment, he could be rendered fit to remain in the service. Men with defective teeth, but willing to undergo dental treatment, could be attested if otherwise fit for general service; a recruit could be passed as 'fit, subject to dental treatment'. Practically all the dental treatment at home for recruits and serving soldiers was carried out by civilian dentists until the middle of 1916 but it was realised that there was no effective control over the work of the civilian dentists, many of whom possessed no dental qualification, with the result that many men had their teeth extracted unnecessarily and too little attention was given to the restoration of repairable teeth. The appointment of an Inspecting Dental Officer to the staff of the deputy directors of medical services at commands became essential to advise on all dental matters. The importance of dentistry as a 'special branch of army medical organisation' was thus recognised and the nucleus of an Army Dental Service established. The War Office agreed to provide dental treatment for troops both at home and overseas and at the end of hostilities, in November 1918, there were 831 dental surgeons serving in the Army at home and overseas.

The formation of The Army Dental Corps (ADCorps) was authorised by Royal Warrant on 4th January 1921 and the Special Army Order, signed by Winston Churchill, was published on 11th January. There was no shortage of applicants for the new ADCorps. The peacetime establishment was to be 107 dental officers, 107 dental clerk-orderlies and 25 dental mechanics. However, the post-war period in the Army was not an ideal time for instituting a new corps as it had to manage on a very small budget for several years. The Corps served in all Home Commands, also with the Army of the Rhine and with the British Forces in Turkey, Gibraltar, Malta, Egypt, Palestine, India, Burma, Iraq, North China and the Caribbean. The small strength of British garrisons at some stations prevented the full-time employment of a dental officer and dental treatment was carried out by civilian dental practitioners in Bermuda, Ceylon, Jamaica, Malaya, Hong Kong, Mauritius and West Africa.

By 1939, the dental condition of the Army had been vastly improved. This had been achieved by an understaffed ADCorps despite the very poor dental condition of recruits, due to the lowered standard of dental health required. Fortunately for the efficiency of the soldier on active service, the ADCorps had raised the standard of dental health in all branches of the Regular Army and had made maintenance of it a part of army life. General Mobilisation was declared in September 1939 and by the close of the year the total officer strength was 581, and at the end of 1940 it was 1,368 and the estimated requirement by 1st October 1941 was 2,000 dental officers. At it's peak wartime strength there were 3,653 soldiers, of whom 1,753 were dental mechanics, and 2,160 dental officers, all of whom had passed through the ADCorps School of Instruction in Aldershot.

At the end of WW2 personnel of The ADCorps had acquitted themselves with great honour and distinction not only in their clinical work but also in their military roles for which many were decorated for bravery in action – a high accolade for a non-combatant Corps. It is difficult to describe just how much the availability of dental treatment contributed to the health, efficiency and morale of the Army in action. However, the value of the Corps was recognised when His Majesty King George VI approved the change of title and The Army Dental Corps became the Royal Army Dental Corps (RADC) in 1946.

The Roll of the Army Dental Personnel who died in the service of their country are commemorated in the Royal Army Dental Corps Roll of Honour 1939–1945. Eighty-one names are recorded in the Corps Book of Remembrance, which is displayed in the Royal Garrison Church Aldershot. The Corps War Memorial in Aldershot was consecrated in 1948. In 1973 the Corps, as part of the Army Medical Services, was granted the Honour of the Freedom of Aldershot and exercised their right to march through the town with drums beating and band playing.

With the rest of the Armed Forces the RADC has reduced in size as the world wide commitment has grown smaller, however, the standards of clinical and military excellence have been enhanced. In recent years RADC dental teams have seen action in the Falkland and Gulf Wars and have been employed extensively in 'Hearts & Minds' operations providing much needed medical relief to peoples ravaged by war or natural disasters.

Today the RADC works in close co-operation with its' colleagues in the Navy and RAF and is the major partner in the tri-Service Dental Defence Agency (DDA). The DDA is responsible for providing primary dental care in some 200 locations for approximately 235,000 Service personnel and a further 55,000 entitled civilians and dependants oveseas.

MOD retains the capacity to deploy on military operations fully trained and combat ready RADC staff whose operational commitment is to provide trained dental personnel in support of the National Contingency Force.

Right, top: Modern emphasis on Preventive Dentistry, Challenger crew in the desert.

Right, bottom: Dental care in the Front Line, Gulf War 1991.

THE INTELLIGENCE CORPS

Military Intelligence has been an important aspect of every war ever fought including, of course, those fought by the British Army. Despite this, there was no Intelligence Corps as such until its formation was found to be a necessity with the outbreak of the First World War. 27 years before this the post of Director of Military Intelligence was created and in 1899 the appointment was held by Sir John Ardagh. His forecasts and assessments of Boer capabilities and intentions were meticulous and accurate – and completely ignored by the Cabinet. However, the Intelligence Corps traces its origin from the campaign in South Africa and by the end of 1901 the Field Intelligence Department, as it was then known, had grown into a force of 132 officers and 2,321 men. It was disbanded at the end of the war.

In 1912 the mobilization plan for the Army did include 'an intelligence element' which crossed to France on 12 August 1914 as The Intelligence Corps. At the end of the war the Corps consisted of some 3,000 officers and men, many of whom were experienced specialists in one or more intelligence functions. After the war the service dwindled rapidly and ceased to exist in December 1929.

At the outbreak of the Second World War in 1939 no attempt had been made to put in place an Army intelligence organisation of any sort. However, due to the efforts of a Major Templer (subsequently Field Marshal Sir Gerald Templer) in MI 1(a) at the War Office, thirty-one Field Security Sections were deployed with the British Expeditionary Force in France. The actual formation of the Intelligence Corps was notified in Army Order No 1 dated 19 July 1940 after being approved by King George VI when the Corps was awarded its own cap badge.

During the Second World War, members of the Intelligence Corps were employed in operational intelligence, counter-intelligence, technical intelligence, air photo interpretation, censorship, travel control, special operations and as interpreters. The list of Honours and Awards includes 1,194 names and, of the 9,000 members of the Corps, 217 lost their lives on active service.

Immediately post-War, the prejudice against a permanent Intelligence Corps remained and it was not until 1948 that the Standing Committee on Army Post-War Problems decided that 'there was a need for a permanent Intelligence Corps in the Regular Army'; but only in July 1957 was authority given for a cadre of 100 officers to hold commissions in the Intelligence Corps. Since the end of the Second World War the Corps has repeatedly provided effective intelligence in all theatres; from the Korean War and the troubles in Palestine to the emergencies in Malaya, East Africa, Cyprus, Borneo and Aden. In 1966 the Government proposed to disband the Corps once again unless it could show good reason for its existence. It did, and the situation changed radically three years later when the 'troubles' began in Northern Ireland. In 1972, in a telegram to the Colonel Commandant, the GOC Northern Ireland praised the

work done by members of the Corps and admitted that 'without them our operations would have come to a halt'. More recently, members of the Corps have had an important part to play in the Falklands War, the Gulf War and in the Former Yugoslavia whilst continuing to maintain a large and important presence in the Province.

The appointment of His Royal Highness, The Prince Philip, Duke of Edinburgh, as Colonel-in-Chief of the Intelligence Corps in the summer of 1977 was another milestone on the road to permanence.

The Intelligence Corps has had a number of homes. Its first 'assembly point' in the First World War was at Southampton and in the Second the Officers' Wing was raised at Oxford with the Field Security personnel going to Mychett near Aldershot. The first Depot of the Corps was at Sheerness and then at Winchester from 1940 to 1942. After short periods at Wentworth, Woodhouse and Oudenarde Barracks, Aldershot, the Corps was established at Maresfield in Sussex from 1948 until 1966. From January 1966 to March 1997 the home of the Corps was Templer Barracks, Ashford, Kent until it moved to its current location in Chicksands, Bedfordshire.

The present role of the Intelligence Corps is to supply specialist intelligence units and personnel for current operations and to provide continuity in the direction, training and management of Army intelligence and security. The Corps is now approximately 1100 strong, of whom 250 are commissioned officers. Soldiers are trained in one of two main trades; the Operator Intelligence and Security and the Operator Special Intelligence (Analyst), a large proportion of whom are also trained as linguists.

The majority of Intelligence Corps soldiers work in the Operator Intelligence and Security trade simply because the variety of tasks is so great. As well as the basic intelligence and security roles, operators can find themselves involved in such things as interrogation and debriefing, computer security, covert surveillance and imagery analysis working, in some cases, in support of the Security Service, the civilian police and Special Branch and with members of the security services and military intelligence units of other countries.

The principle task of the Operator Special Intelligence is to analyse signals intelligence and he or she would normally be employed with military units whose equipment is designed to intercept enemy radio transmissions and locate enemy positions on the battlefield.

In an increasingly uncertain world the future of the Intelligence Corps appears secure. Greater use of technology in information gathering is now an important aspect of how the Corps carries out its role and the recent introduction of the Phoenix remotely piloted vehicle and the forthcoming deployment of the ASTOR airborne radar imaging system are just two examples of the expanding roles of the Intelligence Corps.

SIMROD OPTRONICS LTD

An Intelligence Corps Officer briefs one of his Operators.

Top: An Operator employed in combat intelligence uses a vehicle-borne battlefield computer.

Left: Computer security is an ever-increasing aspect of Corps work.

THE ARMY PHYSICAL TRAINING CORPS

After Crimean War and Indian Mutiny there was outcry over the inadequate training of soldiers, it was believed that some form of physical training should be introduced.

1860 Major Hammersley and 12 NCOs (the Apostles) went to Oxford University for a six months course. The Army Gymnastic Staff was born and the first gymnasium was set up at Wellington Lines Aldershot.

1862 Order was given for gymnasiums to be built in all garrisons with an officer in charge of each.

1865 Regulations for Physical Training published. Recruits to do no more than one hour per day. Trained soldiers up to the age of 30 to do annual course of three months, one hour each day.

1871 Major Hammersley made Lt Col director of Gymnasia.

1876 New ideas from Scandinavia. Hammersley succeeded by Maj Gildea the founder of the Royal Tournament.

1890 Col Fox becomes Inspector of PT. Boxing and Fencing gain in popularity. Value of fitness training now becoming noticeable and appreciated.

1894 Cranbrook Gym built, later to become Fox Gym.

1897 Col Napier became Inspector of PT and had swimming pool built next to Fox gym, paid for by receipts of the Royal Tournament, £12,000.

1906 Training altered drastically with introduction of the Ling system.

1908 First Manual of Physical Training published by Major Charles Moore. Public and private schools copy Army methods of PT, Swedish drill.

1914 Start of the Great War; AGS credited with excellent fitness of that 'Contemptible Little Army' of the BEF.

1914–1918 At home PT instructors returned to their units, but mistake recognised and a new staff quickly assembled. Colonel Couper recreates AGS with 80 NCOs, courses held at ASPT Aldershot right through the War. bayonet fighting taught by PT instructors, several PT schools established in France and instructors served in all theatres of War, Italy, Salonika, Mesopotamia and American Army.

1916 Command PT schools set up 6000 PT certificates issued from these schools during the war. 33 members of the AGS were killed in action. Many were decorated for their work.

1919–1939 After Great War run down was rapid, by Nov 1918 strength was 2299. By 1919 this was reduced to 200, by 1922 to 150, now known as the Army Physical Training Staff (APTS).

Work at the School at Aldershot increased with often over 400 students on courses at any one time. APTS became the leaders in physical training in the country, providing members in the British Olympic team in Fencing, Boxing and Modern Pentathlon. Vocational training for instructors leaving the service were held at ASPT and most of the large public schools employed ex APTS instructors. Meanwhile instructors were sent to all overseas stations to serve with garrisons or schools.

1928 New PT tables were introduced. 1929 the numbers on the Staff had shrunk to 148.

1930 Territorial Army and officers Training Corps PT was carried out in Command and Staff Officers for PT were establishing close liaison with units and schools. The first Senior Officers course was held at ASPT.

1931 Manual of Physical Training introduced, this remained basis of PT in the Army until 1939.

First two blocks of Hammersley Barracks for the accommodation of other ranks, staff and NCOs on courses were completed.

May 1932 School visited by The Emir Feisal and his son. New set of Cavalry training tables carried out at Aldershot by APTS.

April 1934 Visit by Their Majesties King George V and Queen Mary.

1935 Alarm at the poor standard of fitness of the nation compared with other nations. One half of recruits turned down by Army as not fit.

1936 British Medical Association recommended that PE in schools should be on the Army model and advice was sought from the School at Aldershot.

Large numbers of men were sub standard and could not be accepted for service. It was decided to run experimental courses for their development and Physical Development Courses came into being and were run right through the War and post War.

1939–1945 Strength Sep 3rd was 280 instructors, by Nov 520, Dec 750, continued to increase up to about 3000 by end of War.

1940 Army Physical Training Staff became Army Physical Training Corps. Revised forms of unarmed combat were perfected, refresher course for Staff was started.

Spring 1940 21 instructors were posted to France. They were all evacuated at Dunkirk except SI Campbell, our first casualty, who was killed there. Instructors served in all the War theatres. 26 dropped with the Airborne Forces at Arnhem, four were killed and sixteen taken prisoner. War ended with about 2000 instructors – this number was rapidly reduced by the demobilisation of the Army to its present figure of around 400. Staff were continued to be deployed world wide in Headquarters, Garrisons and with units. APTC heavily involved in Rehabilitation of sick and wounded.

1950–1960's Instructors were being qualified as Remedial Gymnasts at Pinderfields Hospital and the original AMRUs were absorbed into two joint service remedial centres at RAF Chessington and Headley Court. Instructors were deployed with major units in the Korean war and WO2 Strong served with distinction with the Glorious Glosters, especially in their long march to captivity from Imjin to Pyongyang. Other trouble spots as Aden, Suez, Malay, Borneo and Northern Ireland involved APTC staff with the units concerned.

In mid 1970's Adventurous Training experts from other Corps and Regiments were inducted into the APTC to provide the specialised nucleus of instructors who were to take courses in the subject as it was added to Corps's responsibilities. Schools were established at York and Ripon to cater for this and later the venues were increased as the interest in the Army became greater.

In the post War period the APTC excelled in sport by holding the Adams Shield team gymnastic trophy for nine consecutive years and several instructors became national coaches in gymnastics. Their participation over the whole range of sporting activities had become widely acknowledged and respected.

In 1962 The rebuild of the new Hammersley Barracks was completed, but it was not until the seventies that any additional structures were built at the School location, that being the Fielder Centre, designed to accommodate a laboratory for the measurement of fitness, which was being pursued by the APTC with the introduction of the Army Personal Fitness Assessment (APFA).

Training at the School tended to move away from strict gymnastically orientated achievement to a wider application and at one stage instructors were having to qualify in over thirty separate subjects.

1973 Following the Turkish invasion of Cyprus and the indifferent performance of certain elements of the Army the Adjutant General ordered a study into Army fitness and the Fit to Fight working party was set up, which culminated in a new set of PT pamphlets being written and tests which measured basic fitness evolved. A revised directive in April 1982 set out the mandatory tests for all personnel.

In mid 1980's A Training Development team was set up at ASPT to define the role of the APTC, to update its training methods and review the total concept of physical and recreational training in the Army. This was done just in time to receive the changes brought about by the cut back of the armed forces in the government's 'Options for Change' policy.

With the disbandment of the Womens Royal Army Corps women were to undergo the same training as men for induction into the various instructional levels of PT in the Army, which includes transfer into the APTC. The first woman officer in the APTC entered in **1992.**

Negotiating Grade 3 Rapids

Right: Fox Gymnasium: high horse exercise

Right: Battle swimming, Aldershot, Spring 1940.

QUEEN ALEXANDRA'S ROYAL ARMY NURSING CORPS (Q.A.R.A.N.C.)

Historical Background

Military campaigns from the earliest civilisations have required a range of health care and first aid provision appropriate to their needs and development. An important element of this has been the nursing care given to soldiers, and others caught up in the fighting, suffering from disease or injury.

Formal arrangements for the nursing of soldiers in Britain can be traced to the English Civil War, particularly within the Parliamentary forces, and largely in several static hospitals in major cities. However, it was not until the disastrous experiences of casualties and disease from the Crimean War in 1854 that the need for a recognised nursing service for the Army was established. Instrumental in this was the influential Florence Nightingale who was central in organising improved health care in the Crimea, and also campaigned tirelessly to establish women nurses in all military hospitals. In 1860 she established the Army Training School for military nurses at the Royal Victoria Hospital, Netley.

The Army Nursing Service was formed in 1881, and Princess Christian's Army Nursing Reserve in 1897. Both received their first real test during the Anglo-Boer War (1899–1902) where around 1,400 nurses were sent to work in the 22 General Hospitals. At this time the Regular Army Nursing Service was very small, and the bulk of the Army nurses deployed were reservists, as well as 80 colonial military nurses from Australia, Canada and New Zealand. Unlike their colonial colleagues British nursing Sisters were not granted military rank, although they were considered officer status, and they continued to wear the same cumbersome and impractical uniform worn in general hospitals at home. Conditions were unpleasant and uncomfortable and disease was rife, particularly enteric fever which accounted for significantly more deaths among the troops than did battle wounds. British and colonial Army nurses worked tirelessly throughout the South African Campaign, and for the first time were frequently employed forward with Field Hospitals and hospital trains, gaining considerable praise for their unselfish efforts. Several were ultimately awarded the Order of the Royal Red Cross, and many more were mentioned in the dispatches.

During early 1901 the Report of the Royal Commission on the *Care and Treatment of the Sick and Wounded during the South African Campaign* was presented and in July a Committee was established to consider the reorganisation of the Army Medical and Nursing Services. As a result, the Army Nursing Service and the Indian Nursing Service were amalgamated and the Presidency adopted by the new Queen; Victoria having died in the January. Thus the Royal Warrant was signed on 27 March 1902 and the Queen Alexandra's Imperial Nursing Service was established. Sydney Jane Browne, a veteran of South Africa, was appointed Matron-in-Chief, and Miss Loch the first Senior Lady Superintendent in India. The inaugural Nursing Board meeting took place on 21 April where Surgeon-General Taylor recognised both the important peacetime role of nurses in military hospitals, and their proven utility in war.

They were to prove their worth again during the First World War. In 1914 there were barely 300 regular Nursing Sisters, and these were bolstered by almost 2,000 reservists at the outset of the war. This was clearly insufficient to cope with the drastic casualty rates that British forces were to suffer, and by the end of the war there were over 10,400 qualified nurses in uniform at home and abroad. In addition Voluntary Aid Detachments were established, under command of the QAIMNS, totalling 9,000 unqualified nursing assistants, as well as a significant number from the recently formed Territorial Force Nursing Service. The war was to present a vast array of challenges to QAs ranging from lice and trench foot to horrendous shrapnel wounds, shell shock and the awful effects of gas warfare. Moreover nurses were called to apply their skills in grossly different environments; from the fields of France and Flanders, the harsh Balkans to the severe heat of the Middle East. Nearly two hundred QAs and VADs were to lose their life between 1914 and 1918.

At the start of the Second World War the compliment of Regular QA nurses was around 700. Once again this was supplemented significantly by Reserves and volunteers. QAs found themselves in a wider range of environments including the Far East, North Africa and far more frequently aboard hospital ships and trains than had previously happened. During the early stages of the war they continued to work in their traditional grey dresses and white veils despite the tactical and climatic environment, only donning tin hats as the bombs started to fall; later, however, a sensible move into battle dress was taken. Many QAs found themselves in Japanese POW camps in 1942 but were treated as civilian women, having 'equivalent' status only rather than actual military rank. Perhaps the most harrowing experience, however, befell those QAs who's task it was to care for the victims of the concentration camps which the British forces were to liberate.

Following the war the QAIMNS underwent further reorganisation to better integrate it into the established Army structure, and in February 1949 was renamed Queen Alexandra's Royal Army Nursing Corps with Queen Mary as its Commandant-in-Chief. The official Corps Day remained as 27 March and this is celebrated annually to this day. Full military ranks and the entry of the first non-commissioned servicewoman were to follow in 1950. Male nurses were subsequently trained under the RAMC cap badge, commissioning began in the early 1970s, and all were transferred to the QARANC in 1992.

Since WW2 QAs have undertaken a wide range of peacetime and conflict roles at home and world-wide including Hong Kong, Germany, Cyprus, Belize and Northern Ireland, as well as numerous humanitarian operations in the Third World. They work in hospitals, Field Ambulances, Field Hospitals and small medical centres in both specialist and general duties, and with infantry battalions as independent Regimental Nursing Officers. QAs were directly involved in the Falklands and Gulf Wars and are certain to remain an integral and important part of medical support to the British Army – as shown in Kosovo at the millennium.

Army nurses receive the King's South African War Medal, Bloemfontein 1905.

Right, top: Comforting a grief-stricken Kosovan refugee after the receipt of bad news.

Right, bottom: Deep in Serb-held Kosovo – treating a civilian mine casualty; under guard by the Paras.

MEDIA OPS HQ LAND COMMAND

ELIDA FABERGÉ LTD   NEXT plc

THE EARL OF STOCKTON

123

THE ROYAL HOSPITAL
Governor: General Sir Brian Kenny, GCB CBE

The Governor, General Sir Brian Kenny, contributes to ABF collection by Chelsea Pensioner Joe Britton, age 87, formerly of The Royal Regiment of Fusiliers, (see Page 50).

It is my privilege to be both Governor of the Royal Hospital and Chairman of the Army Benevolent Fund (ABF). It is very fitting that the two appointments should go together as in many ways the Royal Hospital Chelsea is the home of Army benevolence, and the link between the ABF and the In-Pensioners is very strong. It was very appropriate that the Royal Hospital should have been the setting in the Summer of 1994 for the marvellous 50th Anniversary celebration of the ABF held in the presence of Her Majesty Queen Elizabeth The Queen Mother.

Each year at the Chelsea Flower Show, which is one of the ABF's main fund raising events, the Chelsea Pensioners can be seen rattling their collecting tins on behalf of the ABF, standing alongside serving soldiers, wives and friends who make up the collecting team. Those visiting the Flower Show find it hard to bypass a Chelsea Pensioner without making a donation! Chelsea Pensioners can also be seen at many other ABF events across the country.

The Royal Hospital Chapel is the venue for the annual ABF Carol Service which helps to raise a considerable sum at Christmas towards Army benevolence which last year totalled £10m in support of those in need among our past and present service men and women. The Fund also contributes to improving the quality of life for Chelsea Pensioners with various grants; for example to purchase motorised wheelchairs and to assist with convalescent holidays. This is some reward for the work which they do for the Fund.

It is fitting that this very complete account of the British Army, as it is at the Millennium, should feature the Royal Hospital Chelsea as almost certainly *every* regiment and corps, including their antecedents, must have seen a Chelsea Pensioner here at some time over the last three centuries. The Pensioner of today takes as much pride as his forebears in wearing his corps or regimental cap badge. This book will give enormous pleasure to them all.

The Life Guards

The Blues and Royals
(Royal Horse Guards and 1st Dragoons)

CAP BADGES
OF
THE BRITISH ARMY

The Royal Horse Artillery

1st The Queen's Dragoon Guards

The Royal Scots Dragoon Guards
(Carabiners and Greys)

The Royal Dragoon Guards

The Queen's Royal Hussars
(The Queen's Own and Royal Irish)

9th & 12th Royal Lancers
(Prince of Wales's)

The King's Royal Hussars

The Light Dragoons

The Queen's Royal Lancers

The Royal Tank Regiment

Royal Regiment of Artillery

Corps of Royal Engineers

Royal Corps of Signals

Grenadier Guards

Coldstream Guards

Scots Guards

Irish Guards

Welsh Guards

The Royal Scots
(The Royal Regiment)

The Royal Highland Fusiliers
(Princess Margaret's Own Glasgow
and Ayrshire Regiment)

The King's Own Scottish Borderers

The Black Watch
(Royal Highland Regiment)

The Highlanders
(Seaforth, Gordons and Camerons)

The Argyll and Sutherland Highlanders
(Princess Louise's)

Princess of Wales's Royal Regiment
(Queen's and Royal Hampshires)

The Royal Regiment of Fusiliers

The Royal Anglian Regiment

The King's Own Royal Border Regiment

The King's Regiment

The Prince of Wales's Own Regiment
of Yorkshire

The Green Howards
(Alexandra, Princess of Wales's Own
Yorkshire Regiment)

The Queen's Lancashire Regiment

THE BEST 4x4xFAR